Honoré de Balzac

LA COMÉDIE HUMAINE

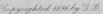

O'Cain del.   Gaujean sc.

BARONESS HULOT DISCOVERS
THE BARON

---

*A heavy step shook the little wooden staircase,
and Adeline could not restrain a piercing cry as she
recognized her husband, Baron Hulot, in a gray
knitted vest, gray swanskin trowsers much worn,
and slippers.*

*"What can I do for you, madame?" said Hulot
courteously.*

Works
" cv.4>

THE NOVELS

OF

ONORÉ DE BALZAC

NOW FOR THE FIRST TIME
COMPLETELY TRANSLATED INTO ENGLISH

THE POOR RELATIONS FIRST EPISODE
   COUSIN BETTE
               BY GEORGE B. IVES

PIERRE GRASSOU
               BY WILLIAM WALTON

THE GIRL WITH THE GOLDEN EYES
               BY E. P. ROBINS

TH TEN ETCHINGS BY GÉRY-BICHARD, EUGÈNE GAUJEAN
AND R. DE LOS RIOS, AFTER PAINTINGS BY
GEORGES CAIN AND LOUIS-EDOUARD
FOURNIER

VOLUME II

PRINTED ONLY FOR SUBSCRIBERS BY
GEORGE D. SPROUL, NEW YORK

THE POOR RELATIONS

FIRST EPISODE

COUSIN BETTE

Continued

*

In Paris, each department is a little city whence women are banished; but there is as much gossiping and underhand scheming going on as if the whole feminine population were admitted there. After three years Monsieur Marneffe's position had been made clear, exposed to the sunlight, so to speak, and the clerks in the bureaus were wondering: "Will Monsieur Marneffe be Monsieur Coquet's successor or will he not?" just exactly as deputies formerly used to wonder in the Chamber: "Will the estimates pass, or not?" The slightest sign of life in the office of the Superintendent of Employés was noted, and everything that took place in Baron Hulot's division was closely watched. The shrewd Councilor of State had enlisted on his side the victim of Marneffe's promotion, a capable official, by telling him that if he chose to do Marneffe's work he would infallibly succeed him, and he pointed to Marneffe as a man on the brink of the grave. This clerk, therefore, was scheming in Marneffe's interest.

When Hulot passed through his audience-room,

(3)

which was filled with visitors, he saw Marneffe's pallid face there in a corner, and Marneffe was the first one summoned.

"What have you to ask me, my dear fellow?" said the baron, concealing his uneasiness.

"Monsieur le Directeur, they are making sport of me in the bureaus, for they have just learned that the Superintendent of Employés went away on leave this morning for his health, to be gone a month. Everybody knows what it means to wait a month. You make me the laughing-stock of my enemies, and it's quite enough to be drummed on on one side; with two at work at once, Monsieur le Directeur, the drum may burst."

"My dear Marneffe, we must be patient in order to attain our object. You cannot be chief of bureau, if at all, in less than two months. I can't request a scandalous promotion, just when I am going to be obliged to strengthen my own position."

"If you are kicked out, I shall never be chief of bureau," said Marneffe coolly; "have me appointed, it won't make any difference."

"So I must sacrifice myself to you?" demanded the baron.

"If it were otherwise I should lose many of my illusions concerning you."

"There's too much Marneffe about you, Monsieur Marneffe!—" said the baron, rising and showing the deputy-chief the door.

"I have the honor to salute you, Monsieur le Baron," rejoined Marneffe humbly.

"What an infernal rascal!" said the baron to himself. "This is much like a summons to pay in twenty-four hours on pain of expropriation."

Two hours later, just as the baron had finished schooling Claude Vignon, whom he proposed to send to the Department of Justice in search of information concerning the judicial functionaries in whose jurisdiction Johann Fischer was, Reine opened the door of his office and handed him a note, requesting an answer.

"To send Reine!" said the baron to himself. "Valérie's mad; she'll compromise us all and endanger that hideous Marneffe's appointment."

He dismissed the minister's private secretary, and read what follows:

"Ah! my dear, what a scene I have just gone through; if you have made me happy for three years, I have paid dearly for it! He returned from his office in a furious rage, that was enough to make one shudder. I knew that he was ugly, but he was positively revolting. His four natural teeth fairly shook, and he threatened me with his hateful company if I continued to receive you. My poor pet, alas! our door will be closed to you henceforth. You can see my tears, they are falling upon my paper, and drenching it! can you read my heart, dear Hector? Ah! to see you no more, to give you up, when I have within me a little of your life as I believed that I had your heart, is enough to kill me. Think of our little Hector! don't abandon me; but do not discredit yourself for Marneffe or give way to his threats! Ah! I love you as I have never loved! I remember all the sacrifices you have made for your Valérie; she is not, and never will be ungrateful; you are, you shall be my only husband. Think no more of the twelve hundred francs a year I asked you to

give the dear little Hector who will come in a few months;—
I don't propose to be any further expense to you. But my
fortune will always be at your disposal.

"Ah! if you loved me as I love you, my Hector, you would
retire on a pension, we would both leave our families, our
worries, our surroundings, where hatred is the prevailing
sentiment, and go, with Lisbeth, to some pleasant spot in
the provinces to live,—Bretagne or wherever you choose.
There we should see no one, and should be happy together,
away from all this crowd. Your retiring pension, and the little
property I have in my own name, will be enough for us.
You are jealous; very well, your Valérie's whole time shall
be given to her Hector, and you will never have to shout at
me as you did the other day. I shall have but one child, and
that will be ours, rest assured of that, my darling old
grumbler. No, you can't imagine my frenzy, for to do that
you must know how he treated me, and the vile things he
vomited out upon your Valérie! such words would soil the
paper, and a woman like myself, Montcornet's daughter,
ought never to have been compelled to listen to a single one
of them in her whole life. Oh! I would have liked you to
be there to punish him by the spectacle of the insane passion
for you that seized upon me. My father would have cut
down the miserable wretch; I can do only what lies in a
woman's power : love you to distraction! And so, my love,
in my present state of exasperation it is impossible for me to
give up seeing you. Yes! I propose to see you secretly,
every day! We are like that, we women; I espouse your
anger. For heaven's sake if you love me don't make him
chief of bureau, but let him die deputy-chief!—At this moment, I haven't any head left; I can hear his insults still.
Bette, who was determined to leave me, has taken pity on
me and will remain a few days longer.

"My dearest love, I do not yet know what to do. I can
think of nothing but flight. I always adored the country—
Bretagne, Languedoc, wherever you choose, provided I can
love you without hindrance. Poor dear, how I pity you! you

are forced to return to your old Adeline, that urn of tears, for he probably told you, the monster, that he should watch me night and day ; he talked about the commissioner of police! Don't come here! I know that he is capable of anything, ever since he made me the victim of a most degrading speculation. For that reason I would that I could return you all that I owe to your generosity. Ah! my dear Hector, I may have flirted, and have seemed fickle to you, but you don't know your Valérie ; she loved to torment you, but she prefers you to all the world. No one can prevent you from coming to see your cousin, and I can invent with her some way by which we can talk together. My dear one, for pity's sake write me a line to comfort me, as I can not have your dear presence—oh! I would give my hand to have you in my arms on our divan. A letter will work upon me like a talisman ; write me something in which I can read your dear heart ; I will send back your letter, for we must be prudent ; I shouldn't know where to conceal it, for he ferrets everywhere. Comfort your Valérie, your wife, the mother of your child. That I, who have seen you every day, should be obliged to write you! ' I did not appreciate my good fortune,' I say to Lisbeth. A thousand kisses, my pet. Always love

" YOUR VALÉRIE."

"Tears!"—said Hulot to himself, when he had finished the letter ; "tears that make her name undecipherable.—How is she?" he asked Reine.

"Madame is in bed with hysterics," was the reply. "The nervous attack twisted madame up like a stick; it took her after she wrote. Oh! how she cried!—She heard monsieur's voice on the stairs."

The baron, in his excitement, wrote the following letter on his official paper with a printed head:

" Never fear, my angel, *he* shall die a deputy-chief ! Your idea is an excellent one ; we will go and live far away from

Paris, and be happy with our little Hector ; I will go on the retired list, and I can find a good position on some railroad. Ah! my sweet love, I feel that your letter has made me young again! I will begin life anew, and make a fortune for our dear little one, as you shall see. As I read your letter, a thousand times more glowing than those in the Nouvelle Héloïse, it worked a miracle! I did not believe that my love for you could grow greater. This evening at Lisbeth's you will see

" Yours for life,

" HECTOR."

Reine took this letter, the only one the baron had ever written to his *sweet love.* Such keen emotion formed a counterpoise to the storms that were rumbling on the horizon; but, at that moment, the baron, feeling sure that he could ward off the blows aimed at his uncle Johann Fischer, thought only of the deficit.

One of the peculiarities of the Bonapartist character is faith in the power of the sword, the certainty of the continued pre-eminence of the military over the civil administration. Hulot laughed at the idea of the king's attorney in Algeria, where the War Department reigned supreme. Man remains what he has been. How could the officers of the Imperial Guard forget that they had seen the mayors of the good cities of the Empire, the Emperor's prefects, emperors themselves on a small scale, coming to receive the Imperial Guard and to compliment them at the confines of the departments they passed through, and in short rendering them sovereign honors?

At half-past four the baron went straight to Madame Marneffe's; his heart was beating like a young man's as he ascended the stairs, for he was asking himself this question: "Shall I see her, or not?" How could he remember the scene of the morning, when his whole family in tears was at his feet? Did not Valérie's letter, folded away forever in a little pocket-book over his heart, prove that she loved him more dearly than the most lovable of young men?

After he had rung, the wretched baron heard the dragging feet and disgusting cough of the invalid Marneffe. Marneffe opened the door, but immediately struck an attitude and pointed to the staircase with a gesture precisely like that with which Hulot had pointed to the door of his office.

"There's too much Hulot about you, Monsieur Hulot!—" said he.

The baron tried to pass, but Marneffe took a pistol from his pocket and cocked it.

"Monsieur le Conseiller d'État, when a man is so vile as I am,—for you think me a vile creature, don't you?—he would be the worst of criminals, if he did not collect all the profits of his bartered honor. You choose war, and it will be a hot one and without quarter. Don't come again and don't try to pass; I have informed the commissioner of police of my relations with you."

Taking advantage of the baron's stupefaction, he pushed him out and locked the door.

"What a deep rascal!" Hulot said to himself as

he went on upstairs to Lisbeth's. "Ah! now I understand the letter. Valérie and I will leave Paris. Valérie is mine for the rest of my life; she will close my eyes."

Lisbeth was not at home. Madame Olivier informed Hulot that she had gone to the baroness's, expecting to find the baron there.

"Poor girl! I wouldn't have believed she could be so cunning as she was this morning," said the baron to himself, recalling Lisbeth's performance as he walked from Rue Vanneau to Rue Plumet.

At the corner of Rue Vanneau and Rue de Babylone, he looked back at the Eden whence Hymen, with the sword of the law in his hands, had driven him forth. Valérie was at her window looking after him; when he raised his head she waved her handkerchief, but the villainous Marneffe struck his wife on the head and roughly pulled her away from the window. A tear came to the Councilor's eyes.

"To be so dearly loved! to see a woman abused, and to be almost seventy years old!" he muttered.

Lisbeth had gone to announce the good news. Adeline and Hortense already knew that the baron, having refused to degrade himself in the eyes of the whole department by nominating Marneffe chief of bureau, would be turned out of door by that gentleman, the baron's enemy. Wherefore Adeline in her joy had ordered dinner on such a scale that her Hector should find it superior to Valérie's, and the devoted Lisbeth was assisting Mariette to achieve that difficult result. Cousin Bette was a sort of idol; the mother and daughter kept kissing her hands, and had told her with a delight that was touching to see, that the maréchal consented to take her for his housekeeper.

"And from that, my dear, to becoming his wife is but a step," said Adeline.

"Indeed he didn't say no when Victorin mentioned it to him," said Countess Steinbock.

The baron was welcomed by his family with such warm and touching demonstrations of affection, which told of such boundless depths of love, that he was obliged to conceal his chagrin. The maréchal came to dinner. After dinner Hulot did not go away. Victorin and his wife came in, and they made up a whist table.

"It's a long while, Hector," said the maréchal gravely, "since you gave *us* such an evening!—"

This remark, coming from the old soldier, who was accustomed to spoil his brother, and yet reproved him thus implicitly, made a deep impression. It disclosed the long, deep wounds of a heart, in which all the others' sorrow, which he had divined, had echoed loudly.

At eight o'clock the baron himself volunteered to escort Lisbeth home, promising to return.

"Well, Lisbeth, *he* abuses her!" he said as soon as they were in the street. "Oh! I never loved her so dearly!"

"And I wouldn't have believed that Valérie was so fond of you!" replied Lisbeth. "She is free and easy, she likes to flirt and to be courted, to have the

comedy of love played for her, as she says; but you
are the only one to whom she is really attached."

"What did she say for me?"

"This," said Lisbeth. "She has, as you know,
shown some favors to Crevel; you mustn't bear her
ill-will for that, for it was he who put her out of
reach of want for the rest of her days; but she de-
tests him, and it's almost over. Well, she has kept
the key of a suite—"

"On Rue du Dauphin!" cried Hulot in ecstasy.
"For that alone, I would forgive her for Crevel.—
I have been there, and I know—"

"Here's the key," said Lisbeth; "have one
made like it to-morrow, two if you can."

"What then?—" said Hulot eagerly.

"Well, I will come and dine with you again to-
morrow, and you must return Valérie's key to me,
for Père Crevel may ask her for the one he gave her.
Day after to-morrow you will meet there, and agree
upon your plans. You will be quite safe, for there
are two ways out. If by any chance Crevel, who
has the morals of the Regency no doubt, as he says,
should come in by the back street you can go out
through the shop, and vice versa. Well, you old
rascal, you owe this to me. What will you do for
me?"

"Whatever you wish!"

"Well, then, don't oppose my marriage to your
brother."

"You, Maréchale Hulot! you, Comtesse de Forzheim!" cried Hector in blank amazement.

"Adeline's a baroness!—" retorted Bette in a bitter and threatening tone. "Listen, you old rake; you know what a mess your affairs are in! Your family may find themselves without bread and in the gutter.—"

"That's my constant fear!" said Hector in dismay.

"If your brother dies, who will support your wife and daughter? The widow of a maréchal of France can obtain a pension of at least six thousand francs, can't she? Very good, I propose to marry simply to make sure that your wife and daughter will have bread to eat, you old fool!"

"I did not think of that result!" said the baron. "I will preach it into my brother, for we're sure of you. Tell my angel that my life is *hers!*"

And, having seen Lisbeth safely within doors on Rue Vanneau, the baron returned to his whist, and remained at home. The baroness was happy beyond words; her husband seemed to have become one of the family once more; for about two weeks he went to the department every morning at nine, returned home for dinner at six, and passed the evening in the bosom of his family. Twice he took Adeline and Hortense to the theatre. The mother and daughter paid for three masses of thanksgiving, and prayed God to preserve the husband and father He had restored to them. One night, Victorin Hulot said to his mother, when the baron had gone to his bed-room:

"We are very happy, for father has come back

to us; my wife and I don't regret the loss of our money, if this keeps on.—''

"Your father will soon be seventy years old,'' the baroness replied; "he still thinks of Madame Marneffe, I have discovered that; but soon he will think no more of her. The passion for women is not like gambling, speculation, or avarice; we can imagine its coming to an end.''

The lovely Adeline, for she was still lovely despite her fifty years and her sorrows, was mistaken in this respect. Libertines, men whom nature has endowed with the highly-prized faculty of loving beyond the limits it has fixed for loving, almost always seem younger than they are. During this relapse into virtuous ways the baron went three times to Rue du Dauphin, and there he was never seventy years old. Rekindled passion renewed his youth, and he would have placed his honor, his family, everything, in Valérie's hands without a regret. But Valérie had changed her tactics entirely; she never mentioned money to him, nor the twelve hundred francs a year for their son; on the other hand, she offered him money; she loved Hulot as a woman of thirty-six loves a handsome law-student, very poor, very poetic, and very much in love. And poor Adeline thought she had made a new conquest of her dear Hector! The fourth meeting of the lovers was agreed upon, at the last moment of the third, precisely as in old days at the Comédie-Italienne the next day's bill used to be announced at the close of the performance. The hour appointed was nine o'clock in the morning. On the day when this good fortune fell due, the anticipation of which reconciled the passionate old man to life with his family, Reine enquired for the baron about eight o'clock. Hulot, fearing some disaster, went out to speak to her, as she refused to come in. The faithful maid handed him the following letter:

"Don't go to Rue du Dauphin, my old grumbler; our nightmare is ill and I have to nurse him; but be there this evening at nine. Crevel is at Monsieur Lebas's, at Corbeil, so I am sure that he'll bring no princess to his little house. I have made arrangements here to have the night for my own, and I can return before Marneffe is awake. Send me an answer; for perhaps your stately poem of a wife won't give you any more liberty than she used. They say she is so lovely still that you are quite capable of being false to me, you're such a terrible rake! Burn my letter, I distrust everybody."

Hulot wrote these few lines in reply:

" My love, my wife has not interfered with my pleasure for twenty-five years, as I told you before. I would sacrifice a hundred Adelines to you ! I will be at the temple Crevel at nine this evening, awaiting my divinity. May the deputy-chief settle his accounts soon ! then we shall be separated no more; such is the dearest wish of

"YOUR HECTOR."

That evening the baron told his wife that he was going to attend to some business with the minister at Saint-Cloud, and would return at four or five o'clock in the morning; and he went to Rue du Dauphin. It was late in the month of June.

Few men have really experienced in their lives
the fearful sensation of going to meet their death;
those who have returned alive from the scaffold are
among the number; but some dreamers have felt
that agony in a most vivid form in their dreams;
they have gone through the whole performance,
and have even felt the knife against their necks
just as the awakening came, with daybreak, to
rescue them.—But the sensation which the Councilor of State felt at five o'clock in the morning, in
Crevel's dainty and luxurious bed, far surpassed in
horror that of feeling one's neck resting on the fatal
block, in the presence of ten thousand spectators
glaring at you with twenty thousand rays of
flame. Valérie was sleeping in a bewitching pose.
She was beautiful as all women are who are sufficiently so to be lovely in their sleep. It was art in-
vading the province of nature, it was the realization
of the painter's conception. In his horizontal position the baron's eyes were about three feet from
the floor; as they wandered about at random, as
every man's eyes do just as he awakes and collects
his thoughts, they rested upon the door, covered
with flowers painted by Jan, an artist who snapped
his fingers at fame. The baron did not see, like the
condemned man, twenty thousand visual rays;
he saw but a single person, whose glance was in
very truth more piercing than the ten thousand of
the public square. It is unquestionably true that a
great number of splenetic Englishmen would pay a
high price for such a sensation in the midst of their

M. MARNEFFE OPENS THE DOOR FOR BARON HULOT

"Monsieur le Conseiller d'État, when a man is so vile as I am,—for you think me a vile creature, don't you?—he would be the worst of criminals, if he did not collect all the profits of his bartered honor. You choose war, and it will be a hot one and without quarter. Don't come again and don't try to pass; I have informed the commissioner of police of my relations with you."

Copyrighted 1896 by G.B.

G. Cain del.

Géry Bichard sc

pleasure,—a sensation much rarer than that felt by a condemned man. The baron remained in his horizontal position, literally bathed in cold perspiration. He would have liked to doubt the evidence of his senses, but that murderous eye had a tongue. He heard voices whispering behind the door.

"What if it were only Crevel trying to play a joke on me!" said the baron to himself, no longer able to doubt the presence of a stranger in the temple.

The door was thrown open. French law, which comes next to royalty on the placards, appeared in all its majesty, in the guise of a nice little commissioner of police, accompanied by a long-legged justice of the peace, both under the escort of Monsieur Marneffe. The commissioner, whose feet were encased in shoes tied with ribbons which were covered with mud, terminated above in a yellow cranium, poorly supplied with hair, the man's whole aspect denoting a crafty, good-natured, mettlesome blade, who knew all the secrets of life in Paris. The expression of his eyes, as seen through the glasses he wore, was shrewd and bantering. The magistrate, a former lawyer, and a worshipper of the fair sex, of long standing, envied the man who had made himself amenable to the law.

"Pray pardon the harshness of our errand, Monsieur le Baron!" said the officer, "we are requisitioned by a complainant. Monsieur le Juge de Paix was a witness of my entry into the house. I know who you are, and who your companion is."

Valérie opened her eyes wide, in amazement,

2

uttered the piercing shriek invented by actresses to
announce an attack of insanity on the stage, and
writhed in convulsions on the bed, like a demoniac
of the Middle Ages in her chemise of sulphur on a
bed of burning fagots.

"Death!—dear Hector, the police? Oh! never!"

She leaped out of bed, flitted like a white
cloud between the three spectators, and crouched
under the *bonheur-du-jour*, hiding her face in her
hands.

"Lost! dead!—" she shrieked.

"Monsieur," said Marneffe to Hulot, "if Madame
Marneffe should go mad, you would be worse than
a libertine, you'd be a murderer—"

What can a man do or say, when he is taken by
surprise in a bed that does not belong to him, even
as a tenant, and with a woman who also does not
belong to him? This.

"Monsieur le Juge de Paix, Monsieur le Commissaire de Police," said the baron with dignity,
"be good enough to look to the welfare of the unfortunate woman whose reason seems to me in danger,
—and then you can make your report. Of course
the doors are secured and you have no reason to
anticipate flight on her part or my own, considering
the condition we are in."

The two functionaries complied with the Councilor's suggestion.

"Come and speak with me, you vile wretch!"—
said Hulot in an undertone to Marneffe, taking him
by the arm and pulling him to his side. "I should

not be the assassin, but you! You want to be chief of bureau and officer of the Legion of Honor?"

"Above all things, director," Marneffe replied, with an inclination of his head.

"You shall be both; go and reassure your wife and send these men away."

"Nay, nay," Marneffe shrewdly retorted. "These gentlemen must draw up their report that you were caught in the act, for, without that document, which is the foundation of my complaint, what would become of me? They know no end of tricks at headquarters. You stole my wife and didn't make me chief of bureau, Monsieur le Baron, and I give you only two days to redeem yourself. Here are the letters—"

"Letters!" cried the baron, interrupting him.

"Yes, the letters proving that the child my wife is carrying at this moment is yours.—Do you understand? you must give my son an income equal to the portion this bastard takes from him. But I will be moderate, for it's none of my business, and I am not drunk with the joys of paternity, myself! A hundred louis a year will do. I shall be Monsieur Coquet's successor to-morrow morning, and my name placed on the list of those who are to be made officers of the Legion at the July fêtes or—the report will be deposited with my complaint at police headquarters. I'm a generous fellow, am I not?"

"Great God! what a pretty woman!" said the magistrate to the officer. "What a loss to society if she should go mad!"

"She's not mad," the commissioner sententiously replied.

A police officer is always the incarnation of suspicion.

"Monsieur le Baron Hulot has stepped into a trap," he added loud enough to be overheard by Valérie.

She shot a glance at the commissioner which would have struck him dead if glances could transmit the fury they express. The commissioner smiled, for he too had set a trap, and the lady fell into it. Marneffe bade his wife return to the bedroom and dress herself decently, for he had come to an understanding on every point with the baron. The latter took a dressing-gown and withdrew to the adjoining room.

"Gentlemen," said he to the two functionaries, "I need not urge secrecy upon you."

The magistrate and the officer bowed. The latter tapped lightly twice on the door, whereupon his secretary entered, sat down at the *bonheur-du-jour*, and began to write what the commissioner dictated to him in a low voice. Valérie continued to weep bitterly. When she had finished her toilette, Hulot went into the bed-room and dressed. Meanwhile the report was drawn up. Thereupon Marneffe started to take his wife away; but Hulot, believing that it was the last time he should see her, implored by a gesture the favor of speaking with her.

"Monsieur, madame has cost me enough for you to allow me to bid adieu to her,—in the presence of you all, of course."

Valérie came to his side, and Hulot whispered in
her ear:

"There is nothing left for us now but flight; but
how shall we correspond? We have been betrayed—"

"By Reine!" she replied. "But, my dear friend,
after this scandal, we ought to meet no more. I am
dishonored. Besides they will tell you infamous
things about me, and you will believe them—"

The baron made a gesture of denial.

"You will believe them, and I thank heaven for
it, for perhaps you will not regret me."

"*He won't die a deputy-chief!*" said Marneffe in
the Councilor's ear, as he returned to get his wife,
to whom he said roughly: "Enough of this,
madame; if I am weak toward you, I don't propose
to be made a fool of by others."

Valérie left the Crevel establishment with such
a wicked parting glance at the baron, that he believed she still adored him. The magistrate gallantly offered his hand to escort her to the carriage.
The crestfallen baron, who was required to sign the
report, was left alone with the commissioner of
police. When the Councilor of State had written
his name, the official cast a shrewd glance at him
over his spectacles.

"You are very fond of that little lady, Monsieur
le Baron?"

"To my discomfiture, as you see—"

"Suppose she didn't love you?" continued the
official; "suppose she was playing you false?"

"I have seen her before in this place, monsieur.—
Monsieur Crevel and I have an understanding.—"

"Aha! you are aware that you are on Monsieur
le Maire's premises?"

"Perfectly."

The commissioner raised his hat slightly to salute
the old fellow.

"You are very much in love, so I will hold my
tongue," said he, "I have as much respect for invet-
erate passions as physicians have for inve—I have
seen Monsieur de Nucingen the banker suffering
from a passion of that sort—"

"He's a friend of mine," rejoined the baron. "I
have often supped with the fair Esther; she was
well worth the two millions she cost him."

"More," said the commissioner. "The old financier's fancy cost four persons their lives. Oh!
these passions are like the cholera."

"What were you going to say to me?" demanded
the Councilor of State, who took this indirect advice
decidedly ill.

"Why should I deprive you of your illusions?"
replied the commissioner; "a man so seldom retains
them at your age."

"Rid me of them!" cried the Councilor.

"You may curse the physician afterward," the
commissioner answered with a smile.

"I appeal to you, Monsieur le Commissaire.—"

"Well, that woman was in league with her husband."

"Oh!—"

"That happens, monsieur, about twice in ten times.   Oh! I know what I'm talking about."

"What proof have you of her complicity?"

"First of all, the husband!" said the clever official with the tranquillity of a surgeon accustomed to probe wounds.   "Speculation is written upon that ghastly, hideous face.   But do you not value highly a certain letter written by this woman in which something is said about a child?"

"I value that letter so highly that I always carry it about me," replied the baron, feeling in his breast pocket for the little pocket-book that never left him.

"Leave the pocket-book where it is," said the commissioner, in the thundering tones of a public prosecutor; "here's the letter.   I know now all I wanted to know.   Madame Marneffe must be in the secret of the pocket-book's contents?"

"She and nobody else in the world."

"So I thought.—Now, here's the proof you desire of the little woman's complicity."

"Let's have it!" said the baron, still incredulous.

"When we arrived here, Monsieur le Baron, that villain Marneffe came in first and got this letter, which his wife had, without doubt, placed on that piece of furniture," said the commissioner, indicating the *bonheur-du-jour*.   "Evidently that place had been agreed upon between the husband and wife, always supposing that she succeeded in filching the letter while you were asleep; for the letter the lady wrote you, with those you have written her, would be decisive in criminal proceedings.''

The commissioner showed Hulot the letter he received through Reine in his office at the department.

''It's a part of the papers in the case,'' said he; ''give it back to me, monsieur.''

''Well, monsieur,'' said Hulot, with discomposed countenance, ''that woman is libertinage reduced to a science; I am certain now that she has three lovers!''

''That's not uncommon,'' said the commissioner. ''Ah! they're not all on the street. When they practice that profession, Monsieur le Baron, in carriages or in salons or in their own houses, it's no longer a matter of francs and centimes. Mademoiselle Esther, whom you have just mentioned and who poisoned herself, devoured millions.—If you take my advice, you'll cut loose, Monsieur le Baron. This last trick will cost you dear. That beast of a husband has the law on his side. Indeed, but for me the little woman would have hooked you again!''

''Thanks, monsieur,'' said the Councilor of State, trying to maintain a dignified countenance.

''Monsieur, we will close the rooms now, the farce is played out, and you can hand the key to Monsieur le Maire.''

＊

Hulot returned home in a depressed condition very near to prostration, and absorbed by the most gloomy thoughts. He awoke his noble-hearted, pure and saint-like wife, and hurled the story of the last three years into her heart, sobbing like a child deprived of a favorite toy. This confession of an old man still young at heart, this distressing, heart-rending epic, while it moved Adeline deeply, inwardly caused her the keenest joy, and she thanked Heaven for this latest stroke, for she imagined her husband restored for ever to the bosom of his family.

"Lisbeth was right!" said Madame Hulot in a soft voice, and without indulging in useless reproaches, "she told us this beforehand."

"True! Ah! if I had listened to her, instead of losing my temper, the day I urged poor Hortense to return home in order not to endanger the reputation of that—Oh! dear Adeline, we must save Wenceslas! he's in the mire up to his chin!"

"My poor dear, the little bourgeoise succeeded no better with you than the actresses," said Adeline with a smile.

The baroness was terrified at the manifest change in her Hector; when she saw that he was unhappy, suffering keenly, bent beneath the weight of his misfortunes, she was all heart, all compassion, all

(25)

love, and she would have shed her blood to make him happy.

"Stay with us, my dear Hector. Tell me what these women do to attach you to them so; I will try to do the same.—Why did you not form me according to your needs? Was it because I lack intelligence? I am still considered beautiful enough for men to pay their court to me."

Many married women, devoted to their duties and their husbands, may here ask themselves the question why these strong, kindly men, who are so compassionate to the Madame Marneffes, do not take their wives for the objects of their fancy and their passion, especially when they resemble Baroness Adeline Hulot. This is one of the most insoluble mysteries of the human organization. Love, that inordinate carousal of the reason, that manly, serious enjoyment of noble hearts; and sensual pleasure, that vulgar commodity offered for sale upon the streets, are two different phases of a single fact. The woman who satisfies these two boundless appetites of the dual nature is as rare in the sex as is the great general, the great writer, the great artist, the great inventor, in a nation. The man of superior mind as well as the imbecile, a Hulot as well as a Crevel, feels the need of the ideal and the need of the sensual; all alike go about in search of this mysterious hermaphrodite, this *rara avis* which, in a majority of cases, is found to be a work in two volumes. This search is a form of depravity for which society is to blame. Certainly, marriage should be looked upon as a task to be accomplished; it is life, with its toil and its bitter sacrifices, to be made on both sides. The libertines, the seekers after treasure, are as guilty as malefactors who are much more severely punished than they. These reflections are not mere moral patchwork; they furnish the explanation of many incomprehensible disasters. Moreover this Scene inculcates its own moral lessons of more than one variety.

The baron paid an early visit to the Maréchal Prince de Wissembourg, whose exalted patronage was his last resource. Having been for thirty-five years a protégé of the old war-horse, he had the *grande* and *petite entrée*, and was privileged to enter his apartments at his hour for rising.

"Ah! good morning, my dear Hector," said that great and warm-hearted officer. "What's the matter? You seem thoughtful. The session's at an end, however. Still another one gone! I speak of them now, as we used to speak of our campaigns. Faith I believe the newspapers call the sessions parliamentary campaigns."

"Indeed, maréchal, we did have some trouble; but it was due to the prevailing want!" said Hulot. "What can you expect? it's the way of the world. Every period has its drawbacks. The greatest misfortune of the year 1841 is that neither the King nor his ministers are untrammeled in their action as the Emperor was."

The maréchal darted at Hulot an eagle-like glance, proud, piercing, acute, which showed that, despite his years, his great heart was still strong and un-flinching.

"You have a favor to ask of me?" he said, affecting a playful air.

"I find myself compelled to ask of you as a personal favor, the promotion of one of my deputy-chiefs to the rank of chief of bureau, and his nomination as an officer of the Legion of Honor."

"What's his name?" said the maréchal, with a glance like a flash of lightning.

"Marneffe!"

"He has a pretty wife, I saw her at your daughter's wedding.—If Roger—but Roger is no longer here. Hector, my boy, this is a matter connected with your amours. What! are you still at the old game? Ah! you do credit to the Imperial Guard! that's what it is to have been in the administration; you have forces in reserve!—Drop this matter right here, my dear boy, there's too much gallantry about it for it to become a department matter."

"No, maréchal, it's a very bad business, for the police court is mixed up in it; do you want to see me there?"

"Oh! the devil!" cried the maréchal, becoming serious. "Go on."

"You see me in the plight of a fox caught in a trap.—You have always been so kind to me, that you will consent to extricate me from my present disgraceful situation."

Hulot thereupon described his misadventure as wittily and cheerfully as possible.

"Do you want my brother, to whom you are so attached, prince, to die of shame," he said, as he concluded, "and to allow one of your directors, a Councilor of State, to be disgraced? My Marneffe is a miserable rascal, we'll put him on the retired list in two or three years."

"How coolly you talk of two or three years, my dear fellow!—" said the maréchal.

"But the Imperial Guard is immortal, prince."

"I am now the only maréchal left of the first promotion," said the minister. "Hark ye, Hector, you don't know how great my attachment to you is, but you shall see! On the day when I leave the ministry, we will leave it together. Ah! my friend, you are not a deputy. Many men have an eye on your place, and, except for me, you would no longer hold it. Yes, I have broken many a lance to keep you there.—Well, I grant your two requests, for it would be much too hard to see you sitting in the dock, at your age, and holding the position that you do. But you are making too many breaches in your credit. If this nomination raises any row, we shall be taken to account for it. I can afford to laugh at it, but it will be one thorn more in your foot. At the next session you will lose your place. Your office has been held out as a bait to five or six influential men, and you have been retained in it only by the subtlety of my arguments. I have urged that, on the day when you were retired and your place was given to some one else, we should have five malcontents and one content; while by leaving you *shaking in your shoes* for two or three years, we could hold our six votes. They began to laugh in the Council, and concluded that the *vieux de la vieille,* as they say, was coming out strong in parliamentary tactics.—I tell you all this frankly. Besides, you are growing gray.—What a lucky dog you are to be able still to get yourself into such a fix! Where are the days when Sub-lieutenant Cottin had mistresses!"

The maréchal rang.

"We must have that report destroyed!" he said.

"You are like a father to me, monseigneur! I didn't dare speak of my anxiety."

"I still wish that Roger was here," cried the maréchal, as Mitouflet, his orderly, entered the room, "and I was just going to send for him.—You may go, Mitouflet.—And do you, old comrade, go and draw up the nomination, and I'll sign it. But that infernal schemer sha'n't long enjoy the fruit of his crimes; he will be watched, and broken at the head of his company, at the slightest shortcoming. Now that you are saved, Hector, take heed to yourself. Don't tire out your friends. The appointment will be sent you this morning, and your man shall be an officer of the Legion!—How old are you now?"

"I shall be seventy in three months."

"What a buck you are!" said the maréchal with a smile. "You're the one who deserves promotion; but, a thousand cannon-balls! we're not living under Louis XV!"

Such is the effect of the good fellowship which unites the glorious relics of the Napoleonic phalanx; they think they are still around the camp-fire, and compelled to protect one another against the whole world.

"Another favor like that," said Hulot to himself as he crossed the courtyard, "and I am ruined."

The unhappy official went to Baron de Nucingen's, to whom he now owed only a trifling sum; he succeeded in borrowing from him forty thousand francs by assigning his salary for two years more; but the baron stipulated that, in case Hulot should be retired, the attachable portion of his pension should be applied to the payment of the loan, principal and interest in full. This last loan, like the former one, was negotiated in the name of Vauvinct, to whom the baron gave his notes for twelve thousand francs. The next day, the fatal report, the husband's complaint, and the letters, all were destroyed. The scandalous promotions of Monsieur Marneffe, hardly noticed amid the excitement of the July fêtes, were not commented on in any newspaper.

Lisbeth, who had, so far as appearances went, broken with Madame Marneffe, was installed at Maréchal Hulot's. Ten days after these occurrences the banns of the old maid's intended marriage to the illustrious veteran were published for the first time. To obtain his consent Adeline told him of her Hector's pecuniary disasters, begging him never to mention it to the baron, who, she said, was in a very gloomy, dejected and feeble state.

"Alas! he shows his age!" she added.

So Lisbeth had triumphed! She was on the point of attaining the goal of her ambition; she was about to see her scheme successful, her hatred satisfied. She enjoyed in anticipation the bliss of reigning over the family which had so long despised her. She promised herself that she would be the protectress of her protectors, the guardian angel who would support the ruined family; she addressed herself in secret as *Madame la Comtesse* or *Madame la Maréchale*, courtesying to herself before the mirror. Adeline and Hortense would end their days in poverty, struggling to drive away want, while Cousin Bette, having the *entrée* at the Tuileries, would be enthroned in society.

A shocking catastrophe hurled the old maid from the social eminence whereon she had so proudly taken her stand.

On the very day on which the banns were first published the baron received another message from Africa. A second Alsatian made his appearance, and delivered a letter after making sure that the recipient was Baron Hulot himself; and, having given his address, he left that dignitary overwhelmed by the perusal of the first lines of the following letter:

"MY NEPHEW:

"You will receive this letter, by my reckoning, on the seventh of August. Assuming that it takes you three days to send us the assistance we require, and two weeks more for it to reach here, it will arrive September first.

" If you can arrange matters thus you will have saved the honor and the life of your devoted Johann Fischer.

" This is what the clerk demands, whom you gave me as a confederate ; for I am, as it appears, liable to be summoned before the Assizes or before a court-martial. You understand that Johann Fischer will never be dragged before any tribunal, but will go of his own motion before that over which God presides.

" Your clerk seems to me to be a wicked rascal, quite capable of compromising you ; but he's as shrewd as any swindler. He claims that you ought to make a louder outcry than anybody, and send us an inspector, a special commissioner with instructions to detect the culprits, unearth abuses, and, in short, put on the screws ; but who will interpose in the first place between the tribunals and us, by raising the question of jurisdiction?

" If your commissioner arrives by September 1, and has the countersign from you, if you send us two hundred thousand francs to replace in the warehouses the supplies that we claim to have in distant localities, we shall be looked upon as honest agents with clean hands.

" You can entrust to the soldier who will hand you this letter a draft to my order on some house in Algiers. He is a reliable man, a relation of mine, and utterly incapable of trying to find out what he is the bearer of. I have taken measures to provide for the boy's return. If you can do nothing I shall gladly die for him to whom we owe our Adeline's happiness."

The agony and the bliss of passion, and the catastrophe which had put an end to his gallant career, had prevented Baron Hulot from giving a thought to poor Johann Fischer, whose first letter, however, definitely foreshadowed the danger which had now become so pressing. He left the dining-room in such distress of mind that he threw himself

3

on the couch in the salon.   He was completely
crushed, overpowered by the deathly torpor caused
by a violent fall.   He stared vacantly at a rose in
the carpet, heedless of the fact that he held Johann's
fatal letter open in his hand.   Adeline from her
bed-room heard her husband fall upon the couch
like a lifeless mass.   The sound was so unusual
that she thought he must have had an apoplectic
stroke.   She looked through the door into the mirror, trembling with the deadly terror which checks
the respiration, and roots one to the spot where one
stands, and she saw her Hector lying as if he had
been thrown down.   She stole into the room on
tiptoe; Hector heard nothing, so that she was able
to approach him; she saw the letter, took it, read
it, and trembled in every limb.   She passed through
one of those violent nervous upheavals, of which
the body always retains the marks.   When the first
shock had passed away, the necessity of acting
promptly gave her the strength which is drawn
from the very well-springs of vitality; but, a few
days later, she became subject to constant attacks
of nervous trembling.

"Hector, come to my room," said she in a voice
which resembled a sigh.   "Don't let your daughter
see you thus!   Come, my dear, come."

"Where can I obtain two hundred thousand
francs?   I can arrange to have Claude Vignon sent
as commissioner.   He's a bright, intelligent fellow.
—That's a matter of a day or two only.—But two
hundred thousand francs!   My son hasn't them, his

house is mortgaged for three hundred thousand.
My brother has laid by thirty thousand francs at
the outside. Nucingen would laugh at me!—Vauvinet?—he consented with very bad grace to loan
me ten thousand francs to make up the amount for
that infernal Marneffe's son. No, it's all over; I must
go and throw myself at the maréchal's feet, confess
to him how things stand, hear myself called a vile
dog, and receive his broadside so that I can go under
decently."

"But, Hector, this is not ruin simply, it's dis-
honor!" said Adeline. "My poor uncle will kill
himself. Kill only us; you have the right to do that,
but don't be a murderer. Take courage, there must
be some way of escape."

"Not one!" said the baron. "Not a man
in the government could put his hand on two
hundred thousand francs, even if it were a question of saving a ministry!—O Napoleon, where
art thou?"

"My uncle! poor man! Hector, we cannot let him
commit suicide in disgrace!"

"There might be one resource," said he; "but—
it's very uncertain.—Yes, Crevel is at daggers
drawn with his daughter.—Ah! he has plenty of
money, he alone could—"

"Well, Hector, it's far better that your wife
should die, than that we should let our uncle, your
brother and the honor of the family die together!"
said the baroness, as an idea flashed suddenly
through her mind. "Yes, I can save you all.—

O my God! what a degrading thought! how could
it have come to me?''

She clasped her hands, fell on her knees, and
prayed. When she arose she saw a look of such
insane joy on her husband's face, that the diabolical
idea returned, and Adeline thereupon fell into a
sort of idiotic melancholy.

"Go, my dear, run to the ministry," she cried,
rousing herself from her torpor, "try to arrange for
sending a commissioner; you must do it. *Wheedle
it out of the maréchal!* And when you return, at
five o'clock, perhaps you will find,—yes! you shall
find two hundred thousand francs. Your family,
your honor as a man, as a Councilor of State, as a
government official, your reputation for honesty,
your son, all will be saved; but your Adeline will
be lost, and you will never see her again. Hector,
my love,'' said she, kneeling at his feet, taking his
hand and kissing it, "give me your blessing and
bid me adieu!''

His wife's words and manner were so heartrending that Hulot said, as he raised her from the floor
and kissed her:

"I don't understand you!''

"If you did,'' she replied, "I should die of shame,
or else I should not be strong enough to carry
through this last sacrifice.''

"Madame, breakfast is served,'' said Mariette.

Hortense came in to bid her father and mother
good-morning. They were forced to conceal their
emotions and go to breakfast.

"Sit down to breakfast without me; I will join you in a moment!" said the baroness.

She sat down at her table and wrote the following letter:

"MY DEAR MONSIEUR CREVEL:

" I have a favor to ask of you; I shall look for you this morning, and I rely upon your gallantry, which is well known to me, not to keep me waiting too long.

" Your devoted servant,
"ADELINE HULOT."

"Louise," said she to her daughter's maid, who was waiting at the table, "take this letter down to the concierge, and tell him to carry it immediately to its address and ask for an answer."

The baron, who was looking over the newspapers, handed a republican sheet to his wife, and pointed out an article in it.

"Will it be in time?" he said.

The article in question, one of those terrible political tirades with which the newspapers flavor their political bread and butter, was as follows:

"One of our correspondents writes us from Algiers that such abuses have been unearthed in the commissary service in the province of Oran, that a judicial investigation has been set on foot. The malversations are unquestionable, and the guilty parties are known. If severe repressive measures are not taken we shall continue to lose more men by extortions which cut down their rations, than by the swords of the Arabs or the heat of the climate. We shall await further information before pursuing this deplorable subject. We are no longer surprised at the dismay caused by the establishment of the press in Algeria, as provided by the Charter of 1830."

"I must dress and go to the department," said the baron, leaving the table; "time is too precious, there's a man's life in every minute."

"O mamma, I have no more hope!" exclaimed Hortense.

Unable to restrain her tears, she handed her mother a *Revue des Beaux-Arts*. Madame Hulot's eye fell upon an engraving of the *Delilah* group by Count Steinbock, beneath which was printed: *Belonging to Madame Marneffe*. The first few lines of the article, which was signed V, revealed the talent and the complaisance of Claude Vignon.

"Poor darling!" said the baroness.

Dismayed by the almost indifferent tone in which her mother spoke, Hortense looked up at her, and saw in her expression the evidence of a sorrow, beside which her own was as nothing. She went to her and kissed her.

"What's the matter, mamma? what has happened?" she said; "can we be more wretched than we are?"

"My child, it seems that my terrible sufferings in the past have been nothing compared to what I bear to-day. When shall I cease to suffer?"

"In heaven, mother!" said Hortense gravely.

"Come, my angel, you shall help me dress.— But no,—I prefer that you should have nothing to do with my toilette to-day. Send Louise to me."

*

When she returned to her bed-room Adeline went
and scrutinized herself in the mirror. She gazed at
herself sadly and curiously, asking herself the question:

"Am I still beautiful?—Can I still arouse desire?
—Have I any wrinkles?"

She pushed back her lovely blond hair, and un-
covered her temples—all was as fresh as in a young
girl. Adeline went farther; she bared her shoulders
and was content. She felt a momentary thrill of
pride. The beauty of shoulders which are really
beautiful, is the last to leave a woman, especially
when she has led a virtuous life. Adeline selected
with care the elements of her toilette; but the
chaste, pious creature was chastely dressed, despite
her little attempts at coquetry. Why wear new
gray silk stockings and satin buskins, when she was
entirely unversed in the art of putting out her little
foot at the decisive moment, a few inches beyond
the skirt half-raised so as to open a vast field to
desire? She donned her prettiest flowered muslin,
with low neck and short sleeves; but she was so
dismayed at the sight of her bare flesh that she covered her lovely arms with gauze sleeves, and veiled
her breast and shoulders with an embroidered fichu.
The English fashion of arranging the hair seemed
too suggestive, so she destroyed its alluring effect

with a very pretty cap; but with or without a cap
would she have known how to play with her golden
curls, so as to exhibit her slender hand to be admired?—This was her paint; the certainty that
she was about to commit a crime, the deliberate
preparations therefor threw the saintly woman into
a violent fever, which restored the bloom of youth
for the moment. Her eyes shone, her skin fairly
glowed. Instead of assuming a seductive expression she viewed with horror what seemed to her
her dissolute appearance. At Adeline's request
Lisbeth had told her the circumstances of Wenceslas' infidelity, and the baroness then learned to her
unbounded amazement that Madame Marneffe had
made herself the bewitched artist's mistress in a
single evening, in a moment.

"How do these women do it?" she asked Lisbeth.

There is nothing to equal the curiosity of virtuous
women on this subject, for they long to possess
the fascinating powers of vice and remain pure.

"Why they seduce men, it's their business,"
Cousin Bette replied. "You see, my dear, Valérie
was lovely enough that night to damn an angel."

"Pray tell me how she went about it?"

"There's no theory in that trade, it's all practice,"
said Lisbeth jocosely.

The baroness, as she recalled this conversation,
would have liked to consult Cousin Bette; but time
was lacking. Poor Adeline, incapable of inventing
a *patch*, of placing a rose-bud in the middle of her
corsage, of devising wiles of the toilette calculated

to reawaken in men deadened passion, was dressed
with great care, nothing more. Wishing doesn't
make one a courtesan! "Woman is man's soup,"
as Molière jocosely remarks by the mouth of the
sage Gros-René. This simile imagines a sort of
culinary science in love. The virtuous, dignified
wife would then be the Homeric repast, the flesh
thrown upon burning coals. The courtesan on the
other hand would be the repast Carême, with its
condiments, its spices and its dainty appointments.
The baroness could not, did not know how to *serve
up* her white breast in a magnificent dish of guipure
lace, after the style of Madame Marneffe. She did
not know the secret of certain poses, the effect of
certain glances. In short, she had not her secret
thrust. The noble woman might have turned and
turned a hundred times without learning how to
attract the libertine's practised eye.

To be a virtuous *prude*, in the eyes of the world,
and a courtesan to one's husband, is to be a woman
of genius, and there are few such. Therein lies
the secret of long attachments, inexplicable to
women who are not endowed with these two-fold,
sublime qualities. Imagine Madame Marneffe virtuous!—you have the Marquise de Pescara! These
grand and noble women, these lovely and virtuous
Dianes de Poitiers can be counted on one's fingers.

The scene with which this serious and painful
Study of Parisian Morals begins was to be reproduced, with this singular difference that the distress
predicted by the captain of the citizen militia played

a different part therein. Madame Hulot was awaiting Crevel with the purpose in view which had
brought him to her, smiling on the Parisians from
his milord, three years before. And strange to say,
the baroness was faithful to herself, and to her love,
while abandoning herself to the basest of all acts of
infidelity, an act which even the mad ardor of
passion does not condone in the eyes of some
judges.

"What must I do to be a Madame Marneffe?"
she said to herself as she heard the bell ring.

She forced back her tears, the fever imparted
animation to her features, and she promised herself,
poor, noble-hearted creature, that she would act the
courtesan to the life.

"What the devil can good Baroness Hulot want
of me?" Crevel was wondering as he ascended the
broad staircase. "Bah! she wants to talk with me
about my quarrel with Célestine and Victorin; but
I'll not yield an inch!—"

As he entered the salon in following Louise, he
said to himself, taking note of the bareness of the
surroundings—à la Crevel—:

"Poor woman!—here she is like a lovely picture
stowed away in the garret by a man who knows
nothing about painting."

Crevel, who had seen Comte Popinot, Minister of
Commerce, buying pictures and statues, aimed to
make himself illustrious among those Parisian
Mæcenases, whose love for the arts consists in trying to change twenty-sou pieces for twenty-franc

pieces. Adeline welcomed Crevel with a gracious smile, and pointed to a chair near her own.

"Here I am, fair lady, at your service," said he.

The mayor, having become a politician, had adopted black broadcloth. His face appeared above that garb like a full moon surmounting a curtain of dark clouds. His shirt, studded with three huge pearls worth five hundred francs each, gave an exalted idea of his—thoracic capacity, and he seemed to say: "You see in me the future athlete of the tribune!" His great plebeian hands were encased in yellow gloves from early morning. His spotless boots betrayed the little one-horse brown coupé in which he had come. Ambition had somewhat modified his attitude in three years. Like the great painters he had reached his second manner. In society, when he went to the Prince de Wissembourg's, to the prefecture, to Comte Popinot's, etc., he held his hat in his hand in a careless fashion taught him by Valérie, and inserted the thumb of the other hand in the armhole of his waistcoat with a jaunty air, coquetting with his head and eyes. This latest *attitude* was attributable to the mischievous Valérie, who, on the pretext of rejuvenating her mayor, had endowed him with one absurd habit more.

"I asked you to come, dear, kind Monsieur Crevel," said the baroness in a trembling voice, "on business of the utmost importance.—"

"I can guess what it is, madame," said Crevel with a knowing look; "but you ask what is impossible.—Oh! I am not a barbarous father, a man, as

Napoléon said, *of the same length, breadth and height*
in his avarice. Listen to me, dear madame. If
my children ruined themselves for themselves, I
would go to their assistance; but to become surety
for your husband, madame?—why, it's like trying
to fill the cask of the Danaïdes! A house mortgaged
for three hundred thousand francs for an incorrigible
father! They have nothing now, poor creatures!
and they don't seem to find it amusing! Now
they'll have to live on what Victorin can earn at the
Palais. How your precious son does jabber!—Ah!
he ought to be a minister, the little wiseacre! the hope
of us all. A pretty little tug-boat that is idiotically
running aground; for, if he had borrowed money
to help himself along, if he had run in debt for entertaining deputies, or to obtain votes and increase
his influence, I would say to him: 'Here's my purse,
draw on it freely, my boy!' But to pay for papa's
foibles, foibles that I predicted to you! Ah! his
father has thrown him where he'll never come
into power.—I'm the one that's going to be a
minister.—"

"Alas! *dear Crevel*, it's not a question of our
children, poor, devoted creatures!—If your heart is
closed to Victorin and Célestine, I will love them so
dearly that perhaps I can allay the bitter sorrow
your anger has caused them. You punish your
children for a kind action!"

"Yes, for a kind action ill-done! It was a half-
crime!" said Crevel, well pleased with the expression.

"To do well, my dear Crevel," rejoined the baroness, "is not to take money from an overflowing purse! but to endure privation because of one's generosity, to suffer for one's well-doing! to anticipate ingratitude! Heaven takes no account of the charity that costs nothing."

"Saints, madame, are permitted to go to the hospital; they know that it is for them the gate of heaven. I am a worldly creature, I fear God, but I am even more afraid of the hell of poverty. To be penniless is the last degree of misfortune in our present social order. I am of my own time, and I honor money!—"

"You are right," said Adeline, "from the worldly point of view."

She found herself a hundred leagues away from the real question, and when she thought of her uncle she felt like Saint Lawrence on the gridiron; for she fancied that she saw him aiming a pistol at himself. She lowered her eyes, then raised them to Crevel's face, filled with angelic gentleness, and not with the tantalizing lewdness, so seductive in Valérie. Three years before she would have fascinated Crevel with that adorable glance.

"I have known you to be more generous," said she.—"You used to speak of three hundred thousand francs as a great nobleman would.—"

Crevel looked at Madame Hulot, who appeared to him like a lily near the close of its blooming; a vague idea passed through his mind; but he honored the saintly creature so much that he crowded the suspicion back to the libertine side of his heart.

"Madame, I am still the same, but a former merchant is, and should be, a great nobleman with method and economy; he carries his idea of order into everything. He opens an account with his follies, gives them a certain amount of credit, and devotes the profits of certain speculations to that account; but encroach upon his capital!—that would be downright madness. My children will have all that belongs to them: their mother's and mine; but of course they don't want their father to be bored to death, to turn monk or mummy!—I lead a joyous life! I am sailing gayly down the river! I perform all the duties imposed upon me by the law, my heart and my family, just as exactly as I used to take up my notes at maturity. Let my children do as I do in my household and I shall be satisfied; and, so far as the present is concerned, so long as my frolics,—for I sometimes indulge in them, cost nobody anything except the *lambs*—I beg your pardon! you don't know that word; it's used on the Bourse—they will have no right to reproach me, and will still have a handsome fortune at my death. Your children can't say as much of their father, who gambols about, ruining his own son and my daughter.—"

The further she went, the further removed she was from her object.—

"You are very ill-disposed toward my husband, my dear Crevel, and yet you would be his best friend, if you had found his wife a weak woman.—"

She darted a burning glance at Crevel. But in that she was like Dubois, who under the table kicked the Regent too often,—she disguised her real character too much, and his former licentious thoughts returned with such force to the mind of the Regency-perfumer, that he said to himself:

"Would she like to revenge herself on Hulot?— Does she think better of me as mayor than as National Guardsman?—Women are so odd!—"

And he struck an attitude in his second manner, looking at the baroness with a Regency expression.

"One would say," she continued, "that you were revenging yourself upon him for a virtue which held out against you, for a woman whom you loved enough to—to buy her," she added in an undertone.

"For a divine creature," replied Crevel with a meaning smile at the baroness, who lowered her eyes, the lashes wet with tears; "for you have swallowed many a mortfication these last three years,—eh, my dear?"

"Don't speak of my suffering, *dear Crevel;* it has been too much for mere human strength. Ah! if you still loved me you might lift me out of the abyss I am in! Yes, I am in hell! The regicides whose flesh was torn with red-hot pincers, who were drawn and quartered, were on a bed of roses compared to me, for only their bodies were dismembered, and my heart has been torn apart by four horses!—"

Crevel's hand left the armhole of his waistcoat, he laid his hat on the work-table, he abandoned his attitude, he smiled! His smile was so idiotic that the baroness misinterpreted it and took it for an expression of kindliness.

"You see before you a woman, not in despair, but suffering the death agony of honor, and resolved to do anything, *my dear*, to prevent crimes. —"

Fearing lest Hortense should come, she bolted her door; then threw herself impulsively at Crevel's feet, took his hand and kissed it.

"Be my savior!" said she.

She imagined that there might be some generous fibres in his tradesman's heart, and had a sudden gleam of hope that she might obtain the two hundred thousand francs without dishonoring herself.

"You who sought to buy my virtue, buy my heart!—" she continued, gazing wildly into his face. "Trust to my woman's probity, to my honor, well-known to you to be unswerving! Be my friend! Save a whole family from ruin, from disgrace, from despair; save it from wallowing in a slough where the mire will be made of blood! Oh! do not ask me to explain!—" she exclaimed at a gesture from Crevel, who tried to speak. "Above all don't say to me: 'I told you so!' like the fortunate friends of misfortune. Come!—obey her whom you once loved, a woman whose groveling at your feet is perhaps the height of nobleness; ask nothing at her hands, but expect everything

from her gratitude!—No, give me nothing; but lend
to me, lend to her whom you called Adeline!—"

At this point the tears came in such abundance,
and Adeline sobbed so bitterly, that they moistened
Crevel's gloves. The words: "I must have two
hundred thousand francs!" were hardly distinguish-
able in the torrent of tears, just as the stones, thrown
into an Alpine torrent swollen by the melting snow,
however large, make no sound.

Such is the inexperience of virtue. Vice asks for
nothing, as we have seen in the case of Madame
Marneffe, but leads one on to offer everything.
Women of that stamp do not become exacting until
the time comes when they have made themselves
indispensable, or when it is a question with them
of making all they can out of a man, as is done
with a quarry where the stone is becoming scarce,
in ruins, the quarrymen call it. When he heard
the words: "two hundred thousand francs!" Crevel
understood the whole thing. He gallantly raised
the baroness from the floor with this insolent remark: "Come, let's be calm, *my little mother*,"
which Adeline in her excitement did not hear. The
scene changed. Crevel became, to use his own
expression, master of the situation. The enormity
of the amount made such a strong impression upon
him, that his keen emotion on seeing this lovely
woman in tears at his feet melted away. Moreover,
however angelic and saintlike a woman may be,
when she weeps hot tears, her beauty disappears.
The Madame Marneffes snivel a little sometimes,

4

as we have seen; they allow a tear or two to glide
down their cheeks; but as for melting away in tears
and making their eyes and nose red!—they never
make such a mistake as that.

"Come, *my child*, be calm, *sapristi!*" said Crevel
taking lovely Madame Hulot's hands in his and
patting them. "Why do you ask me for two hundred thousand francs? What do you propose to do
with them? who are they for?"

"Don't ask me for any explanation, but give
them to me!—You will have saved the lives of
three people, and our children's honor."

"And do you suppose, my little mother," said
Crevel, "that you will find a man in Paris, who, on
the word of a woman who is almost mad, will go,
hic et nunc, here and now, and take from a drawer
or from somewhere else, no matter where, two hundred thousand francs, which are simmering softly
there, waiting for her to come and skim them? Is
that all you know of life and business, my beauty?
—Your people are very ill, send them the sacraments; for none in Paris, except Her Divine High-
ness Madame la Banque, the illustrious Nucingen,
or some miser who loves gold as madly as we other
men love a woman, can perform such a miracle!
The Civil List, however civil it may be, the Civil
List itself would request you to call again to-morrow.
Every one puts his money out at interest and does
his best to make a profit. You make a mistake,
dear angel, if you think that Louis-Philippe reigns,
and he makes no such mistake himself. He knows,

as we all do, that above the Charter there is the
holy, the venerated, the substantial, the lovable,
the gracious, the lovely, the noble, the young, the
omnipotent hundred-sou piece! Now, my lovely
angel, money demands interest, and is always busy
collecting it! 'God of the Jews, thou rulest!'
said the great Racine. In short, it's the immortal
allegory of the golden calf!—In the time of Moses,
there was stock-jobbing in the desert! We have
gone back to the biblical days! The golden calf
was the first known register of public loans,"
he continued. "You live far too much on Rue
Plumet, my Adeline! The Egyptians owed the
Hebrews enormous sums for borrowed money, and
they did not run after God's people but after their
capital."

He looked at the baroness with an expression
which said: "What a witty creature I am!"

"You don't realize the love of every citizen for
his "little-all!" he resumed after this brief pause.
"I beg your pardon. Mark well what I say!
Try to grasp my argument. You want two hundred thousand francs?—No one can let you have
them without changing investments. Reckon it
up!—In order to get two hundred thousand francs
cash, one must sell what brings in about seven
thousand francs a year at three per cent. Well, you
couldn't get your money in less than two days.
That's the shortest possible time. To induce anyone to part with a fortune—for two hundred thous-
and francs is the whole fortune of many people!—

you ought surely to tell him where it's all going,
for what purpose—''

"My dear, kind Crevel, the lives of two men are
at stake, one of whom will die of grief, the other
will kill himself! And it concerns me, too, for I
shall go mad! Am I not partly so already?''

"Not so mad after all,'' said he taking Madame
Hulot by the knees; "Père Crevel has his price, since
you have deigned to think of him, my angel.''

"It seems that one must allow herself to be taken
by the knees!'' thought the saintly, noble woman,
hiding her face in her hands.—"You offered me a
fortune before,'' she said with a blush.

"Ah! my little lady, that was three years
ago!—'' retorted Crevel. "Oh! you are lovelier
than I have ever seen you!'' he cried, seizing the
baroness's arm and pressing it against his heart.
"*Sapristi!* you have a good memory, dear child.—
Oh! well, just see what a mistake you made in playing the prude! for the three hundred thousand francs
you so nobly refused are in another woman's purse.
I loved you and I love you still; but let us go back
to three years ago. When I said to you: 'I shall
have you!' what was my motive? I wanted to be
revenged on that villain Hulot. Now, my beauty,
your husband took for his mistress a jewel of a
woman, a pearl, an artful little minx, twenty-three
years old at that time, for she's twenty-six to-day.
I concluded that it would be more amusing, more
complete, more Louis XV., more Maréchal de Richelieu, more Corsican, to whisk that charming creature

away from him; besides she never loved Hulot, and for three years she has been mad over your humble servant.—"

As he harangued thus, Crevel, from whose hands the baroness had withdrawn hers, struck his attitude once more. He clung to his armholes, and flapped his arms against his sides like a pair of wings, thinking that he was a desirable and charming object. He seemed to say: "This is the man you turned out of doors!"

"So there we are, my dear child; I had my revenge and your husband knew it. I proved to him categorically that he was duped, what we call *hoist with his own petard.*—Madame Marneffe is *my* mistress; if Monsieur Marneffe die, she will be my wife.—"

Madame Hulot stared at Crevel almost wild-eyed. "Hector knew that?"

"And he went back to her!" replied Crevel, "and I put up with it, because Valérie wanted to be the wife of a chief of bureau; but she swore to me that she would so arrange matters that he should be so thoroughly *mauled* that he would not appear again. And my little duchess—for the woman was born a duchess, on my word of honor!—has kept her word. She has given your Hector back to you, madame, as she wittily said, *virtuous in perpetuity!*—It was a kindly lesson, after all, and the baron has had some harsh ones; he won't keep any more ballet-dancers nor women *comme il faut;* he is radically cured, for he's been rinsed out like a beer-glass. If you had listened to Crevel instead of humiliating him, instead of showing him the door, you would have four hundred thousand francs, for my revenge has cost me all that. But I shall get my money back, I trust, at Marneffe's death.—I have banked on my future. That's the secret of my prodigalities. I have solved the problem of how to be an aristocrat cheaply."

"You would give your daughter such a step-mother?—" cried Madame Hulot.

"You don't know Valérie, madame," replied Hulot gravely, striking an attitude in his earlier manner. "She is well-born, and at the same time a woman who enjoys the highest consideration. For instance the vicar of the parish dined with her yesterday. We have presented the church with a superb monstrance, for she is very devout. Oh! she's a clever, bright, delightful, well-informed woman, and she has everything on her side. As for myself, dear Adeline, I owe the charming creature everything: she has sharpened my wits, as you see, and refined my language; she corrects my flights of fancy and suggests words and ideas to me. I no longer offend propriety by my remarks. People see a great change in me; you must have noticed it. In short she has aroused my ambition. I might be a deputy and I wouldn't make a fool of myself, for I consult my Egeria in the most trivial matters. All the great politicians, including Numa, our present illustrious minister, have had their Cumean Sibyl. Valérie receives a score or so of deputies, she is becoming very influential, and now that she's going to take up her abode in a delightful house with a carriage of her own, she'll be one of the unseen sovereigns of Paris. Such a woman as she, is a great one to get ahead! Ah! I have often thanked you for your harsh treatment!—''

"This would make one doubt the virtue of God Himself," said Adeline, indignation having dried her tears. "But no, the divine justice must hover over that head!—''

"You don't know the world, fair lady," retorted Crevel the great politician, deeply hurt. "The world, my Adeline, loves success! Tell me, does it come in search of your sublime virtue, which you appraise at two hundred thousand francs?''

These words fairly made Madame Hulot shudder, and she was taken with another attack of nervous trembling. She realized that the retired perfumer was taking his revenge on her in a despicable way, as he had taken his revenge on Hulot; her heart rose in disgust, and she was so choked by that sentiment that she could not speak.

"Money!—always money!'' she exclaimed at last.

"You touched me deeply,'' rejoined Crevel, reminded by that exclamation of the woman's abasement, "when I saw you weeping here at my feet!— You don't believe me perhaps, but if I had had my pocket-book it would have been at your service. Tell me, must you have that amount?—''

At this question, pregnant with two hundred thousand francs, Adeline forgot all the outrageous insults of this cheap aristocrat, in face of this enticing hint of possible success held out with such Machiavelian ingenuity by Crevel, who simply wished to get to the bottom of Adeline's secrets in order to laugh over them with Valérie.''

"Oh! I will do anything!'' cried the wretched woman. "Monsieur, I will sell myself,—I will become, if need be, a Valérie.''

"That would be a difficult thing for you to do,'' rejoined Crevel. "Valérie is perfection in her class. My little mother, twenty-five years of virtue always repel a man, like a disease not properly cared for. And your virtue has grown sadly musty here, my dear child. But I'll show you how much I love you. I am going to let you have your two hundred thousand francs.''

Adeline seized Crevel's hand and pressed it against her heart, unable to utter a word, while tears of joy stood in her eyes.

"Oh! wait a bit! there'll be some work to do! I, for my part, am a high liver, a good sort of fellow, without prejudices, and I'm going to tell you frankly just how things stand. You want to be a Valérie—well and good. That isn't enough; you must have a *gogo*, a broker, a Hulot. I know an old fat retired grocer, no he's a hosier. He's a dull, thick-headed creature without an idea in his head; I am forming him and I don't know how soon he will be able to do me credit. My man's a deputy, vain as a peacock and an idiot; kept hitherto in the depths of the provinces by the tyranny of some sort of a creature in a turban, in absolute virginity so far as regards the pleasures and dissipations of Parisian life; but Beauvisage—his name is Beau-visage—is a millionaire, and he would give three hundred thousand francs for the love of a woman *comme il faut,* as I would have done three years ago, my dear little woman.—"Yes," he continued, thinking that he had accurately interpreted Adeline's gesture, "he's jealous of me, you see!—yes, jealous of my good fortune with Madame Marneffe, and he's just the boy to sell a good property to become the proprietor of a—"

"Enough, Monsieur Crevel!" said Madame Hulot, no longer disguising her disgust, and allowing her shame to appear upon her face. "I am punished now more severely than my sin required. My conscience, with such difficulty restrained by the iron hand of necessity, cries out to me at this last insult that such sacrifices are impossible. I have no pride left, I do not lose my temper as I used, and I will not say to you: 'Go!' after receiving this mortal blow. I have lost the right, for I have offered myself to you like a prostitute.—Yes," she continued, replying to a gesture of denial, "I have besmirched my life, hitherto pure, by a degrading purpose; and I have no excuse, I know!—I deserve all the insults with which you crush me! May God's will be done! If He desires the death of two beings who are worthy to go to Him, let them die; I will weep for them, I will pray for them! If He desires the humiliation of our family, let us bow

our heads beneath His avenging sword, and kiss it,
Christians that we are! I know how to expiate
this momentary degradation, which will be the torment of my declining years. Monsieur, it is no
longer Madame Hulot who speaks to you, but the
poor, humble sinner, the Christian whose heart
will contain henceforth but a single sentiment—
repentance; and whose life will be given to charity
and prayer. The power of my sin makes me the
lowest of women and the first of penitents. You
have been the means of my return to reason, and
by the voice of God which now speaks within me,
I thank you!—"

She was trembling with a nervous affection,
which from that moment, never left her. Her sweet
voice was in strong contrast to the feverish words
of the woman who had resolved upon her own dis-
honor to save a family. The blood left her cheeks,
she became pale as death, and her eyes were dry.

"Besides, I played my part very badly, did I
not?" she resumed, looking at Crevel with an expression of such gentleness as the martyrs must
have assumed when looking upon the proconsul.
"True love, the holy and devoted love of a wife,
has other pleasures than those which are sold in the
market of prostitution!—But why these words?"
said she, changing her tone and advancing one step
further toward perfection; "they seem like sarcasm,
and I have none in my heart! forgive me for them.
Indeed, monsieur, it may have been only myself
whom I wished to wound—"

The majesty of virtue, its celestial radiance, had swept away the momentary unchastity of the woman, and now, resplendent with the beauty which was all her own, she seemed vastly greater in Crevel's eyes. At that moment Adeline was as sublime as the figures of Religion, upheld by a cross, which the old Venetians painted; but she made manifest all the grandeur of her own misfortune and that of the Catholic Church, to which she turned for refuge like a wounded dove. Crevel was dazzled, abashed.

"Madame, I am at your service unconditionally!" said he in a burst of generosity. "We will look into the matter, and—What do you want?—is it the impossible?—I will do it. I will deposit consols at the Bank, and within two hours you shall have your money."

"My God, what a miracle!" exclaimed poor Adeline, falling on her knees.

She repeated a prayer with a fervor which affected Crevel so deeply that Madame Hulot saw tears in his eyes when she rose, having finished her prayer.

"Be my friend, monsieur!—" said she. "Your heart is kinder than your acts and your words. God gave you your heart, and you get your ideas from the world and your passions! Oh! I will love you dearly!" she cried with angelic warmth, in strange contrast with her wretched little coquetries.

"Don't tremble so," said Crevel.

"Am I trembling?" asked the baroness, who had

not noticed the infirmity that had come upon her so rapidly.

"Yes, look," said Crevel, taking her arm and pointing out to her how it was shaking. "Come, madame," he added respectfully, "calm yourself; I am off to the Bank.—"

"Return quickly! Consider, my friend," said she, disclosing her secrets, "that it's a question of preventing the suicide of my poor Uncle Fischer, whom my husband has got into trouble; for I have confidence in you now and tell you everything! Oh! if we do not act in time, I know the maréchal so well, he is so sensitive that he would die very soon."

"I go then," said Crevel, kissing the baroness's hand. "But what has poor Hulot done?"

"He has stolen from the State!—"

"Oh! my God!—I fly, madame; I understand you now and admire you."

Crevel bent his knee, kissed the hem of Madame Hulot's dress, and disappeared, saying:

"I will see you again soon!"

*

Unluckily, on his way from Rue Plumet to his
own quarters to get his certificates, Crevel passed
through Rue Vanneau, and he could not resist the
temptation to call upon his little duchess. His face
still bore traces of emotion when he arrived. He
entered Valérie's bedroom and found her having her
hair dressed. She looked at Crevel in the glass,
and like all women of her class, was put out, without knowing why, to see him under the influence
of a strong emotion of which she was not the
cause.

"What's the matter, my buck?" said she. "Is
this the way for a man to come into his little
duchess's room? I wouldn't be a duchess for you,
monsieur, unless I was still your *little louloute*, old
monster!"

Crevel replied with a sad smile, and pointed to
Reine.

"Reine, my girl, enough for to-day; I'll finish
my hair myself. Give me my Chinese silk dressing-gown, for *my gentleman* acts amazingly like *a
Chinaman.—*"

Reine, a maiden whose face was punctured like a
sieve, with the small-pox, and who seemed to have
been made expressly for Valérie, exchanged a smile
with her mistress, and brought the dressing-gown.
Valérie removed her *peignoir*, appeared in her

(61)

chemise, and in a moment was as comfortable in
her dressing-gown as an adder under its tuft of grass.

"Madame is at home to no one?"

"What a question!" said Valérie.—"Come, my
fat old puss, tell me, has the Left Bank gone down?"

"No."

"Somebody's overbid you for the house?"

"No."

"You don't believe you're the father of your little
Crevel?"

"What nonsense!" replied the man who was
sure that she loved him.

"Faith, I'm done then!" said Madame Marneffe.
"When I ought to draw my friend's troubles out of
him, as one draws the cork from a bottle of Bordeaux, I have to leave them all there.—Go away,
you pre—"

"It's nothing," said Crevel.   "I must have two
hundred thousand francs in two hours."

"Oh! you'll find them!   By the way, I haven't
used the fifty thousand francs for the Hulot report,
and I can ask Henri for fifty thousand."

"Henri! always Henri!—" cried Crevel.

"Do you think, you great fat budding Machiavel,
that I'll send Henri away?   Does France disarm
her fleet?—Henri,—why he's the dagger hanging
in its sheath on a nail.   The boy," she continued,
"helps me to find out whether you love me.—And
you don't love me this morning!"

"I don't love you, Valérie!" cried Crevel; "I
love you like a million!"

"That's not enough!—" she retorted, jumping
on his knees and throwing her arms about his neck,
as she might have clung to a *patera*. "I want to be
loved like ten millions, like all the gold in the
world, and more too. Henri would never stay with
me five minutes without telling me what he has in
his heart. Come, what's the matter, my chubby
dear? Let's unload our little cargo.—Let's tell our
little louloute everything, and do it quickly!"

She brushed Crevel's face with her hair and
twisted his nose.

"Can a man have a nose like that," she went on,
"and keep a secret from his Vava-lélé-ririe!—"

At *Vava*, the nose went to the right; at *lélé* to the
left; at *ririe* it resumed its normal position.

"Well, I have just seen—"

Crevel checked himself and looked at Madame
Marneffe.

"Valérie, my bijou, you must promise me on
your honor,—our honor, you know?—not to repeat
a word of what I am going to tell you."

"Stop there, mayor! I hold up my hand, see!—
and my foot!"

She struck an attitude well calculated to make
Crevel, as Rabelais says, *barefoot from his head to
his heels,* so mischievous was she, and so sublime
the charms half visible through the mists of fine
lawn.

"I have just seen virtue in despair!"

"Does virtue ever despair?" said she, shaking
her head and folding her arms à la Napoléon.

"It was poor Madame Hulot; she must have two hundred thousand francs! otherwise the maréchal and Père Fischer will blow their brains out; and as you are in a measure the cause of it all, my little duchess, I propose to repair the evil. Oh! I know her well, she's a saint, and she'll return it all."

At the words "Hulot" and "two hundred thousand francs," Valérie darted a glance between her long lashes, that gleamed like the flash of a cannon through its smoke.

"For God's sake what did the old lady do to arouse your pity? She showed you what? her—her religion?"

"Don't make fun of her, dear heart, for she's a perfect saint, a noble, pious woman, worthy of respect!—"

"So I am not worthy of respect, eh?" said Valérie, with a threatening glance at Crevel.

"I said nothing of the kind," he replied, realizing how much any eulogium of virtue must wound Madame Marneffe.

"I am pious, too," said Valérie, sitting down in an easy-chair; "but I don't make a trade of my religion, I go to church secretly."

She said no more, and paid no more attention to Crevel. Becoming excessively uneasy he went and posed in front of the chair in which she had thrown herself, and found her absorbed by the thoughts he had so idiotically awakened.

"Valérie, my little angel!—"

Absolute silence. An enigmatical tear was furtively wiped away.

"One word, my *louloute.*—"

"Monsieur!"

"What are you thinking about, my love?"

"Ah! Monsieur Crevel, I am thinking of the day of my first communion! How lovely I was! how pure! how like a saint!—immaculate!—Oh! if anyone had come to my mother that day and had said to her: 'Your daughter will be *a harlot,* she will deceive her husband. Some day a police officer will find her in a *petite maison;* she will sell herself to a Crevel to be false to a Hulot, two villainous old men,—' God help me! she'd have died before the end of the sentence, she loved me so dearly, poor woman."

"Calm yourself!"

"You don't know how much one must love a man to silence the remorse that gnaws at the heart of an adulteress. I am sorry Reine has gone; she'd have told you that she found me this morning with tears in my eyes and praying. You see, Monsieur Crevel, I don't make sport of religion. Did you ever hear me say a word I should not have said on that subject?"

Crevel shook his head.

"I forbid people to speak of it in my presence.— I'll chatter away on any subject you please: kings, politics, finance, everything that society holds sacred, judges, marriage, love, young girls, old men!—But the Church!—and God!—Oh! I draw

5

the line at that.   I am well aware that I am doing wrong, that I am sacrificing my future to you.— And you don't even suspect the extent of my love!"

Crevel clasped his hands.

"Ah! you must look into my heart, and measure the depth of my convictions, to realize all that I sacrifice to you!—I feel within me the stuff of which Magdalens are made. Why, see how respectfully I treat the priests! Count up the presents I have made to the church. My mother brought me up in the Catholic faith, and I understand the power of God. We wicked creatures are the ones to whom he speaks in the most awful tones."

Valérie wiped away two tears which were rolling down her cheeks. Crevel was in dismay. She rose to her feet in a state of intense excitement.

"Calm yourself, my *louloute!*" said he; "you frighten me!"

Madame Marneffe fell upon her knees.

"My God! I am not bad at heart!" she cried, clasping her hands. "Deign to gather thy wandering sheep into the fold, strike her and wound her to rescue her from the hands which make of her an infamous adulteress; with joy she will hide her face upon thy shoulder! she will return to the fold the happiest of women!"

She rose and gazed at Crevel, and Crevel was afraid of her white eyes.

"And do you know, Crevel, there are times when I am afraid,—God's laws are enforced in this world as strictly as in the other. What consideration can

I expect at God's hands? His vengeance is wreaked upon the guilty in all sorts of ways; it borrows all the characteristics of misfortune. All the misfortunes which fools can not explain are expiations. That is what my mother told me on her death-bed, speaking of her old age.—And if I should lose you!" she added, seizing Crevel and embracing him with savage energy,—"oh it would kill me!"

Soon she released him, knelt again in front of her chair, clasped her hands—and in what a ravishing attitude—and repeated with incredible fervor the following prayer:

"And you, Sainte Valérie, my kindly patron saint, why do you not more frequently visit her bedside who was entrusted to your care? Oh! come to-night, as you came this morning, to inspire me with righteous thoughts, and I will leave the crooked path; like Magdalen I will renounce the empty joys, the factitious splendor of the world, yes, even the man I love so well!"

"My *louloute!*" said Crevel.

"There is no *louloute* now, monsieur!"

She turned about with the haughty air of a virtuous wife; and confronted him with a cold, dignified, indifferent face, her eyes wet with tears.

"Leave me," she said, repelling him. "What is my duty?—to devote myself to my husband. The man is dying, and what am I doing? I am deceiving him as he stands on the brink of the grave! He believes that your son is his.—I am going to tell him the truth, to begin by purchasing his forgiveness, before seeking God's.   Let us part!—Adieu, Monsieur Crevel!—" she continued standing before him and offering him an ice-cold hand. "Adieu, my friend, we shall meet again only in a better world.—You are indebted to me for some enjoyment, very criminal, it is true; but now I long for,—yes, I will have your esteem."

Crevel was weeping copiously.

"You great donkey!" she burst out, with a shriek of infernal laughter, "that's the way your pious women go to work to do you out of a paltry two hundred thousand francs! And you talk about the Maréchal de Richelieu, the prototype of Lovelace, and then allow yourself to be taken in by such trumpery balderdash! as Steinbock says. I would screw two hundred thousand francs out of you if I wanted them, you great gaby!—So keep your money! If you have any too much, the too much belongs to me! If you give two sous to that respectable dame, who plays at piety because she's fifty-seven years old, we shall see each other no more, and you can take her for your mistress; you'll come back to me the next day all sore from her angular fondlings; and surfeited with her tears, her *skimpy* little caps, and her whimpering, which must make her favors resemble a heavy shower!—"

"The fact is," said Crevel, "that two hundred thousand francs is a tidy sum."

"These pious women have a hearty appetite!— Ah! *microscope!* they sell their sermons at a better price than we get for the rarest and most reliable

thing on earth,—pleasure. And they write novels!
No?—ah! but I know them, I've seen some of them in
my mother's house! They think they're at liberty
to do anything for the Church, for—Why, you
ought to be ashamed of yourself, my buck! you,
who are so little inclined to give—for you haven't
given me two hundred thousand francs in all!''

"Oh yes!'' said Crevel, "the little house alone
will cost that.''

''So you have four hundred thousand francs,
have you?'' she asked pensively.

"No.''

''Very well, monsieur! you proposed to lend that
old horror the two hundred thousand francs that
were to pay for my house, did you? That's *lèse-
loulvule!*''

''But just listen to me!''

''If you were giving the money to some absurd
philanthropical fad, you would be looked upon as a
man of the future,'' said she warming to her subject,
''and I would be the first to advise you to do it; for
you're too innocent to write thick volumes on politics, that would make your reputation; you haven't
style enough to write pamphlets filled with nothing
at all; you might pose as other men do who are in
your position, and who cover their names with
glory by putting themselves at the head of some
social, moral, national or general undertaking.
Benevolence you've been anticipated in; it's
thought but little of now.—Ex-convicts who meet
with a better fate than poor, honest devils, are

played out. I would like to see you think up something harder, something really useful, for your two hundred thousand francs. You would be talked about as if you were a *little blue cloak*, as a Montyon, and I should be proud of you! But to throw two hundred thousand francs into a holy-water vase, to loan them to a devotee abandoned by her husband for some reason or other—there's always a reason, you know, for am I abandoned, pray?—would be a crazy idea which, in these days, could take root nowhere else than in the skull of an ex-perfumer! It smells of his counting-house. Two days after you wouldn't dare look at yourself in your mirror! Go and deposit your money in the sinking-fund; hurry, for I won't receive you again without a receipt for the amount. Go! go at once and quickly!"

She pushed Crevel out of the room by the shoulders, when she saw avarice blooming again upon his face. When the outer door of the suite was secured, she said to herself:

"Lisbeth's more than revenged now!—What a pity she's at the old maréchal's; how we would have laughed! Aha! so the old lady wants to take the bread out of my mouth!—I'll give her a good shaking for you!"

*

Being obliged to occupy apartments in keeping
with the highest military dignity, Maréchal Hulot
had taken up his quarters in a superb mansion on
Rue du Mont-Parnasse, where the establishments of
several princes were located. Although he had
hired the whole house he occupied only the ground-
floor. When Lisbeth came to keep house for him
she at once wanted to sub-let the first-floor, which,
she said, would pay the whole rent, so that the
count could have his own quarters for almost nothing;
but the old soldier refused. For several months the
maréchal's mind had been much troubled. He had
divined his sister-in-law's distress; he suspected
that things were going wrong without detecting the
cause. The old fellow, usually so cheerful in his
deafness, became taciturn; he imagined that his
house would some day become a place of refuge for
Baroness Hulot and her daughter, and he was re-
serving the first floor for them. Comte de Forzheim's moderate circumstances were so well known,
that the Prince de Wissembourg, Minister of War,
had insisted upon it that his old comrade should
accept an allowance to defray the expense of setting
up his establishment. Hulot used this allowance to
furnish the ground-floor, where everything was in
harmony with his rank, for, as he himself expressed
it, he did not want his maréchal's baton in order to

carry it on foot. The mansion having been the
property of a Senator under the Empire, the salons
on the ground-floor were decorated with great magnificence, all white and gold, with much carved
work, and were well preserved.   The maréchal had
furnished them with handsome old furniture in
keeping with the decorations.   He kept a carriage
in the carriage-house, with the two crossed batons
painted on the panels, and he hired horses when he
had to go out in state, to the ministry or the châ-
teau, for some ceremonial, or some holiday. For
thirty years he had had as a servant an old soldier,
now sixty years old, whose sister was his cook, so
that he was able to save something like ten thous-
and francs a year, which he added to a little hoard
intended for Hortense.   Every day the old man
went on foot from Rue du Mont-Parnasse to Rue
Plumet by the boulevard; every veteran, when he
saw him approaching, invariably drew up as if on
parade and saluted him, and the maréchal as invariably rewarded him with a smile.

"Who is that man you drew yourself up so
straight for?" a young mechanic one day asked an
old captain of the Invalides.

"I'll tell you, boy," was the reply.

The young fellow assumed the pose of a man who
resigns himself to listen to a garrulous old dotard.

"In 1809," said the veteran, "we were covering
the flank of the *Grande Armée*, commanded by the
Emperor, who was marching upon Vienna. We
came to a bridge defended by a triple battery of

cannons terraced on a sort of cliff, three redoubts one above the other, which raked the bridge. We were under Maréchal Massena. That man yonder was colonel of the grenadiers of the Guard, and I was marching with — Our columns were on one side of the river, the redoubts on the other. Three times they attacked the bridge and three times they were driven back. 'Send for Hulot!' said the maréchal; 'no one but he and his men can swallow that tid-bit.' We came up. The last general to be driven back from the bridge stopped Hulot under fire to tell him how to go to work, and he blocked up the road. 'I don't need advice, but room to pass,' said the general coolly, crossing the bridge at the head of his column—And then, hurrah! thirty guns opening fire on us—"

"Ah! bless my soul!" cried the workman, "that must have been where you got those crutches!"

"If you had heard him say that in the coolest way, as I did, my boy, you would salute that man till your hat touched the ground! That little affair isn't so well known as the Bridge of Arcola, but it was even finer perhaps. And in due course we were in among the batteries with Hulot. Honor to those who remained there!" exclaimed the officer removing his hat. "The *kaiserlicks* were taken by surprise. So the Emperor made the old man you see a count; he honored us all in our leader, and these new fellows have done very well to make him a maréchal."

"Vive le maréchal!" exclaimed the workman.

"Oh! you can shout as loud as you please; the maréchal's deaf from listening to the cannon."

This anecdote will give an idea of the respect with which the veterans treated Maréchal Hulot, whose unchanging republican opinions won for him the popular regard throughout the quarter.

It was a heart-rending spectacle to see that pure and calm and noble heart suffering so intensely. The baroness could only lie and, with a woman's skill, conceal the whole terrible truth from her brother-in-law. During this disastrous morning, the maréchal, who like all men of his years slept but little, had obtained some information as to his brother's situation from Lisbeth, by promising to marry her as the reward of her indiscretion. Every one will understand the old maid's delight in allowing confidences to be extorted from her, which she had fully intended to make to her future spouse ever since she came beneath his roof; for in this way she would the better assure her marriage.

"Your brother is incurable!" Lisbeth shouted into the maréchal's good ear.

The Lorrainer's strong, distinct voice made it possible for her to talk with the old man. She tired out her lungs, so intent was she upon demonstrating to her future consort that he would never be deaf with her.

"He has had three mistresses," said the old man," and he had an Adeline!—Poor Adeline!"

"If you take my advice," cried Lisbeth, "you

will use your influence with the Prince de Wissembourg to obtain an honorable position for my cousin;
she will need it, for the baron's salary is assigned
for three years."

"I will go to the department," he said, "see the
maréchal, find out what he thinks about my brother,
and ask his active protection for my sister. The
idea of finding a place worthy of her!"

"The ladies who distribute alms in Paris have
formed benevolent associations with the arch-
bishop's concurrence; they need women to serve as
inspectors, who are employed to find out those
really in need, and are handsomely paid. Such
duties would suit my dear Adeline, they would be
after her own heart."

"Send for the horses," said the maréchal; "I am
going to dress. I'll go to Neuilly if necessary!"

"How he loves her! So I am to find her in my
way, always and everywhere!" muttered the Lorrainer.

Lisbeth was already queen of the household, but
out of the maréchal's sight. She had inspired the
three servants with dread. She had taken unto
herself a maid, and exerted her old-maid energy in
requiring a strict account of everything, peering
into everything, and seeking to promote her dear
maréchal's well-being in every respect. As strong
a republican as her spouse that was to be, Lisbeth
pleased him mightily with her democratic notions,
and she flattered him too with amazing talent; so
that within the last two weeks, the maréchal, finding

that he lived better, and was as carefully looked after as a child by its mother, had at last concluded that Lisbeth was part of his dream.

"My dear maréchal," she screamed, accompanying him out to the steps, "put up the windows; don't sit in a draught, for my sake!—"

The maréchal, who had never been coddled, old bachelor that he was, smiled at Lisbeth as he drove away, although his heart was broken.

At that very moment Baron Hulot left the offices of the War Department, and bent his steps to the cabinet of the Maréchal Prince de Wissembourg, who had sent for him. Although there was nothing extraordinary in the mere fact of the minister's sending for one of his directors-general, Hulot's conscience was so ill at ease, that Mitouflet's face seemed strangely cold and forbidding.

"How's the Prince, Mitouflet?" he asked, closing his office, and overtaking the usher, who had gone on before.

"He must have a rod in pickle for you, Monsieur le Baron, for his voice and look and face are set for storms."

Hulot turned pale and said no more; he passed through the reception-room and the salons, and reached the door of the cabinet, with his heart beating tumultuously. The maréchal, at this time seventy years old, with snow-white hair, and the swarthy face common to men of his age, commanded respect by a brow of such amplitude that the imagination could see a whole battle-field thereon.

Beneath that snow-laden cupola, and shadowed by
the very pronounced projection of two overhanging
eyebrows, gleamed eyes of a Napoleonic blue,
ordinarily sad, because of the bitter thoughts and
regrets reflected therein. This rival of Bernadotte
had hoped to find repose upon a throne. But those
eyes became two awe-inspiring lightning flashes
when any intense emotion called on them for expression. The voice, almost always cavernous, at
such times came forth in sharp, strident tones. In
his wrath the prince became a soldier once more,
and spoke the language of Sub-lieutenant Cottin;
he paid no heed to anything or anybody.

Hulot d'Ervy espied the old lion, whose hair was
as scanty as a horse's mane, standing near the
fire-place with his back against the mantel, his eyebrows drawn together, and his eyes apparently gazing into space.

"I am here at your command, my prince," said
Hulot gracefully and with an unconcerned demeanor.

The maréchal gazed fixedly at the director without
speaking a word while he walked from the door to
within a few steps of him. This leaden glance was
like the glance of God; Hulot could not meet it, but
lowered his eyes in confusion.

"He knows all," he thought.

"Has your conscience nothing to say to you?"
asked the maréchal in his deep, grave voice.

"It tells me, my prince, that I probably did
wrong to make *razzias* in Algeria without mentioning it to you. After forty-five years of service I

am without fortune, at my age and with my tastes.
You know the principles that guide the four hundred elect of France. These gentlemen are envious
of every office-holder; they pare down the salaries
of ministers, that tells the story!—go and ask them
for money for an old servant!—What is one to
expect from people who pay in such niggardly
fashion as they pay the magistracy to-day? who
give thirty sous a day to mechanics in the port of
Toulon, when it's a physical impossibility to live
there for less than forty sous for a family? who
do not reflect on the atrocity of paying clerks six
hundred, a thousand, and twelve hundred francs a
year in Paris, and who want our places for themselves when the salary is forty thousand?—lastly,
who refuse to give up to the crown a parcel of
crown-property, confiscated to the crown in 1830,—
and a purchase made with Louis the Sixteenth's
money at that!—when they were asked to do it for
the benefit of a needy prince!—If you had no fortune, prince, they would leave you, as they have
my brother, high and dry, with nothing but your
salary, without remembering that you saved the
Grande Armée, with me by your side, in the
marshy plains of Poland."

"You have robbed the State! you have put yourself in a position where you're liable to be dragged
before the Assize Court, as the cashier of the
Treasury was," exclaimed the maréchal, "and you
take it as flippantly as this?"

"But what a difference, monseigneur!" cried

Hulot. "Have I plunged my hands in a treasure-chest that was placed in my charge?"

"When a man commits such infamous crimes," said the maréchal, "he is guilty twice over, occupying the position you occupy, if he does things bunglingly. You have compromised most shamefully, the responsible administration of our department, which hitherto has been the purest in Europe! —And that, monsieur, for two hundred thousand francs and a strumpet!—" roared the maréchal in a voice of thunder. "You are a Councilor of State, and the private soldier who sells the property of his regiment is punished with death. Listen to what Colonel Pourin of the Second Lancers told me one day. At Saverne one of his men fell in love with a little Alsatian girl, who was very anxious to have a shawl; the hussy was so persistent that the lancer, who was on the point of being promoted to be sergeant-major after twenty years' service, and was the pride of his regiment, sold the company property in order to give her the shawl. Do you know what the lancer did, Baron d'Ervy? He pounded up the glass out of his window and ate it, and died of the trouble in the hospital, in eleven hours.—Do your best to die of apoplexy, so that we can save your honor."

The baron looked at the old war-horse, with haggard eyes; and the maréchal, observing his expression, which betrayed a coward, felt the color mount to his cheeks, and his eyes gleamed.

"Would you abandon me?" stammered Hulot.

At that moment Maréchal Hulot, having learned that his brother and the minister were closeted together, took the liberty of walking in, and went as a deaf man would, straight to the prince.

"Oh!" cried the hero of the Poland campaign, "I know what you have come for, my old comrade!—But it's all useless."

"Useless?—" repeated Maréchal Hulot, who heard only the last word.

"Why, yes, you have come to speak in your brother's behalf; but do you know what your brother is?"

"My brother?—" demanded the deaf man.

"Well, he's a damned scoundrel, unworthy of your affection!" cried the maréchal.

And his wrath caused his eyes to send forth lightning-like glances, similar to those with which Napoléon shattered men's minds and brains.

"You lie, Cottin!" retorted Maréchal Hulot, pale as death. "Throw away your bâton as I do mine! —I am at your service."

The prince walked up to his old comrade, gazed earnestly in his face, and said in his ear as he pressed his hands:

"Are you a man?"

"You shall see."

"Well then, be strong! for you have to endure the greatest misfortune that can happen to you."

The prince turned, took a bundle of papers from his table, and put it into Maréchal Hulot's hands.

"Read!" he shouted.

The Comte de Forzheim read the following letter, which was within the package:

"TO HIS EXCELLENCY THE PRESIDENT OF THE COUNCIL.

"*Confidential.*

"MY DEAR PRINCE:

"ALGIERS, * * * *

"We have an extremely unpleasant business on our hands, as you will see by the documents I send you herewith:

"In brief, Baron Hulot d'Ervy sent one of his uncles to the province of Oran to dabble in grain and forage, and furnished him with a storekeeper for confederate. This storekeeper confessed, in order to make himself notorious, and ended by running away. The king's attorney pushed the affair somewhat roughly, seeing only two subordinates concerned; but Johann Fischer, your director-general's uncle, finding that he was on the point of being brought before the Court of Assizes, stabbed himself in prison with a nail.

"That would have been the end of the incident, had not that upright and respectable man, who was probably deceived both by his nephew and his confederate, undertaken to write to Baron Hulot. His letter, which fell into the hands of the prosecuting authorities, so astounded the king's attorney, that he came to me. The arrest and prosecution of a Councilor of State, a director-general, who has such a record of faithful and valuable service,—for he saved us all after the Bérésina by reorganizing the administration,—would be such a terrible blow, that I caused all the papers to be sent to me.

"Must the affair take its course? Or, the principal apparent culprit being dead, shall we stifle the prosecution by convicting the storekeeper by default?

"The *procureur-général* consents that the papers be sent to you; and as Baron d'Ervy has his domicile at Paris, the prosecution will properly be carried on in your Royal Court.

6

We have invented this method, somewhat devious, I admit, of getting rid of the difficulty for the moment.

"But, my dear maréchal, make up your mind promptly. There is already too much gossip about this deplorable business, which would be a vastly more serious matter for us, if the complicity of the principal culprit, who is as yet known only to the king's attorney, the examining magistrate, the *procureur-général* and myself, should be bruited abroad."

The paper fell from Maréchal Hulot's hands; he glanced at his brother and saw that it was useless to examine the other papers; but he took out Johann Fischer's letter, and handed it to him after running his eye over it.

"FROM THE PRISON AT ORAN.

"My nephew, when you read this letter I shall have ceased to live.

"Have no fear, for they will find no evidence against you. With me dead and your jesuit of a Chardin out of the way, the prosecution will come to an end. The face of our Adeline, made happy by you, makes death very sweet to me. You need not send the two hundred thousand francs. Adieu.

"This letter will be handed you by a prisoner whom I think I can trust.

"JOHANN FISCHER."

"I beg your pardon," said Maréchal Hulot, with touching pride, to the Prince de Wissembourg.

"Come, come, let things be as always between us, Hulot!" replied the minister pressing his old friend's hand.—"The poor lancer killed nobody but himself," he added, with a withering glance at Hulot d'Ervy.

"How much have you taken?" the Comte de Forzheim sternly demanded of his brother.

"Two hundred thousand francs."

"My dear friend," said the comte, addressing the minister, "you shall have the two hundred thousand francs within forty-eight hours. It shall never be said that a man bearing the name of Hulot cheated the public out of a sou."

"What childish nonsense!" said the maréchal. "I know where the two hundred thousand francs are, and I propose to compel restitution.—Send in your resignation, and ask to be placed on the retired list!" he continued, tossing a double sheet of foolscap across the table to where the Councilor of State had taken a seat, for his legs refused to support him. "Your prosecution would disgrace us all, so I have obtained the consent of the Council of Ministers to act as I am acting. As you accept life without honor, without my esteem, a life of degradation, you shall have the retiring pension which is your due. But blot yourself out of everybody's memory."

He rang.

"Is Marneffe here?"

"Yes, monseigneur," said the usher.

"Send him to me."

"You and your wife," cried the minister as Marneffe entered, "have designedly ruined Baron d'Ervy here."

"Monsieur le Ministre, I beg your pardon, but we are very poor; I have only my salary to live on, and I have two children, the last one of whom will have been brought into my family by Baron Hulot."

"What a gallows-bred face!" said the prince to Maréchal Hulot.—"Enough of your snivelling," he continued; "you will return two hundred thousand francs, or go to Algeria."

"But, *Monsieur le Ministre,* you don't know my wife; she has spent it all. Monsieur le Baron invited six people to dinner every day.—They spent fifty thousand a year at my house."

"Go," said the minister in the thundering tone with which he sounded the charge in the midst of a battle; "you will receive notice of your transfer in two hours. Go."

"I prefer to resign," said Marneffe impudently; "for it's too much to be what I am, and be beaten; I shouldn't be satisfied."

And he left the room.

"What an impudent rascal!" said the prince.

Maréchal Hulot, who had remained standing throughout this scene, motionless as a statue and pale as a corpse, covertly glancing at his brother, took the prince's hand, and said again:

"In forty-eight hours the material wrong will be repaired; but honor!—Adieu, maréchal! it's the last blow that kills.—Yes, it will kill me," he whispered.

"Why the devil did you come this morning?" replied the prince, deeply moved.

"I came on his wife's account," replied the comte, pointing to Hector; "she is without bread,—now more than ever."

"He has his retiring pension!"

"It's assigned!"

"He must have the very devil in him!" said the prince, with a shrug. "What sort of a love draught do these women give you to take your mind away?" he asked the baron. "How could you, knowing as you do the minute exactness with which the French government makes a record of everything, requires reports of everything and uses up reams of paper in verifying the receipt or disbursement of a few centimes,—you, who used to deplore the necessity of obtaining a hundred signatures for the merest trifles, to liberate a soldier, or buy a curry-comb,—how could you hope to conceal such a theft for any length of time? And the newspapers? And the men who envy you? And the men who'd like a chance to steal? Do the hussies take away your common sense? do they put walnut-shells over your eyes? or are you made differently from us? You should leave the government the minute you cease to be a man, and become a mass of sentiment! If you have been guilty of so many idiotic performances in addition to your crime, you'll end,—I don't want to tell you where."

"Promise me to look out for her, Cottin, won't you?—" said the Comte de Forzheim, who heard nothing of what was said, and was thinking of his sister-in-law alone.

"Never fear!" said the minister.

"Very well; thanks, and adieu!—Come, monsieur," he said to his brother.

The prince cast an apparently unmoved glance at the two brothers, so strongly contrasted in attitude, in build and character, the brave man and the coward, the man of rigid virtue and the voluptuary, the upright man and the peculator,—and he said to himself:

"That dastard will not know enough to die! and my poor, incorruptible Hulot has death in his pocket!"

He sat down at his desk and resumed his perusal of the despatches from Africa, with a gesture which expressed at once the sang-froid of the brave captain, and the profound pity caused by the sight of a battle-field; for there is no class of men so tender-hearted in reality, as are the soldiers, who seem so unfeeling, because familiarity with war imparts to them the cold, unmoved demeanor that is so essential on the battle-field.

The next morning some of the newspapers contained the following articles under various headings:

" Monsieur le Baron Hulot d'Ervy has asked to be retired. The irregularities in the accounts of the Algerian administration, which have been disclosed by the death of one clerk and the flight of another, had much to do with the step taken by this prominent member of the administration. Upon being informed of the crimes committed by employés, in whom unfortunately he had placed his confidence, Monsieur le Baron Hulot was stricken with paralysis in the minister's cabinet.

" Monsieur Hulot d'Ervy, the brother of the maréchal, has been in the service of the nation forty-five years. His present resolution, which he has been urged to reconsider, but to no purpose, is viewed with much regret by all those who know

Monsieur Hulot, whose private qualities equal his administrative talents. No one has forgotten the devoted service of the Commissary-in-Chief of the Imperial Guard at Warsaw, nor the marvelous activity with which he organized the different branches of the army hastily got together by Napoléon in 1815.

"Another of the glories of the Imperial era is about to leave the stage. Since 1830 Monsieur le Baron Hulot has constantly been one of the indispensable luminaries in the Council of State and the Ministry of War."

"ALGIERS.—The affair known as the forage affair, to which certain newspapers have attributed an absurdly disproportionate importance, is concluded by the death of the principal culprit. Monsieur Johann Wisch committed suicide in prison, and his confederate has fled; but he will be convicted by default.

"Wisch, formerly an army contractor, was an honest man and highly esteemed, and could not endure the thought that he had been the dupe of Chardin, the fugitive storekeeper."

And among the Parisian news appeared the following:

"Monsieur le Maréchal, Minister of War, to avoid all future irregularity, has determined to create a bureau of subsistence in Africa. Monsieur Marneffe, chief of one of the bureaus, is appointed to organize this new department."

"The question of the succession to Baron Hulot excites the keenest rivalry. The directorship has been promised, so it is said, to Monsieur le Comte Martial de la Roche-Hugon, a deputy and brother-in-law of Monsieur le Comte de Rastignac. Monsieur Massol, Master of Requests, will be appointed Councilor of State, and Monsieur Claude Vignon Master of Requests."

Of all varieties of *canards*, the most dangerous to opposition newspapers is the official canard. However shrewd journalists may be, they are sometimes the dupes, voluntary or involuntary, of the skill of those men, who have risen, like Claude Vignon, from the newspaper office to the exalted regions of power. The newspaper, it may be said, can be put down by the newspaper man, and by no one else. So we might say, paraphrasing Voltaire:

The news of Paris is simply what a vain people think.

*

Maréchal Hulot drove back to his own house with his brother, who sat in the front seat of the carriage, respectfully leaving the back seat to his elder. The two did not exchange a word. Hector was completely crushed. The maréchal sat in deep thought, like a man who was collecting all his forces and binding them together to sustain a crushing weight. When they reached the house he led the way to his study, without a word but with an imperative gesture. The comte had received from the Emperor Napoléon a superb pair of pistols from the factory at Versailles; he took the case, on which this inscription was engraved: *Presented by the Emperor Napoléon to General Hulot,* from the secretary in which he kept it, and showed it to his brother.

"There's your doctor," he said.

Lisbeth, who was peeping through the half-opened door, ran out to the carriage, and ordered the coachman to drive at full speed to Rue Plumet. In about twenty minutes she brought back the baroness, telling her on the way of the maréchal's threat to his brother.

The comte, meanwhile, without looking at his brother, rang for his factotum, the old soldier who had been in his service thirty years.

"Beau-Pied," said he, "bring my notary here, also Comte Steinbock, my niece Hortense, and the

(89)

transfer clerk from the Treasury. It is half-past
ten and I must have them all here at noon. Take
carriages,—and go *quicker than that!*"—he added,
resorting to a republican phrase which at one time
was often in his mouth.

And he made the awe-inspiring grimace which
used to keep his soldiers attentive to their duties
when he was searching the thickets of Brittany in
1799.—See *The Chouans.*—

"You shall be obeyed, maréchal," said Beau-Pied,
putting the back of his hand to his forehead.

Without paying any heed to his brother, the
veteran returned to his cabinet, took a key that
was concealed in a secretary, and opened a casket
made of malachite laid upon steel, a present from
the Emperor Alexander. By order of the Emperor
Napoléon, he had gone to return to the Russian
Emperor certain private property taken at the battle of Dresden, in exchange for which Napoléon
hoped to obtain Vandamme. The Czar rewarded
General Hulot handsomely by the gift of this
casket, and said to him that he hoped to be able
some day to perform a similar act of courtesy to
the Emperor of the French,—but he kept Vandamme.
The Imperial arms of Russia in gold were on the
cover, and all the trimmings of the box were gold.
The maréchal counted the bank-notes and gold,
which the casket contained; he possessed one hundred and fifty-two thousand francs! He allowed a
gesture of satisfaction to escape him. At that
moment Madame Hulot entered in a state to move

even political judges to compassion. She threw herself upon Hector, glancing from the box of pistols to the maréchal, with a wild look in her eyes.

"What have you against your brother? What has my husband done to you?" she demanded in so piercing a voice that the maréchal heard it.

"He has disgraced us all!" replied the veteran of the Republic, reopening one of his wounds by the effort. "He has stolen from the State! He has made my name odious; he makes me long to die, he has killed me.—I have strength enough left to make restitution and no more!—I have been humiliated before the Condé of the Republic, before the man whom I esteem above all others, and to whom I unjustly gave the lie,—the Prince de Wissembourg!—Is all that nothing? That's his account with his country!"

He wiped away a tear.

"And now for his family!" he continued. "He snatches from your mouths the bread I was saving for you, the fruit of the savings of thirty years, the hoard amassed by the old soldier's privations! There's what I intended for you!" he added, pointing to the bank-notes. "He has killed his uncle Fischer, a noble, worthy son of Alsace, who could not, as he can, endure the thought of a stain upon his peasant's name. And last of all, God with unspeakable kindness allowed him to make choice of an angel among all the women in the world! he had the incredible good fortune to take for his wife an Adeline! and he has betrayed her, he has made her drink the cup of sorrow, he has deserted her for strum-pets, for street-walkers, for dancing-girls, actresses, Joséphas, Cadines, Marneffes!—And that's the man whom I looked upon as my child, who was my pride!—Begone, unhappy man, if you accept the infamous life you have made for yourself, leave this house! I haven't the strength to curse a brother I have loved so dearly; I am as weak where he is concerned as you are, Adeline; but let me never see his face again. I forbid him to attend my funeral, to follow my coffin. May he have the shame of crime, if he has no remorse."

The maréchal, deadly pale, fell upon the couch in his study, exhausted by this solemn harangue. And, for the first time in his life perhaps, two tears fell from his eyes and made a furrow down his cheeks.

"My poor uncle Fischer!" cried Lisbeth with a handkerchief at her eyes.

"Brother!" said Adeline, kneeling at the mar-échal's feet, "live for me! Help me in the task I will undertake of reconciling Hector to life, of mak-ing him atone for his sins!"

"He!" cried the maréchal; "if he lives, he's not at the end of his crimes yet! A man who has failed to appreciate an Adeline, and who has extinguished in his heart those sentiments which make the true republican, the love of country, of his family, and of the poor, which I strove to inculcate in him,— that man is a monster, a hog.—Take him away if you still love him, for I hear a voice within me

crying to me to load my pistols and blow his brains
out! By killing him I should save you all, and I
should save him from himself."

The old maréchal sprang to his feet with such an
alarming gesture that poor Adeline, crying "Come,
Hector!" seized her husband, and left the house,
almost dragging the baron, whom she was obliged
to put in a carriage to transport him to Rue Plumet,
where he took to his bed. He remained there several days without speaking, completely prostrated
and refusing all nourishment. Adeline, by dint of
much weeping, induced him to swallow a little soup;
she nursed him, sitting constantly by his bedside,
and feeling, of all the sentiments that formerly filled
her heart, naught but profound pity.

At half-past twelve Lisbeth, who dared not leave
her dear maréchal, so terrified was she by the change
that had taken place in him, ushered in the notary
and Comte Steinbock.

"Monsieur le Comte," said the maréchal, "I beg
you to sign the necessary document to authorize my
niece, your wife, to sell a certificate of stock, in
which she now has a reversionary interest only.—
Mademoiselle Fischer, you will surrender your interest in the income and acquiesce in this sale?"

"Yes, dear comte," said Lisbeth without hesita-
tion.

"Very well, my dear," said the veteran. "I
hope to live long enough to reward you. I did not
doubt you; you are a true republican, a daughter of
the people."

He took the old maid's hand and deposited a kiss upon it.

"Monsieur Hannequin," he said to the notary, "prepare the necessary document in the form of a power of attorney, so that I may have it two hours hence and be able to sell the stock on the Bourse to-day. My niece, the comtesse, holds the title; she is coming, and will sign the power when you bring it, as will mademoiselle. Monsieur le Comte will go with you to your office to affix his signature."

The artist, at a signal from Lisbeth, bowed respectfully to the maréchal and went away.

The next morning at ten o'clock the Comte de Forzheim sent in his name to the Prince de Wissembourg, and was at once admitted.

"Well, my dear Hulot," said Maréchal Cottin offering his old friend the newspapers, "we have saved appearances, you see. Read."

Maréchal Hulot laid the papers on the minister's desk, and held out the two hundred thousand francs.

"Here's the amount my brother took from the State," said he.

"What folly" cried the minister. "It's impossible," he added, taking the ear-trumpet the maréchal handed him, and speaking into his ear, "for us to manage a restitution. We should be compelled to admit your brother's peculations, and we have done everything under heaven to conceal them."

"Do what you choose with it; but I don't propose that there shall be a liard that has been stolen from

the State in the coffers of the Hulot family," said
the comte.

"I will take the king's orders on this subject.
Let us say no more about it," replied the minister,
realizing the impossibility of overcoming the old
man's sublime obstinacy.

"Adieu, Cottin," said he, taking the prince's
hand, "I feel as if my heart were frozen."

He took a step or two, then turned and looked at
the prince, and seeing that he was deeply moved,
opened his arms, and the two veterans embraced.

"It seems to me that I am bidding adieu to the
whole *Grande Armée* in your person. Farewell, my
dear old comrade!" said the minister.

"Yes, farewell, for I am going where all our old
comrades for whom we have wept have gone."

At that moment Claude Vignon came in. The
two old relics of the Napoleonic phalanxes bowed
gravely, banishing all traces of emotion.

"You ought to be satisfied with the tone of the
newspapers, my prince," said the future master of
requests. "I arranged matters so as to make the
opposition sheets believe that they were publishing
our secrets."

"Unfortunately, it's all of no avail," replied the
minister looking after Hulot, as he walked away
through the salon. "I have just bade that man
adieu for the last time, and it has nearly broken my
heart! Maréchal Hulot hasn't three days to live; I
saw it yesterday plainly enough. That man,
whose sturdy honesty is almost divine, a soldier

respected by the cannon-balls; despite his gallantry
—see! in that chair, yonder—received his death-
blow, at my hand, from a paper!—Ring and order
my carriage. I am going to Neuilly," he said, placing the two hundred thousand francs in his minis-
terial portfolio.

Notwithstanding Lisbeth's devoted care, Maréchal Hulot died three days later. Such men are the
honor of the parties they espouse. To republicans
the maréchal was the ideal of patriotism; so they
were all at his funeral, which was followed by an
immense crowd. The army, the government, the
court, the people, all ranks and classes assembled
to do homage to his exalted virtue, his unswerving
probity, his spotless renown. May not any man
who desires it have the people at his funeral?
These obsequies were signalized by one of those
outbursts of delicacy, good taste, and kindness of
heart, which come at long intervals, to recall the
great virtues and the glory of the nobility of France.
Behind the coffin of the maréchal walked the aged
Marquis de Montauran, brother of the man, who, when
the Chouans took up arms in 1799, was the adversary, and the unsuccessful adversary, of Hulot. The
marquis, when dying from wounds received at the
hands of the Blues, entrusted his young brother's
interests to the soldier of the Republic—See *The
Chouans*.—

Hulot accepted the nobleman's verbal legacy
in good faith, and succeeded in saving the property
of the young man, then an *émigré*. So it was that

the homage of the old French nobility was not wanting at the obsequies of the soldier, who, nine years before, had vanquished MADAME.

The maréchal's death, happening as it did four days before the last publication of her marriage, was to Lisbeth the lightning stroke which burns the crop after it is safely housed, with the barn that contains it. The Lorrainer, as often happens, had succeeded too well. The death of the maréchal was due to the blows aimed at the family by herself and Madame Marneffe. The old maid's hatred, which seemed to have been glutted by success, became more intense with the defeat of all her hopes. Lisbeth went to weep out her rage at Madame Marneffe's; for she was without a home, the maréchal having limited the duration of his lease to that of his life. Crevel, to console Valérie's friend, took her savings, increased them considerably, and invested the whole amount at five per cent in Célestine's name, the income to be paid to Lisbeth. By virtue of this transaction Lisbeth had two thousand francs a year for her life. When the inventory of the property of the maréchal was taken, they found a line addressed to his sister-in-law, his niece Hortense, and his nephew Victorin, charging them to pay, between them, twelve hundred francs a year for life to her who was to have been his wife, Mademoiselle Lisbeth Fischer.

Adeline, seeing that the baron was between life and death, succeeded in concealing the death of the maréchal from him for several days; but Lisbeth

7

came to see him, dressed in mourning, and the fatal truth was revealed to him eleven days after the funeral. This terrible blow restored the sick man's energy, he left his bed and found all his family assembled in the salon, dressed in black; they all ceased speaking when he appeared. Hulot had become as thin as a ghost in the fortnight that had passed, and appeared to his family as but a shadow of his former self.

"We must come to some resolution," he said in a weak voice, sitting down in an armchair and looking around upon the family party, from which Crevel and Steinbock were missing.

"We can stay here no longer," Hortense was saying just as her father appeared, "the rent is too high.—"

"As far as lodgings are concerned," said Victorin, breaking the painful silence, "I offer *my mother*—"

At these words, which seemed to exclude him, the baron raised his eyes, which were gazing at the flowers in the carpet without seeing them, and cast a piteous glance at the advocate. A father's rights are always so sacred, even when he is an infamous scoundrel and bereft of honor that Victorin stopped short.

"Your mother—" the baron repeated. "You are right, my son!"

"The suite above ours in our pavilion," said Célestine, finishing her husband's sentence.

"Am I a burden to you, my children?" said the baron with the gentle manner characteristic of those

who are convicted by their own consciences.
"Oh! have no anxiety for the future; you will
have no more cause to complain of your father, and
you will never see him again until the time when
you will not have to blush for him."

He went to Hortense and kissed her on the brow.
He opened his arms to his son, who threw himself
into them despairingly, divining his father's inten-
tions. The baron made a sign to Lisbeth, who
came to him, and he kissed her on the brow. Then
he withdrew to his bed-room, whither Adeline followed him in the keenest of anxiety.

"My brother was right, Adeline," said he, taking
her by the hand. "I am unworthy to live with my
family. I did not dare bless, otherwise than in my
heart, my poor children, whose whole conduct has
been noble; tell them that I could do nothing more
than kiss them; for the blessing of a dishonored
man, of a father who becomes the assassin, the
scourge of his family, instead of being its protector
and its glory, might bring misfortune upon them;
but I will bless them from afar every day. As for
yourself, God alone, for He is omnipotent, can reward you in proportion to your deserts!—I ask you
to forgive me," he said, kneeling at his wife's feet,
taking her hands, and wetting them with his tears.

"Hector! Hector! your sins are great; but the
Divine pity is infinite, and you can atone for everything by remaining with me.—Stand erect in the
faith of a Christian, my dear.—I am your wife and
not your judge. I am your chattel, do with me

whatever you choose, take me wherever you go, for I feel that I have the strength to comfort you and to render life supportable to you, by my love and care and respect.—Our children are taken care of, they no longer need me. Let me try to be your diversion, your amusement. Allow me to share the hardships of your exile, of your poverty, so that I may lighten them. I shall always be good for something, if it were nothing more than to save the expense of a servant."

"Do you pardon me, my dear, beloved Adeline?"

"Yes; but pray get up, my dear!"

"With your forgiveness I shall be able to live!" he continued, rising to his feet. "I came into our room so that our children should not witness their father's abasement. Ah! it's a frightful thing, it degrades the paternal authority, and destroys the family, for children to have before their eyes every day a father who is a criminal like myself. So I can not stay among you, I leave you to spare you the hateful spectacle, of a father bereft of a father's dignity. Do not urge me not to go, Adeline. It would be equivalent to loading the pistol for me to blow my brains out. Lastly, do not follow me in my flight, or you will deprive me of my only remaining source of strength,—remorse."

Hector's earnestness imposed silence on the heartbroken Adeline. Great amid so much ruin and desolation, she derived her courage from her happy reunion with her husband; she thought that he was hers again, she assumed the divine mission of consoling him, of wooing him back to live contentedly with his family, of reconciling him to himself.

"Hector, do you mean to leave me to die of despair and anxiety?" said she, seeing that the main source of her strength was about to be withdrawn.

"I will come back to you, my angel, sent from heaven expressly for me, I verily believe; I will return to you, in comfortable circumstances at least, if not rich. Listen, dear Adeline; I cannot stay here for a multitude of reasons. In the first place, my pension, which will be six thousand francs, is assigned for four years, so that I have nothing. That is not all! in a few days I shall be subjected to arrest, on a suit upon certain notes of hand held by Vauvinet.—So I must go away until my son, with whom I shall leave precise instructions, has taken them up. My disappearance will assist greatly in that operation. When my retiring pension is free, and Vauvinet paid, I will come back to you. You would disclose the secret of my hiding-place. Have no fear, Adeline, don't weep.— It's only a matter of a month."

"Where will you go? what will you do? what will become of you? who will take care of you, for you're no longer young? Let me disappear with you, and we will go abroad together," said she.

"Well, we'll see about it," he replied.

The baron rang, and ordered Mariette to get his things together, and pack them secretly and quickly. Then he begged his wife, after kissing her with a demonstration of affection to which she was not accustomed, to leave him alone a moment to write out the instructions Victorin required, promising not to leave the house until night and with her. As soon as the baroness returned to the salon, the cunning old fellow went through the dressing-room to the reception-room and left the house, handing Mariette a scrap of paper on which he had written: "Send my trunks to Monsieur Hector, *bureau restante*, Corbeil, by the Corbeil railroad." The baron had taken a fiacre, and was already driving rapidly through Paris, when Mariette entered the salon and showed the baroness the paper, telling her that monsieur had gone. Adeline darted into the bed-room, trembling more violently than ever; her children heard a piercing shriek and followed her, in terror. They found the baroness unconscious; she was at once put to bed, for she was taken with a nervous fever which kept her hovering between life and death for a month.

"Where is he?" were the only words they could induce her to utter.

*

Victorin's search for his father was without result. For this reason. The baron was driven to the Place du Palais-Royal. In possession once more of all his faculties, which were restored to him for the accomplishment of a plan thought out during the days he had passed in bed, worn out with sorrow and chagrin, he passed through the Palais-Royal and hired a magnificent hackney carriage, on the Rue Joquelet. Following the orders given him the coachman turned into Rue de la Ville-l'Évêque, in the rear of the mansion occupied by Josépha, whose gates were thrown open for this superb equipage at the call of the coachman. Josépha's curiosity brought her to the window; her footman informed her that a feeble old man, who was unable to leave his carriage, entreated her to come down to him for an instant.

"Josépha! it's I!—"

The famous cantatrice recognized Hulot by his voice alone.

"What, you, my poor old man!—On my word you look like the twenty-franc pieces clipped by German Jews, that bankers won't accept!"

"Alas! yes," Hulot replied; "I am just out of the arms of death! But you are still lovely! will you be kind to me?"

"That depends, everything is relative," said she.

"Listen," rejoined Hulot. "Can you put me up in one of your servant's rooms under the eaves for a day or two? I am without a sou, without hope, without bread, without a roof to cover me, without a wife, without children, without a place of refuge, without honor, without courage, without a friend, and worse than all! I have certain notes hanging over me."

"Poor old man! there's a fine lot of *withouts!* Are you without breeches—*sans-culotte*—also?"

"You laugh at me, I am lost!" cried the baron. "And yet I relied upon you, as Gourville did upon Ninon."

"It's a society woman, so I've been told, who's brought you into this condition," said Josépha. "The *pulcinellas* know how to pluck a turkey better than we do!—Why, you're like a carcass abandoned by the crows,—I can look right through you!"

"Time flies, Josépha!"

"Come in, old boy! I am alone and my people don't know you. Send your carriage away. Is it paid for?"

"Yes," said the baron, stepping down, leaning on Josépha's arm.

"You shall pass for my father if you choose," said the singer compassionately.

She led Hulot to the superb salon where he had seen her before, and bade him be seated.

"Is it true, old man," said she, "that you have killed your brother and your uncle, ruined your family, mortgaged your children's house beyond its value, and fed on the government frogs in Africa with the princess?"

The baron bowed sadly.

"Well, do you know, I like that!" cried Josépha, springing to her feet, overflowing with enthusiasm. "It's a general *conflagration!* It's Sardanapalus! it's great! it's complete! You may be a sad dog, but you have heart, for my own part I prefer a spendthrift, mad after women as you are, to those cold heartless bankers, supposed to be virtuous, who ruin thousands of families with their railroads, which are gold for them, but iron for the *gogos!* You ruined nobody but your own people, you made way with none but yourself! and then you have an excuse, both physical and moral.—"

She assumed a theatrical pose and exclaimed:

"''Tis Venus herself who has seized her prey.' And here she is!" she added, with a pirouette.

Thus Hulot received absolution from vice, vice smiled upon him from the midst of its boundless luxury. There, as in the eyes of jurors, the magnitude of the crime was an extenuating circumstance.

"Your society woman is pretty, at least?" queried the singer, trying to begin her alms-giving by distracting Hulot's attention, for his grief tore her heart.

"Faith, almost as pretty as you!" the baron cunningly replied.

"And—very cunning, so I've been told. Pray what did she do to you? Is she more amusing than I am?"

"Let's not talk about her any more," said Hulot.

"They say she has trapped my Crevel, and little Steinbock, and a magnificent Brazilian?"

"It's very possible."

"She lives in a house as pretty as this, given her by Crevel. The hussy is my provost, she finishes off the men I've taken the first slice of! That's the reason I'm so curious to find out about her; I saw her in a calèche at the *Bois*, but at a distance. She's *a shrewd thief*, so Carabine told me! She tried to swallow Crevel, but she could only get a nibble at him. Crevel's a skin-flint! a good-humored one, who always says *yes*, but acts only with his head. He is vain and passionate, but his money's cold. One can get no more than one to three thousand francs a month from such duffers, and they draw back from any considerable expenditure like a donkey when he comes to a river. You're not that kind, old man; you're the slave of your passions, and a woman could make you sell your country! So you see I'm ready to do anything for you. You are my father, you gave me my start in life! that makes you sacred to me. What do you want? A hundred thousand francs? we'll pull the skies down to get them for you. As to giving you the grub and the nest to lie in, that's nothing. You shall have a cover laid for you every day, you can have a fine room on the second floor, and a hundred crowns a month in your pocket."

The baron, touched by this reception, exhibited a last spark of noble feeling.

"No, little one, no, I didn't come here to have you keep me," said he.

"At your age it's quite a triumph!"

"This is what I do want, my child. Your Duc d'Hérouville has vast estates in Normandy, and I would like to be his manager under the name of Thoul. I am capable and honest,—for though a man may take money from the government it doesn't follow that he'll steal private property."

"What's that?" exclaimed Josépha; "who has drunk will drink!"

"Well, I simply ask to be enabled to live out of sight for three years."

"That will take but a moment to arrange; tonight, after dinner," said Josépha, "I need do no more than mention it. The duke would marry me if I chose; but I have his fortune and I want something more!—his esteem. He's a duke of the old school. He is noble, distinguished, great as Louis XIV. and Napoléon, placed one on top of the other, although he's a dwarf. And then I have done as the Schontz did with Rochefide: by following my advice he has made two millions. But, look you, my old pistol. I know you; you are fond of women, and you'd run about down yonder after the little Normans, who are fine girls; you'd get your bones broken by their sweethearts or their fathers, and the duke would be forced to turn you off. Don't you suppose I can see by the way you look at me that *the young man* isn't dead within you yet, as Fénelon says! That sort of business isn't the thing for you. A man can't break with Paris and with us women at will, old fellow! You would die of ennui at Hérouville!

"What can I do?" demanded the baron, "for I only want to stay with you long enough to settle my plans."

"Well, do you want me to pick out a place for you according to my ideas? Listen, old satyr!— You can't get along without women. They can console for everything. Now attend to what I say. At the foot of the Courtille, Rue Saint-Maur-du-Temple, I know a poor family possessing a rare treasure : a little daughter prettier than I was at sixteen!—Aha! your eye begins to sparkle already!—She works sixteen hours a day embroid-ering rich stuffs for silk merchants, and earns six-teen sous a day, one sou an hour, a wretched pittance!—And she eats potatoes, like the Irish, but fried in rat-grease, bread five times a week, and drinks Ourcq water from the city pipes, because Seine water is too dear ; and she can't set up in business on her own account for lack of six or seven thousand francs. She would do the *hundred hor-rors* to get seven or eight thousand francs. Your wife and family bore you, don't they?—Besides you can't stand it to be nobody where you used to be a god. A father without money or honor should be stuffed and put in a glass-case."

The baron could not help smiling at this irrever-ent pleasantry.

"Well, little Bijou is coming to-morrow to bring me an embroidered dressing-gown, a perfect love ; they have spent six months on it, nobody will have anything like it. Bijou is fond of me, for I give

her nice things to eat and my old dresses. Then I
send presents of bread and wood and meat to the
family, who would break both legs for me at a
wink, if I chose. I try to do a little good. Ah! I
remember what I suffered when I was hungry!
Bijou has poured her little secrets into my heart.
There's the making of a *figurante* at the Ambigu-
Comique in that little creature. Bijou dreams of
wearing lovely dresses like mine, and above all
things, of riding in a carriage. I'll say to her:
'Little one, would you like a gentleman—' How
old are you anyway?" she asked, interrupting herself,—"seventy-two?"

"I haven't any age!"

"'Would you like a gentleman of seventy-two,'
I'll say to her, 'neat as a pin, who doesn't use
tobacco, sound as my eye, and worth any young
man of them all? you'll be married to him in the
thirteenth arrondissement*; he'll do the handsome
thing by you, give you seven thousand francs to do
what you please with, and furnish apartments for
you in mahogany throughout; then, if you're a good
girl, he'll take you to the play now and then. He'll
give you a hundred francs a month for yourself and
fifty for expenses!' I know Bijou, she's just myself
at fourteen over again. I jumped for joy when
that disgusting Crevel made these same shocking
propositions to me! Well, old man, you'll be

---

* "To be married in the thirteenth arrondissement" was an expression used
at the time Paris had but twelve arrondissements as a synonym for taking a
mistress.

packed away there for three years. It's a wise
plan, and honest, and the illusion will last three or
four years, not more.''

Hulot did not hesitate, he had made up his mind
to refuse; but he pretended to waver between vice
and virtue in order to thank the kind-hearted, good-
natured songstress who was doing the best she knew.

"Come, come! you're as cold as the pavement in
December!" she continued in amazement. "Just
think! you will bring happiness to a family that
consists of an old tottering grandfather, a mother
who's wearing herself out with work, and two sisters, one very ugly, who earn thirty-two sous a day
together, by murdering their eyes. That will make
up for the harm you've done at home, you can atone
for your sins, and at the same time enjoy yourself
like a lorette at the Mabille.''

Hulot, to put an end to these seductive sugges-
tions, went through the motion of counting money.

"Have no fear as to ways and means," Josépha
went on. "My duke will loan you ten thousand
francs: seven thousand for an embroidery establishment in Bijou's name and three thousand to furnish
her apartment; and every three months you will
find six hundred and fifty francs here with a note.
When your pension is free again you must pay
back the seventeen thousand francs. Meanwhile
you'll be as happy as a pig in clover, and out of
sight in a hole where the police can't possibly find
you! You can wear a great beaver overcoat, and
you'll look like a well-to-do householder of the

quarter. Call yourself Thoul if that suits you. I'll
turn you over to Bijou as an uncle of mine come
from Germany after failing in business there, and
you'll be looked up to as a god.   There you are,
papa!—Who knows? perhaps you won't find reason
to regret anything.   If by chance you do get bored,
keep one of your dress suits, and then you can come
here and ask me to keep you to dinner and to pass
the evening."

"And I intended to become a virtuous, reformed
man!—Come, arrange a loan of twenty thousand
francs for me, and I'll go off to America and make
my fortune, like my friend d'Aiglemont when Nucingen ruined him."

"You!" cried Josépha; "for God's sake leave
morals to the grocers, the simple clodhoppers, the
Fr-r-r-rench citizens, who have nothing but their virtue to travel on!   You! Why, you were born to be
something better than a simpleton; as a man you
are just what, as a woman, I am, a *vagabond*
genius!"

"The night brings counsel, we'll talk of all this
to-morrow."

"You'll dine with the duke to-night.   My d'Hérouville will receive you as cordially as if you had
saved the State! and to-morrow you can make up
your mind. Come, cheer up, old man! Life's a
suit of clothes; when it's dirty, we brush it; when
it's torn we mend it; but we stay clothed as long
as we can!"

This philosophy of vice and the enthusiasm with

which it was put forward made Hulot forget his poignant suffering.

The next day, at noon, after a succulent breakfast, Hulot's eyes were attracted by the appearance of one of those living chefs-d'œuvre which Paris alone, in all the world, can produce, because of the incessant concubinage of luxury and poverty, of vice and virtue, of repressed desire and recurring temptation, which makes that city the legitimate heir of Nineveh and Babylon and imperial Rome. Mademoiselle Olympe Bijou, a young girl of sixteen, possessed the same sublime countenance that Raphaël conceived for his Virgins; innocent eyes, made melancholy by overwork, black, dreamy eyes, provided with long lashes, and in which the natural moisture was dried up by the wearing labors of the night,—eyes clouded with fatigue; a complexion like porcelain, almost unhealthy in its whiteness; a mouth like a half-opened pomegranate; a throbbing bosom, well-rounded figure, pretty hands, beautiful white teeth, luxuriant black hair,—the whole enveloped in calico at seventy-five centimes the metre, adorned with an embroidered neckerchief, her feet encased in leather shoes without nails, and her hands in gloves at twenty-nine sous. The child, who was ignorant of her worth, had made her finest toilet to visit the great lady's house. The baron, seized anew by the claw-like hand of lust, felt that all his life was escaping through his eyes. He forgot everything in the presence of this sublime creature. He was like the hunter when he catches sight of the game; even in an emperor's presence, he takes aim at it.

"And its warranted fresh," said Josépha in his ear, "and virtuous! and no bread. That's Paris! I've been there!"

"It's agreed," rejoined the old man, rising and rubbing his hands.

When Olympe Bijou had taken her leave, Josépha cast a mischievous glance at the baron.

"If you don't want to have trouble, papa," said she, "be as stern as a *procureur-général* on his bench. Keep the little one in leash; be another Bartholo! 'Ware the Augustines and Hippolytuses, the Nestors and Victors and all the other *ors.*—Damme, when, she is once well clothed and well-fed, if she raises her head, you'll be led by the nose like a Russian. —I am going to see about furnishing your rooms. The duke does things handsomely; he loans you, that is to say he gives you, ten thousand francs, and he will place eight thousand in his notary's hands, who will be instructed to pay you six hundred francs every quarter, for I'm afraid of you.— Am I a good girl?"

"Adorable!"

Ten days after his desertion of his family, when they stood, a tearful group, about the bedside of the dying Adeline, who constantly asked in a feeble voice: "What is he doing?" Hector, under the name of Thoul, was with Olympe at the head of an embroidery establishment on Rue Saint-Maur, under the absurd firm-name of Thoul and Bijou.

8

*

The unremitting ill-fortune of his family was to Victorin Hulot the last touch that perfects or demoralizes a man. He became perfect. In the great storms of life man imitates the sea-captain who lightens his ship in a hurricane by throwing the more cumbersome freight overboard. The advocate lost his internal pride, his palpable self-conceit, his oratorical pomposity, and his political pretensions. In short he became, as a man, what his mother was as a woman. He determined to make the best of his Célestine, who certainly did not come up to his dreams; and reached the sound, sensible conclusion that the common law of life requires man to content himself with an *almost* in everything. He took a solemn oath to himself that he would fulfil his duty, so horrified was he by his father's conduct. These sentiments acquired new strength at his mother's bedside on the day that her life was saved. This first stroke of good fortune did not come alone. Claude Vignon, who came every day on behalf of the Prince de Wissembourg to inquire for Madame Hulot's health, requested the newly re-elected deputy to accompany him to the minister's office.

"His Excellency," he said, "desires to confer with you touching your family affairs."

Victorin Hulot and the minister had been long

acquainted; so the former was welcomed with characteristic and auspicious affability. "My friend," said the veteran, "in this very room I swore to the maréchal, your uncle, that I would have an eye to your mother's welfare. That noble woman is convalescent, I am told, and the time has come to cure your wounds. I have two hundred thousand francs here for you and I am going to turn them over to you."

The advocate made a gesture worthy of his uncle the maréchal.

"Don't be alarmed," said the prince with a smile. "It's a trust-fund. My days are numbered; I shall not always be here, so do you take the money, and take my place as trustee in your family. You can use this money to pay off the mortgage with which your house is burdened. These two hundred thousand francs belong to your mother and sister. If I should give such a sum to Madame Hulot, I should be afraid, on account of her devotion to her husband, that it would be squandered; and it is the intention of those who give it that it should be used for the support of Madame Hulot and her daughter Comtesse Steinbock. You are a discreet man, the worthy son of your noble mother, the true nephew of my friend the maréchal, and you are as thoroughly appreciated here as elsewhere, my dear friend. So be the guardian angel of your family, accept our uncle's legacy and mine."

"Monseigneur," said Hulot, taking the minister's hand and pressing it, "men like you know that verbal thanks mean nothing, and that gratitude is proved by deeds."

"Prove yours!" said the old soldier.

"What must I do?"

"Accept my propositions," was the reply. "We propose to appoint you to take charge of all matters in litigation in the War Department, which is overburdened with law-suits, in the engineering branch, growing out of the fortifications of Paris; also consulting advocate of the prefecture of police, and counsel for the Civil List. These three appointments will be worth eighteen thousand francs a year to you, and will not take away your independence. You will vote in the Chamber according to your political opinions and your conscience.—Act with perfect freedom, my boy! we should be much embarrassed if we had no national opposition! The fact is that a line from your uncle, written only a few hours before he breathed his last, marked out the line of conduct he wished me to adopt toward your mother, of whom the maréchal was very fond! —Mesdames Popinot, de Rastignac, de Navarreins, d'Espard, de Grandlieu, de Carigliano, de Lenoncourt and de la Bâtie have created for your mother a position as inspector of benevolent work. These presidents of benevolent associations cannot do everything themselves; they need a reliable lady to support them energetically, to visit the unfortunate, find out whether charity is misplaced in any instance, make sure that the money or supplies have been delivered to those who asked for them, seek out those poor people who are ashamed to ask alms, etc. Your mother will perform the mission of an angel on earth; she will come in contact with none but the curés and the ladies engaged in the charitable work; they will give her six thousand francs a year and her carriages will be paid for. You see, my young friend, that the pure man, the virtuous, noble-hearted man, even from the grave looks out for the welfare of his family. Such names as your uncle's are, and should be, an ægis against misfortune in all properly-constituted society. Follow in your uncle's footsteps; or rather continue in your present course, for you are now following in his footsteps, I know.''

''So great delicacy, prince, does not surprise me in my uncle's friend,'' said Victorin. ''I will strive to fulfil all your hopes.''

''Go at once and comfort your family!—By the way,'' added the prince, exchanging a grasp of the hand with Victorin, ''your father has disappeared?''

''Alas! yes.''

''So much the better. The unhappy man showed his wit in that; indeed, he doesn't lack that quality.''

''There were some notes hanging over him.''

''Aha!'' said the maréchal; ''you will receive six months' salary for your three offices in advance. This will assist you no doubt to take up the notes from the usurer who holds them. I will see Nucingen, too, and perhaps I may be able to release your father's pension, without it's costing you or the Department a sou. The peer of France hasn't buried the banker; Nucingen is insatiable and he's now after some concession or other, I don't know what."

Thus on his return to Rue Plumet Victorin was able to carry out his plan of taking his mother and sister home with him.

The young and famous lawyer's whole fortune consisted in one of the finest pieces of real estate in Paris, a house purchased in 1834, in anticipation of his marriage, and located on the boulevard between Rue de la Paix and Rue Louis-le-Grand. A speculator had built two houses, one on the street and one on the boulevard. Between the two with a courtyard and garden on either side stood a handsome pavilion, the last remnant of the splendors of the magnificent De Verneuil mansion. Hulot junior, sure of Mademoiselle Crevel's dowry, purchased this fine property at auction for a million and paid five hundred thousand down. He established himself on the ground floor, expecting to make up the balance of the purchase-money by renting the other floors; but, although real-estate speculation in Paris may be sure, it is slow and capricious, for it depends upon many circumstances that cannot be anticipated. As Parisian *flâneurs* may have noticed, the boulevard between Rue Louis-le-Grand and Rue de la Paix was built up very slowly; so much care was taken to clean it up and beautify it that it was not until 1840 that commerce began to be in evidence there in the shape of gorgeous shop-fronts, the unrivaled magnificence of the shops themselves, the fairy-like devices of fashion, and

the gold of the money-changers. Notwithstanding
the two hundred thousand francs presented to his
daughter by Crevel at a time when his self-love
was tickled by the marriage and before the baron
had taken Josépha from him; notwithstanding the
fact that Victorin had paid two hundred thousand
francs in seven years, he still owed five hundred
thousand francs on the house because of his devotion to his father.   Luckily the continual advance
in rents and the desirable situation made it possible
for him at this time to rent both houses for all they
were worth.   At the end of eight years the speculation was justified, and meanwhile the advocate had
exhausted his resources in paying interest and
insignificant instalments of the principal.   The
tradespeople themselves made advantageous offers
for the shops, on condition that they were allowed
to take leases for eighteen years.   The apartments
gained in rental value by the change of the business centre, which was at this time between the
Bourse and the Madeleine, thenceforth the centre of
political power and of finance in Paris.   The sum
turned over by the minister, added to the year's
rents paid in advance, and the good-will agreed
to by the tenants, would reduce Victorin's debt to
two hundred thousand francs.   The two buildings
he did not occupy, being entirely let, would bring
in a hundred thousand francs a year.   Two years
more, during which Victorin's professional income
would be doubled by the places the maréchal had
offered him, and he would be in a most enviable

position. It was like the manna falling from heaven. Victorin was able to give his mother the whole first floor of the pavilion and his sister the second, on which Lisbeth would have two rooms. With Cousin Bette for housekeeper the threefold household would be able to pay all expenses, and maintain an honorable position in the eyes of the world, as befitted the celebrated advocate. The stars of the Palais are soon eclipsed; and Hulot junior, being endowed with the art of discreet speech, and a reputation for the strictest probity, had the ear of the judges and councilors; he made a careful study of his cases, he made no statements that he could not prove, he did not accept a retainer in all cases indiscriminately,—in short he did honor to the bar.

Her home on Rue Plumet was so hateful to the baroness that she consented to change her abode to Rue Louis-le-Grand. Thus, through her son's means, Adeline was installed in handsome apartments; she was spared all concern about the material details of existence, for Lisbeth undertook the duty of performing once more the economical miracles she had performed at Madame Marneffe's, seeing an opportunity of wreaking her vengeance upon these three noble creatures, her unrelenting hatred for them being embittered by the overthrow of all her hopes. Once a month she went to see Valérie, being sent to her by Hortense who sought news of Wenceslas, and by Célestine who was extremely anxious about her father's avowed and recognized

liaison with a woman to whom her husband's mother
and sister owed their ruin and their unhappiness.

As may be imagined, Lisbeth took advantage of
their anxiety to see Valérie as often as she desired.

About twenty months passed, during which the
baroness's health constantly improved, although the
nervous trembling did not leave her. She made
herself familiar with her duties, which afforded a
noble means of forgetting her grief for the moment,
and food for the divine aspirations of her heart.
She saw in it, moreover, a possible means of recovering her husband, as her duties took her to every
part of Paris. During this time the Vauvinet notes
were paid, and the pension of six thousand francs,
awarded to Baron Hulot, was almost freed from incumbrance. Victorin paid all his mother's expenses
as well as Hortense's with the ten thousand francs
interest on the fund handed over to him by the
maréchal in trust. As Adeline's salary was six
thousand francs, that sum, added to the six thous-
and of the baron's pension would ere long afford
the mother and daughter an income of twelve thous-
and a year, free of all charges. The poor woman
would have been almost happy, except for her never-
ending anxiety as to the fate of the baron, whom she
would have liked to have by her side to enjoy the
good fortune which was just beginning to smile
upon the family; except for the sad spectacle of
her deserted daughter, and the terrible blows *inno-
cently* dealt her by Lisbeth, whose infernal disposition was no longer under the slightest restraint.

A scene that occurred in the beginning of the month of March, 1843, will serve to explain the effect produced by the persistent though concealed hatred of Lisbeth, always seconded by Madame Marneffe. Two great events had happened at Madame Marneffe's. In the first place, the latter had brought into the world a premature child, whose death was worth two thousand francs a year to her. Then as to Monsieur Marneffe, eleven months previously Lisbeth had imparted the following information to the family on her return from a visit of exploration to the Marneffe mansion:

"This morning," she said, "that horrible Valérie sent for Doctor Bianchon to ask if the doctors who had given her husband up the day before, were not mistaken. This doctor said that, before this night is over, that beast of a man will have gone to the hell that awaits him. Père Crevel and Madame Marneffe went to the door with the doctor, and your father, my dear Célestine, gave him five pieces of gold for the good news. When they returned to the salon Crevel capered about like a ballet-dancer; he kissed that woman, and cried: 'At last then you will be Madame Crevel!'—And when she left us alone to resume her place by the bedside of her husband, who had the death-rattle in his throat, your honorable father said to me: 'With Valérie for my wife, I shall be a peer of France! I'm going to buy an estate I've got my eye on, the estate of Presles which Madame de Sérizy wants to sell. I shall be Crevel de Presles, I shall become a member of the General Council of Seine-et-Oise, and a deputy. I shall have a son! I shall be whatever I choose to be.'—'Very good,' I replied, 'and your daughter?'—'Bah! she's a girl,' he exclaimed, 'and she's become altogether too much of a Hulot, and Valérie has a horror of all those people.—My son-in-law has never been willing to come here; why does he play the mentor, the Spartan, the Puritan, the philanthropist? Besides, I've settled accounts with my daughter, and she has received all her mother's fortune with two hundred thousand francs more! So I am at liberty to go my own way. I shall pass judgment on my daughter and son-in-law when I am married; as they do, so will I do. If they are kind to their mother-in-law, I'll see! I am a man!' All such nonsense as that! and he struck an attitude like Napoléon on the column!''

The ten months of widowhood, formally enjoined by the Code Napoléon, had expired some days. The estate of Presles had been purchased. Victorin and Célestine had sent Lisbeth on the morning in question to Madame Marneffe's in quest of news touching the marriage of that fascinating widow to the Mayor of Paris, now a member of the Council General of Seine-et-Oise.

Célestine and Hortense who had become much more attached to each other since they had lived under the same roof, were almost always together. The baroness, impelled by her unswerving honesty of purpose, which led her to exaggerate the duties of her position, sacrificed herself to the benevolent work in which she was the intermediary, and was away from home almost every day from eleven o'clock till five. The two sisters-in-law, drawn together by their maternal duties, for they took care of their children in common, remained at home and worked side by side. They had acquired the habit of thinking aloud, a touching instance of perfect harmony between two sisters, one of a happy, the other of a melancholy disposition. Beautiful, full of overflowing life, animated, bright and smiling, the unfortunate sister seemed to give the lie to her real situation by her external bearing; just as the melancholy one, gentle and calm, as even-tempered as reason itself, habitually thoughtful and reflecting, would have led one to believe in some secret trouble. Perhaps this contrast contributed to their warm friendship. They loaned to each other whatever either lacked. Seated in a little kiosk, in the middle of the garden which the trowel of speculation had spared by a whim of the builder, who counted upon retaining the hundred square feet for himself, they feasted their eyes upon the first blooming of the lilacs, a spring festival which is enjoyed to its fullest extent only in Paris, where the Parisians have lived for six months in total forgetfulness of all vegetation, amid the stone cliffs against which their living ocean beats.

"Célestine," said Hortense, replying to an observation of her sister-in-law, who was complaining because her husband had to be in the Chamber in such fine weather, "it seems to me that you don't appreciate your good fortune as you ought. Victorin is an angel, and sometimes you worry him."

"My dear, men love to be teased! Certain fault-finding ways are a proof of affection. If your poor mother had been, not exacting, but always on the point of being, I am sure you wouldn't have had so much misery to deplore."

"Lisbeth doesn't come back! I am going to sing *Malbrouck's* song," said Hortense. "How I long for news of Wenceslas!—What is he living on? he has done nothing for two years."

"Victorin saw him the other day with that hateful woman, so he told me, and he fancies that she's supporting him in idleness.—Ah! if you chose, dear sister, you could bring your husband back to you even now."

Hortense shook her head.

"Believe me, your position will soon become intolerable," continued Célestine. "At first, wrath, indignation and despair gave you strength. The incredible disasters which have since overwhelmed our family: two deaths, the ruin and disappearance of Baron Hulot, have filled your mind and heart since; but, now that you are living in tranquillity and peace you will not find it easy to endure the emptiness of your life; as you can not, as you will not deviate from the path of honor, the time will come when you must be reconciled to Wenceslas. Victorin, who loves you so dearly, is of that opinion. There is something stronger than our feelings, and that is nature!"

"Such a coward!" cried the proud Hortense. "He loves that woman because she supports him. — So she has paid his debts, has she?—My God! night and day I think of that man's plight! He is the father of my child, and he is dishonoring himself—"

"Look at your mother, dear—" rejoined Célestine.

Célestine belonged to that class of women who, when you have given them reasons strong enough to convince a Breton peasant, begin upon their original argument again for the hundredth time. Her somewhat expressionless, cold and uninteresting face, her light chestnut hair disposed in stiff plaits, her complexion, everything in her appearance, in short, indicated the woman of good sense, without the power to charm, but also without weakness.

"The baroness would love dearly to be with her disgraced husband, to comfort him and conceal him in her heart from all eyes," continued Célestine. "She has had a room arranged for him upstairs as if she might find him any day, and bring him home."

"Oh! my mother is sublime!" Hortense replied; "she has been sublime every minute in every day for twenty-six years; but I haven't her disposition. —What can I do? sometimes I lose my head when I know I ought not. Ah! Célestine, you don't know what it is to have to palter with infamy!"

"What about my father?" rejoined Célestine calmly. "He is certainly on the road where yours came to grief. My father is ten years younger than the baron, and he's been a business man, to be sure, but how will it end? This Madame Marneffe has made my father her dog, she does as she pleases with his fortune and his ideas, and no one can make him realize what he's doing. Indeed, I am trembling with apprehension lest I hear that the banns are published! My husband is making one last effort, he looks upon it as his duty to avenge society and his family, and to call that woman to account for all her crimes. Ah! dear Hortense, noble minds like Victorin's and hearts like ours learn too late the world and its methods! This is a secret, dear sister; I tell it to you, for it concerns you; but do not reveal it by word or gesture, either to Lisbeth or your mother or anyone else, for—"

"Here's Lisbeth!" said Hortense.—"Well, cousin, how goes the hell on Rue Barbet?"

"Badly for you, children.—Your husband, Hortense, my love, is more intoxicated than ever with that woman, who seems to have a mad sort of passion for him, I admit.—Your father, dear Célestine, is as blind as a king. That's nothing; that's what I see every fortnight, and upon my word I think I'm fortunate never to have known what a man is.— They're absolute beasts! Five days hence you and Victorin, little one, will have lost your father's fortune!"

"Are the banns published?" Célestine asked.

"Yes," replied Lisbeth. "I have pleaded your cause. I said to the monster, who is walking in the footsteps of another, that, if he would relieve you from your embarrassment, by paying off the incumbrance on your house, you would be grateful to him and would receive your mother-in-law—"

Hortense made a gesture of horror.

"Victorin will decide for us," rejoined Célestine coldly.

"Do you know what Monsieur le Maire answered?" continued Lisbeth: " 'I prefer to leave them in trouble; you can't subdue a refractory horse except by hunger, lack of sleep and sugar!' Baron Hulot's a better man than Crevel.—So, my poor child, put on mourning for your inheritance. And such a fortune! Your father paid three millions for Presles, and he has thirty thousand francs a year left! Oh! he has no secrets from me. He talks of buying the Hotel de Navarreins, Rue du Bac. Madame Marneffe has forty thousand a year herself. —Ah! here's our guardian angel, here's your mother!—" she cried as she heard the rumbling of a carriage.

A moment later the baroness ascended the steps and joined the family group. At fifty-five years, Adeline, though she had been so sorely beset by trouble and sorrow, and trembled incessantly as if she were always suffering from fever, though she was pale and wrinkled, still retained a beautiful figure, superb in its outlines, and her natural nobility of carriage. People who saw her would say: "She must have been very beautiful!" Consumed by the misery of knowing nothing of her husband's

9

fate and of his being unable to share the good fortune
the family was about to enjoy in the retirement and
silence of this Parisian oasis, she resembled one of
those majestic ruins upon which the eye loves to
dwell.   As each gleam of hope faded away, as each
new quest proved fruitless, Adeline would have an
attack of black melancholy which drove her children to despair.   As she had left home on this particular morning, with a fresh clue to follow, her
return was impatiently awaited.   A certain *intend-
ant-général*, being under obligations to Hulot, to
whom he was indebted for his official position, said
that he had seen the baron in a box at the Ambigu-
Comique, with a woman of magnificent beauty.
Adeline therefore had gone to call upon Baron Vernier.   That exalted functionary informed her that he
did see his former patron, and asserted that his bearing toward the woman during the performance
seemed to indicate a clandestine marriage; but he
told Madame Hulot that her husband left the theatre
before the end of the performance to avoid meeting
himself.

"He acted like a family man, and his dress be-
spoke the straitened condition he sought to hide," he
added in conclusion.

"Well?" said the three women in one voice to
the baroness.

"Monsieur Hulot is in Paris; and it's a gleam of
happiness for me simply to know that he is near
us," Adeline replied.

"He doesn't seem to have mended his ways!"

said Lisbeth when Adeline had told the story of her interview with Baron Vernier; "he must have taken up with some little work-girl. But where does he get his money? I'll wager that he goes to his former mistresses for it, Mademoiselle Jenny Cadine or Josépha."

The constant agitation of the baroness's nerves redoubled in intensity; she wiped away the tears that came to her eyes, and raised them piteously toward heaven.

"I don't believe that a grand officer of the Legion of Honor can have fallen so low," said she.

"What wouldn't he do for his own pleasure?" retorted Lisbeth; "he has stolen from the State, he'll steal from private individuals, he'll commit murder perhaps—"

"Oh! Lisbeth!" cried the baroness, "keep such thoughts to yourself."

At that moment Louise approached the family group, which had already been increased by the two little Hulots and little Wenceslas, curious to know if there were any sweetmeats in their grand-mother's pockets.

"What is it, Louise?—"

"A man asking to see Mademoiselle Fischer."

"What sort of a man is he?" said Lisbeth.

"He's all in rags, mademoiselle, and he's covered with wool like a mattress-maker; he has a red nose, he smells of wine and brandy. He's one of the workmen that hardly works half the week."

This unalluring description had the effect of

sending Lisbeth in a great hurry out into the court-
yard of the house on Rue Louis-le-Grand, where
she found the man smoking a pipe, the coloring of
which made it clear that he was an artist in the
matter of smoking.

"Why do you come here, Père Chardin?" said
she. "It was agreed that you should be at the
door of the Hôtel Marneffe, on Rue Barbet-de-Jouy
on the first Saturday of every month. I have just
come from there after waiting five hours, and you
didn't come!—"

"I have been there, my respected and charitable
young lady!" replied the mattress-maker; "but there
was a big pool up at the Café des Savants, Rue du
Cœur-Volant, and every man to his passions.
Mine's billiards. Without billiards I should eat
off silver-plate; for just you mark this!" he continued, feeling for a paper in the pocket of his dilapidated breeches, "billiards lead to brandy drinking.
It ruins a fellow by the things that go with it, like
everything else that's decent. I know my orders,
but the old man's in such a pickle that I ventured
to step on the forbidden ground.—If our horsehair
was all horsehair you could lie down and go to
sleep on it; but it's a mixture! God isn't the
same to everybody, as they say; He has His prefer-
ences; that's His right. Here's the hand-writing
of your estimable relative, a good friend to the mattress.—That's his political opinion."

Père Chardin tried to draw zigzag lines in the air
with the forefinger of his right hand.

Lisbeth, paying no heed to him, read these two lines:

"Dear cousin, be my providence!   Give me three hundred francs to-day.

"HECTOR."

"What does he want so much money for?"

"The *landlord!*" said Père Chardin, still trying to design arabesques.   "And then my son has come back from Algeria, by way of Spain, Bayonne and— he didn't take anything, contrary to his custom; for he's a finished rascal, is my son, saving your presence.   What's he to do? he's half-starved; but he'll return you what we let him have, for he means to get himself talked about; he has ideas that may carry him a great way—"

"Into the police court!" retorted Lisbeth.   "He's my uncle's murderer, I'll not forget that!"

"He! why he couldn't bleed a chicken, respected young lady!"

"Here are three hundred francs," said Lisbeth, taking fifteen gold pieces from her purse.   "Off with you now, and never come here again."

She escorted, to the door, the father of the keeper of the forage store-houses at Oran, and called the concierge's attention to the drunken old man.

"Whenever that man comes, if by any chance he does come again, you won't let him in, and you'll tell him that I'm not here.   If he should try to find out whether Monsieur Hulot junior or

Madame la Baronne Hulot lives here, you will reply that you don't know any such persons."

"Very well, mademoiselle."

"Your place will be in danger in case of any blunder, even if it's involuntary," said the old maid in the concierge's ear.—"Cousin, you are threatened with a great calamity," she said to the advocate, who came in at that moment.

"What is it?"

"Your wife will have Madame Marneffe for a step-mother within a few days."

"We'll see about that!" said Victorin.

*

For six months Lisbeth had been paying, and
paying with great promptitude, a small pension to
her former protector, Baron Hulot, whose protectress she had become; she knew the secret of his
abiding-place, and she gloated over Adeline's tears,
saying to her when she found her in good spirits
and filled with hope: "Wait a while and some day
you'll read my poor cousin's name in the police
court news." In this, as on previous occasions,
she went too far in her thirst for vengeance. She
had put Victorin on his guard. Victorin had determined to do away with this sword of Damocles
constantly held over their heads by Lisbeth, and
with the female demon to whom his mother and
the family owed so much misery. The Prince de
Wissembourg, who was made acquainted with
Madame Marneffe, supported the advocate in his
secret undertaking; he promised him, as a president of the Council promises, the secret interven-
tion of the police to enlighten Crevel, and to save
a large fortune from the claws of the diabolical
courtesan, whom he had not forgiven for the death
of Maréchal Hulot nor for the total ruin of the
Councilor of State.

Lisbeth's words: "He goes to his former mistresses for money!" filled the baroness's mind during the whole night. Like those invalids given up

(135)

by their physicians who put themselves in the hands
of charlatans, like those persons who have reached
the last Dantesque stage of despair, or like the
drowning man who clutches at a straw for support,
she ended by believing in the degradation, the mere
suggestion of which had aroused her ire, and she
conceived the idea of calling upon one of those
odious creatures for aid. The next morning, without consulting her children, without a word to anyone, she drove to the house of Mademoiselle Josépha
Mirah, *prima donna* at the Royal Academy of Music,
seeking the fulfilment or the death of the hope which
gleamed before her eyes like a will-o'-the-wisp.
Just at noon the famous songstress's maid handed
her Baroness Hulot's card, saying that the lady was
waiting at her door, having sent up to ask if mademoiselle could receive her.

"Are the rooms in order?"

"Yes, mademoiselle."

"Have you put fresh flowers about?"

"Yes, mademoiselle."

"Tell Jean to take a look round and see that
everything's all right, before showing the lady in,
and tell him that she's to be treated with the
greatest respect. Go! then come back and dress
me, for I want to look my loveliest!"

She went and looked at herself in her mirror.

"I must put on my Sunday best," she said to
herself. "Vice must be under arms to face virtue!
Poor woman! what can she want of me?—It makes
me nervous to see

" The August Victim of Misfortune."

She was just finishing that famous air, when her
maid returned.

"Madame," said she, ''the lady has an attack of
nervous trembling."

"Give her some orange water, rum, a cup of
soup—"

"I have done so, mademoiselle, but she refused
them all; she says it's a little trouble she's subject
to,—nervous excitement—"

"Where did you take her?"

"To the large salon."

"Hurry with me, my girl! Quick, my prettiest
slippers, my flowered robe de chambre by Bijou,
with all its fluttering lace on it. Dress my hair
so as to astonish any woman.—This lady plays a
part the exact opposite of mine! And let some one
tell her—for she's a great lady, my girl! that's still
better; that's something you will never be; a woman whose prayers release souls from your purga-
tory!—let some one tell her that I acted last night
and was in bed, but am getting up."

The baroness took no heed of the time she passed
in the grand salon of Josépha's apartments, although
she waited there a long half-hour. This salon,
which had already been redecorated and refurnished
since Josépha's installation in the little palace, was
now done in *massaca*-colored silk and gold. The
magnificence which great noblemen formerly displayed in their *petites maisons,* and of which so

many examples still bear witness to those *follies*
that fully justify the name applied to them, shone
resplendent with the greater perfection due to more
modern methods in the four rooms opening into one
another, where an equable temperature was maintained by concealed heating apparatus.   The bewildered baroness examined each object of art in the
utmost astonishment.   She found therein the explanation of the melting away of great fortunes in
the crucible, beneath which licentiousness and
vanity kindle a consuming fire.   This woman who,
for twenty-six years, had lived amid the faded
relics of the splendor of the imperial régime, whose
eyes were accustomed to carpets on which the
flowers had become invisible, worn bronzes, and
silk hangings as dilapidated as her own heart,
caught a glimpse of the seductions of vice as she
gazed upon its results.   It was impossible not to
look with envious eye upon these lovely things,
these admirable creations to which the great unknown artists who make Paris what it is to-day,
and the renown of its productions, European, had all
contributed.   One's wonder was aroused by the
perfection of each individual object.   The models
being broken, the figures, the sculptures, the
shapes were all original.   That is the culmina-
tion of the luxury of the present day.   To possess
things which are not vulgarized by two thousand
wealthy ex-tradesmen, who think they are living
luxuriously when they make a parade of the treasures with which the shops are filled,—that is the

stamp of genuine luxury, the luxury of modern great noblemen, ephemeral stars in the Parisian firmament. Upon examining the jardinières filled with the rarest exotic flowers,—jardinières made of bronze with carved ornaments of the so-called Boulle pattern,—the baroness was actually dismayed at the treasures the room contained. Necessarily that sentiment extended to the person upon whom they were showered in such profusion. Adeline concluded that Josépha Mirah, whose portrait by Joseph Bridau beamed upon her from the boudoir adjoining, was a cantatrice of great talent, a Malibran, and she waited in the expectation of seeing a real lioness. She regretted having come. But she was impelled by so powerful and natural a feeling, by a devotion so utterly free from calculating self-interest, that she summoned all her courage to go through with the interview. Then, too, she was to have an opportunity to satisfy the curiosity, which she had felt so keenly, to study the charm possessed by women of this class, which enabled them to extract so much gold from the miserly deposits in the Parisian soil. The baroness looked herself over to see if her appearance did not make a blot upon all this magnificence; but she carried herself nobly in her velvet dress, with a lovely neckerchief of superb lace, and her velvet hat of the same color as her dress was most becoming. Realizing that she was still as imposing as a queen, always a queen even when she is dethroned, she concluded that the nobility born of misfortune might hold its own against the nobility of talent. She heard doors opening and closing, and at last Josépha stood before her. The famous singer resembled Allori's *Judith*, a masterpiece that remains graven for ever on the memory of all who have seen it in the Pitti Palace, near the door of one of the great salons; the same haughty pose, the same sublime features, black hair twisted carelessly into a knot, and a yellow robe de chambre with thousands of embroidered flowers, an exact reproduction of the brocade in which the immortal homicide created by Bronzino's nephew is dressed.

"Madame la Baronne, I am abashed by the honor you confer upon me in coming here," said the cantatrice, who had promised herself to play the rôle of a great lady to perfection.

With her own hand she drew forward an easy chair for the baroness and sat down herself upon a folding-chair. She detected the traces of her visitor's vanished beauty, and was conscious of a feeling of profound compassion when she saw how her whole frame was shaken by the nervous trembling which the least emotion made convulsive. At a glance she read the whole story of the saintly life which Hulot and Crevel had long before described to her; and not only did she thereupon abandon all thought of a contest with her, but she humbled herself before this grandeur of soul, which she could understand. The divine artist admired that of which the courtesan made sport.

"Mademoiselle, I am brought hither by despair, which leads one to resort to any expedient—"

A gesture on Josépha's part gave the baroness to understand that she had wounded her from whom she expected so much, and she looked up into the artist's face. This supplicating glance extinguished the fire in Josépha's eyes, and she smiled. There was a thrilling eloquence in this dumb by-play between the two women.

"It is now two years and a half since Monsieur Hulot left his family, and I do not know where he is, although I know he is living in Paris," said the baroness in a trembling voice. "A dream gave me the idea, an absurd idea perhaps, that you might have interested yourself in Monsieur Hulot. If you could put me in the way of seeing him again if nothing more, oh! mademoiselle, I would pray for you every day so long as I remain on earth."

Two great tears glistened in the singer's eyes as she replied.

"Madame," said she, in a tone of deep humility, "I injured you when I did not know you; but, now that I am fortunate enough to see you, and in you the most perfect image of virtue upon earth, pray believe that I realize the magnitude of my sin, and that I most sincerely repent; you may therefore be sure that I am ready to do anything to repair it!"

She took the baroness's hand before she had time to resist, kissed it most respectfully and carried her self-abasement so far as to bend the knee before her. Then she stood erect again as proudly as when she came upon the stage in the part of Mathilde, and rang.

"Take a horse," she said to her footman, "and
founder him if necessary, but find little Bijou for
me, Rue Saint-Maur-du-Temple; bring her to me,
put her into a carriage and pay the driver to come
at a gallop. Don't lose a minute,—or I'll dismiss
you.—Madame," she continued, returning to the
baroness and addressing her in a most respectful
tone, "you must forgive me. As soon as the Duc
d'Hérouville became my protector I dismissed the
baron, having learned that he was ruining his family for me. What more could I do? To all of us
who adopt a theatrical career a protector is necessary when we make our first appearance. Our
salaries do not pay half of our expenses, so we take
temporary husbands.—I had no great regard for
Monsieur Hulot, who induced me to leave a rich
man, a conceited idiot. Père Crevel would certainly
have married me—"

"He told me so," the baroness interrupted.

"Well, you see, madame! I should be an honest
woman to-day, having but one lawful husband!"

"You have excuses, mademoiselle," said the
baroness, "and God will give you due credit for
them. But I, far from reproaching you, have come
to incur a debt of gratitude to you."

"Madame, nearly three years ago I provided for
Monsieur le Baron's necessities—"

"You did!" cried the baroness, her eyes filling
with tears. "Oh! what can I do for you? I can
only pray."

"Monsieur le Duc d'Hérouville," continued the

cantatrice, "a noble-hearted, true gentleman, and myself,—"

And Josépha told the story of Père Thoul's establishment and marriage.

"And so, mademoiselle, my husband, thanks to you, has had all that he needed?" said the baroness.

"We did all we could, madame, to see that he had."

"And where is he?"

"Monsieur le Duc told me about six months ago that the baron, who was known to his notary under the name of Thoul, had exhausted the eight thousand francs, which were to be handed him in equal quarterly payments," Josépha replied. "Since then neither Monsieur d'Hérouville nor myself has heard of him. Our life, you know, is so full, so busy, that I couldn't run after Père Thoul. It so happens that for the last six months Bijou, who does my embroidering, his—what shall I say?—"

"His mistress," said Madame Hulot.

"His mistress," Josépha repeated, "has not been here. Mademoiselle Olympe Bijou may well have left him. Divorce is very common in our arrondissement."

Josépha rose, looked over the rare flowers in her jardinières, and picked a lovely, fragrant bouquet for the baroness, whose anticipations, we ought to say, were entirely falsified. Like the good bourgeois who look upon men and women of genius as monsters who eat, drink, walk and talk differently from the rest of mankind, the baroness had expected to see Josépha the siren, the cantatrice, the clever

and voluptuous courtesan; and she found a calm and
sedate woman, with the noble bearing suited to her
talent, the simple manners of an actress who knows
that she will be queen when night comes, and, better
than all, a frail woman, who, by her look, her attitude and her whole manner did full and unqualified
homage to the virtuous woman, *à la Mater Dolorosa*
of sacred song, and who strewed flowers upon her
wounds, as the Italian peasants deck their Madonnas.

"Madame," said the footman, returning after an
absence of half an hour, "Mère Bijou's on the way;
but you can not count upon seeing little Olympe.
Madame's embroiderer has become a good bourgeoise, she is married.—"

"With the left hand?" asked Josépha.

"No, madame, really married.   She's at the head
of a magnificent establishment, she has married the
proprietor of a great emporium of novelties on
which millions have been spent, on the Boulevard
des Italiens, and she has left her embroidery establishment to her sister and mother.   She's Madame
Grenouville.   The rich merchant—"

"Another Crevel!"

"Yes, madame," said the footman.   "He acknow-
ledges to thirty thousand a year in Mademoiselle
Bijou's contract.   Her elder sister, they say, is going
to marry a rich butcher."

"Your matter doesn't seem to look very promising," said Josépha to the baroness.   "Monsieur le
Baron isn't where I located him."

Ten minutes later Madame Bijou was announced.

Josépha took the precaution to ask the baroness to go into her boudoir, and drew the portière.

"You would frighten her," said she; "she wouldn't let out anything if she guessed that you were interested in what she might say, so let me confess her! Conceal yourself there, where you will overhear everything. This scene is played as often in real life as on the stage.—Well, Mère Bijou," said she to an old woman enveloped in a dress of the material called *tartan*, and who resembled a concierge in her Sunday clothes, "so you're all in luck, are you? your daughter has had her chance!"

"Oh! in luck!—my daughter gives us a hundred francs a month and she rides in her carriage and she eats off silver; she's a *miyonaire!*—Olympe might have put me out of want. To work, at my age!—Is that a kindness?"

"She does wrong to be ungrateful, for she owes her beauty to you," said Josépha; "but why hasn't she been to see me? I was the one who made life easy for her by marrying her to my uncle."

"Yes, madame, Père Thoul!—But he's pretty old, all used up—"

"What have you done with him, pray? Is he with you?—She did very wrong to leave him, for here he is worth his millions."

"Ah! *Dieu de Dieu!*" exclaimed Mère Bijou; "that's what I used to say to her when she didn't treat him well, and him gentleness itself, poor old man! Ah! she made him step round! Olympe was led astray, madame!"

10

"How?"

"Saving your presence, madame, she got acquainted with a *claqueur*, grand-nephew of an old mattress-maker of Faubourg Saint-Marceau. This *loafer*, for that's what all these pretty boys are, a paid *applauder* of plays, you know! is the darling of the Boulevard du Temple, where he works for the new pieces, and *looks after the entrées* of the actresses, as he says. In the morning, he takes his breakfast; before the play he dines so's to get a little mellow; indeed he's been fond of liquors and billiards ever since he was born. 'That's no business at all!' I used to tell Olympe."

"Unfortunately it is a business," said Josépha.

"At last Olympe lost her head over this scamp, who kept bad company, madame, for didn't he come near being arrested in the tavern where the thieves go? but, for that once, Monsieur Braulard, the head of the *claque*, got him off. The creature wears gold earrings and lives by doing nothing, at the expense of women who go mad over such doll-faced men! He used up all the money Monsieur Thoul gave the little one. The business got in a very bad way. What embroidery brought in went for billiards. The boy, madame, had a pretty sister who was in the same business as her brother, on a small scale, in the students' quarter."

"A lorette of the Chaumière," said Josépha.

"Yes, madame," said Mère Bijou. "So Idamore, —he calls himself Idamore but that's a *nom de guerre*, his real name's Chardin,—Idamore imagined

your uncle must have more money than he'd admit,
and he found a way to send his sister Élodie—he
gave her a stage name—to us, without my daughter's suspecting it, as a workgirl; *Dieu de Dieu!*
how she did turn the place upside down! she de-
bauched all the poor girls and they're all past
soiling, saving your presence.—She did so much
that she took Père Thoul for herself and carried
him off, we don't know where, and that put us in a
mess on account of all the notes that were out. We
ain't able to pay them to this very day; but my
daughter, who's on hand, looks out for them when
they come due.—When Idamore saw that he had
the old man, through his sister, he let my poor girl
drop, and now he's with a *jeune première* at the
Funambules.—And that's how my daughter came
to be married, as you'll see—"

"But do you know where the mattress-maker
lives?—" interposed Josépha.

"Old Père Chardin? Do you call what he does
living?—He's drunk at six o'clock in the morning,
he makes one mattress every month, he spends the
whole day in low tap-rooms, he plays pool—" *

"What! he makes chickens?—he's a fine sort of
rooster!"

"'You don't understand, madame; I mean pool
(*poule*) at billiards; he wins three or four games
every day, and he drinks—"

"Chicken's milk!—" *Des laits de poule!*—said

---

* *Il fait des poules.* This may mean, "he plays pool," or "he makes
chickens"—the word *poule* having both meanings.

Josépha. "But Idamore carries on his business on the boulevard, and we can find him by applying to my friend Braulard."

"I don't know, madame, seeing that this all happened six months ago. Idamore's one of the fellows who's sure to get into the police court, from there to Melun, and then—damme!—"

"To the penitentiary!" said Josépha.

"Ah! madame knows it all," said Mère Bijou with a smile. "If my daughter'd never known that creature, she'd be—But she's had a good chance all the same, you'll tell me; for Monsieur Grenouville got so dead in love with her that he married her."

"How did the marriage come about?"

"Because Olympe was in despair, madame. When she saw that she was deserted for the *jeune première* who she'd often spanked! ah! she boxed her ears!—and that she'd lost Père Thoul who adored her, she swore she'd have no more to do with men. Then Monsieur Grenouville, who used to buy a lot of stuff at our place—two hundred embroidered China sashes a quarter—undertook to console her; but, true or not, she wouldn't hear to anything unless the mayor's office and the church were included. 'I mean to be an honest woman!' she always said, 'or may I die!' And she stuck to it. Monsieur Grenouville agreed to marry her on condition that she gave us up, and we consented—"

"For a money consideration?" inquired the sharp-witted Josépha.

"Yes, madame, ten thousand francs, and a little income for my father, who can't work."

"I asked your daughter to make Père Thoul happy, and she's thrown him into the mud! It isn't fair. I'll never interest myself in anybody again! That's what it is to be guided by a charitable instinct!—Charity's no good except as a speculation, that's sure. Olympe ought at least to have let me know about this muddle! If you find Père Thoul within a fortnight, I'll give you a thousand francs."

"It's a very hard thing to do, my good lady, but there's a many hundred-sou pieces in a thousand francs, and I'll try to earn your money.'

"Adieu, Madame Bijou."

Upon returning to her boudoir the singer found Madame Hulot in a dead swoon; but, although she was unconscious, her nervous affection made her tremble still, just as the fragments of a snake that has been cut in pieces continue to wriggle. Strong salts, fresh water and all the usual remedies, being applied in profusion, restored the baroness to life, or, if you please, to the consciousness of her suffering.

"Oh! mademoiselle, how low he has fallen!" she said as she recognized Josépha and saw that they were alone.

"Have courage, madame," said Josépha, who had seated herself on a cushion at the baroness's feet and was kissing her hands; "we'll find him; and if he's in the mire, why, he'll wash himself clean. My word for it, with well-bred men it's a

matter of clothes. Let me undo the wrong I have
done you, for I see how much you must be attached
to your husband, notwithstanding his conduct, to
have come here! Damme! the poor man! he does
love women.—Now, you see, if you'd had a little
of our *chic*, you could have prevented his running
riot so; for you would have been what we have
the secret of being: *all sorts of women* for one man.
The government ought to set up a school of gym-
nastics for virtuous women! But governments are
so prudish!—they are managed by men whom we
lead by the nose! For my part, I pity the people!
—But the point now is to work for you, and not to
joke.—Have no fear, madame, return home, and
don't worry any more. I'll bring your Hector back
to you as he was thirty years ago."

"Oh! mademoiselle, let us go to this Madame
Grenouville!" said the baroness; "she must know
something; perhaps I shall see Monsieur Hulot to-
day, and I may be able to rescue him at once from
want and shame.—"

"Madame, I will prove to you in advance the
profound gratitude with which I shall always think of
you for the honor you have done me, by not exhibiting Josépha the actress, the Duc d'Hérouville's
mistress, beside the most beautiful, the most saintly
image of virtue. I respect you too deeply to show
myself by your side. It is not the humility of an
actress, but my homage to you. You make me regret, madame, that I did not follow your path, despite the thorns that have torn your feet and hands!

But what would you have? I belong to art as you belong to virtue—"

"Poor girl!" exclaimed the baroness, deeply touched, amid her own sorrows, by a strange feeling of sympathetic commiseration. "I will pray for you, for you are the victim of society, which is sadly in need of plays. When old age comes upon you, repent—you will be forgiven if God will deign to listen to the prayers of a—"

"Of a martyr, madame," said Josépha, kissing the hem of the baroness's dress with deep respect.

But Adeline took her hand, drew her to her side and kissed her on the forehead. Blushing crimson with pleasure, the cantatrice escorted Adeline to her carriage, with demonstrations of almost servile humility.

"It's some one of those charitable women," said the footman to the maid, "for *she* isn't like that to anyone, not even her good friend, Madame Jenny Cadine!"

"Wait a few days, madame," said Josépha, "and you shall see *him*, or I will deny the God of my fathers; and for a Jewess, you know, that's a promise of success."

*

About the time that the baroness arrived at Josépha's home, Victorin received in his office an old woman of some seventy-five years, who, in order to gain access to the celebrated advocate, made use of the awe-inspiring name of the chief of the secret police. The servant announced:

"Madame de Saint-Estève!"

"I have taken one of my *noms de guerre,*" said she as she took a seat.

Victorin felt an internal shudder, so to speak, at the sight of this horrid old woman. Although richly dressed she was a terrifying object on account of the indications of cold-blooded depravity on her hard, deeply-wrinkled, dead-white muscular face. Marat, if a woman, would have been, at that age, like Saint-Estève, a living image of the Terror. The sinister old hag's sharp little eyes gleamed with the blood-thirsty cupidity of the tiger. Her broad flat nose, with nostrils like oval-shaped cavities in her face exhaling the flaming breath of hell, reminded one of the beak of the fiercest of birds of prey. The genius of intrigue was written upon her low, cruel forehead. The long hairs which grew at random in all the furrows of her face betrayed the virility of her mind. One who looked upon the woman might well have thought that every painter who ever

(153)

essayed to portray the face of Mephistopheles had missed his mark.

"My dear monsieur," she began in a patronizing tone, "I haven't had a hand in a job—I have not mixed myself up with anything for a long time. What I am going to do for you I do out of consideration for my dear nephew, whom I love better than I should love my son if I had one.—Now, the prefect of police, after the President of the Council had said a couple of words in his ear, referring to you, upon conferring with Monsieur Chapuzot concluded that the police ought not to appear at all in any matter of this kind. So they gave my nephew carte blanche; but my nephew won't take any part except to give advice, for he can't afford to compromise himself."

"You are the aunt of—?"

"You've hit it, and I'm a little bit proud of him," she replied, cutting the advocate short, "for he's my pupil, a pupil who soon became the master.— We have looked into your matter, and *gauged* it! Will you give thirty thousand francs to be rid of it all? I'll do the business for you, and you needn't pay till it's done."

"Do you know the persons concerned?"

"No, my dear monsieur, I await information from you. They told us: 'There's an old simpleton who's got into the clutches of a widow. This widow, twenty-nine years old, has plied her trade as a *thief* so successfully that she has forty thousand a year wormed out of two fathers of families.

She's on the point of raking in twenty-four thous-
and a year more by marrying an old fellow of sixty-
one; she will ruin a whole virtuous family; she will
soon get rid of her old husband and will give that
immense fortune to her child by some lover.'
There's the problem."

"You have it just right!" said Victorin. "My
father-in-law, Monsieur Crevel,—"

"Formerly a dealer in perfumery, now a mayor;
I live in his arrondissement under the name of
Mame Nourrisson," said she.

"The other person is Madame Marneffe."

"I don't know her," said Madame de Saint-
Estève, "but within three days I'll be able to count
her chemises."

"Could you prevent the marriage?" the advocate
inquired.

"How far along is it?"

"The second publication."

"We should have to kidnap the woman. It's
Sunday to-day, and we have only three days, for
they'll be married Wednesday; no, it can't be done.
But we can kill her for you—"

Victorin Hulot started back with the horror of an
honest man at these seven words, uttered with perfect sang-froid.

"Kill her!" said he. "How will you go about
it, pray?"

"For forty years, monsieur, we have taken the
place of destiny," she replied with aggressive
pride, "and have done whatever we chose in Paris.

More than one family, and in the Faubourg Saint-Germain, too, has told me its secrets. I have made and broken many marriages, I have torn up many wills, I have saved many reputations, I have stowed away here," she said, pointing to her head, " a whole flock of secrets, worth thirty-six thousand francs a year to me; and you will be one of my lambs, you know! Would a woman like me be what I am if she chattered about her methods? I act! Everything that happens, my dear master, will be the work of chance, and you needn't have the slightest remorse. You'll be like people cured by sleepwalkers; who at the end of a month think nature did it all."

The cold sweat stood on Victorin's forehead. The sight of the executioner would have moved him less than this sententious and pretentious sister of the galleys; as he looked at her dress of the color of wine-lees, he fancied that she was dressed in blood.

"Madame, I cannot accept the assistance of your experience and zeal, if success is to be attained at the cost of a life, or if anything in the nature of a crime is to result."

"You're a great baby, monsieur!" replied Madame de Saint-Estève. "You want to remain virtuous in your own eyes, and at the same time you want to see your enemy go under."

Victorin made a sign of dissent.

"Oh! yes," she continued; "you propose that this Madame Marneffe shall release the prey she has in her jaws! And how would you make a tiger let go his piece of beef? By patting him on the back, and saying: 'Pretty puss!—pretty puss!' —You're not logical. You order a battle, but you won't have any wounds! Very good; I'll make you a present of the innocence you have so much at heart. I have always looked upon virtue as the stuff of which hypocrisy is made! Some day, in the course of three months, a poor priest will come and ask you for forty thousand francs for some pious cause, a ruined convent in the East or in the desert! If you are satisfied with your lot, give the good man the forty thousand francs! you'll pay many times that amount into the exchequer. It will be a small matter, God knows, in comparison with what you'll reap."

She stood up on her enormous feet, which her satin shoes could so ill-contain that the flesh overhung them, bowed smilingly to the advocate, and withdrew.

"The devil has a sister," said Victorin to himself, as he rose.

He walked to the door with the horrible unknown, evoked from the caverns of espionage, as a hideous monster rises from the depths below the stage at the opera, in obedience to the magic wand in a fairy ballet.

Having concluded his duties at the Palais, Victorin, in search of information touching his unknown visitor, called upon Monsieur Chapuzot, who was at the head of one of the most important departments in the prefecture of police. Finding Monsieur

Chapuzot alone in his office, Victorin thanked him for his assistance."

"You sent me," said he, "an old woman who might serve to personify Paris, as seen on its criminal side."

Monsieur Chapuzot placed his spectacles on his papers, and stared at the advocate in amazement.

"I should not allow myself to send any person whatsoever to you without notifying you, or without a word of introduction," said he.

"Then it must have been Monsieur le Préfet."

"I don't think it," said Chapuzot. "The last time the Prince de Wissembourg dined with the Minister of the Interior he saw Monsieur le Préfet, and talked with him about the plight you were in, a truly deplorable plight, and asked him if he could not obligingly come to your assistance. Monsieur le Préfet, deeply interested by his Excellency's evident feeling on the subject of this family affair, was kind enough to consult me concerning it. When Monsieur le Préfet took the reins of this department, which is so maligned and at the same time is so useful, he first of all forbade our taking part in any family broils. He was right, both in principle and morally; but he was wrong in practice. The police, during the forty-five years I have been in the department, has rendered services of immense value to families, from 1799 to 1815. Since 1820 the press and the constitutional government have totally changed the conditions of our existence. So my advice was against meddling with an affair of this sort, and Monsieur le Préfet was so kind as to coincide with my opinion. The chief of the secret police received in my presence orders to take no steps; and if, by any chance, you have received a visit from any one sent by him, I shall reprimand him. It would be a case for dismissal. It's easy to say: 'The police will do thus and so!' The police! The police! But, my dear sir, the maréchal and the Council of Ministers have no idea what the police is. Only the police itself knows. The kings, Napoléon and Louis XVIII., knew what their police were about; but in our day, only Fouché, Monsieur Lenoir, Monsieur de Sartines, and some few clever prefects ever suspected.—Now all is changed. We are reduced in numbers, disarmed! I have seen many private disasters sprout and blossom that I might have prevented with five grains of arbitrary power. We shall be regretted by the very men who have wiped us out, when they are brought face to face, as you are now, with some moral monstrosity, which we should be empowered to put out of the way as we remove the mud from the streets! In politics the police are expected to anticipate everything when the public welfare is at stake; but the family is sacred. I would do anything to discover and defeat a plot against the king's life; I would make the walls of a house transparent; but to poke our noses into private households, into family affairs!—never so long as I sit in this office, for I am afraid—"

"Of what?"

"Of the press, Monsieur le Député of the Left Centre!"

"What ought I to do?" said Hulot after a pause.

"Eh! you call yourself the family!" retorted the chief of division; "that's all right, act as you see fit; but to come to your assistance, to make the police the instrument of private passion and private interests,—is such a thing possible?—Therein, you see, lies the secret of the inevitable persecution, which the magistrates deemed illegal, aimed at the predecessor of our present chief of the secret service. Bibi-Lupin ran the police for the benefit of private individuals. This concealed an immense social danger! With the means at his disposal that man would have been formidable, he would have been a sort of *sub-destiny*—"

"But, in my position—?" said Hulot.

"Oh! you, who sell consultations, come and ask for a consultation with me!" retorted Monsieur Chapuzot. "Go to, my dear master, you're laughing at me."

Hulot bowed to the chief of division and took his leave without noticing the almost imperceptible shrug which escaped that official when he rose to show him out.

"And that man claims to be a statesman!" said Monsieur Chapuzot to himself, taking up his reports once more.

Victorin returned home, concealing his perplexity, which he could confide to no one. At dinner the baroness joyfully announced that, within a month,

their father might be sharing their good fortune,
and finishing his days in peace in the bosom of his
family.

"Ah! I would gladly give my thirty-six hundred
francs a year to see the baron here!" cried Lisbeth.
"But, dear Adeline, I beg of you, don't count too
much upon such happiness beforehand."

"Lisbeth is right," said Célestine. "Dear
mother, do wait until he's here."

The baroness, all heart and hope, told of her visit
to Josépha, dilated upon the unhappiness of such
poor creatures in all their good-fortune, and spoke
of Chardin, the mattress-maker, the father of the
store-keeper at Oran, thus proving that she was
not following a false clue.

At seven o'clock the next morning Lisbeth was
on the Quai de la Tournelle, in a fiacre which she
stopped at the corner of Rue de Poissy.

"Go to Number 7 Rue des Bernardins," said she
to the driver; "it's a house on a court, with no
concierge. You will go up to the fourth floor and
ring at the door on the left, on which you will read:
'Mademoiselle Chardin, laces and cashmeres repaired.' When your ring is answered you will ask
for *the chevalier*. The answer will be: 'He has
gone out.'—You will say: 'I know it, but go and
find him, for his *bonne* is down on the quay in a
fiacre, and wants to see him.'"

Some twenty minutes later an old man, who
seemed quite eighty years of age, with snow-white
hair, a nose reddened by the cold wind set in a pallid

11

face as wrinkled as an old woman's, his back bent
double, dressed in an old alpaca overcoat, with list
slippers on his feet, with the sleeves of a knitted
waist-coat protruding at his wrists, an alarmingly
yellow shirt, and wearing no decoration, timidly
made his appearance, dragging one foot after the
other, looked at the fiacre, recognized Lisbeth, and
came to the door.

"Oh! what a state you're in, my dear cousin!"
said she.

"Élodie takes all the money for herself!" said
Baron Hulot.   "These Chardins are a stinking
canaille—"

"Do you want to come back with us?"

"Oh! no, no," said the old man; "I'd like to
cross to America."

"Adeline's on your track."

"Ah! if they could only pay my debts," said the
baron suspiciously, "for Samanon is after me."

"We haven't yet been able to pay up your arrears;
your son still owes a hundred thousand francs."

"Poor boy!"

"And your pension won't be free for seven or
eight months to come.—If you are willing to wait,
I have two thousand francs here!"

The baron put out his hand with an eager gesture
of awful significance.

"Give it to me, Lisbeth! May God reward you!
Give it to me!   I know where to go!"

"But you'll tell me, old monster?"

"Yes, I can wait eight months, for I've discovered

a little angel, a dear, innocent creature who isn't old enough to be depraved yet."

"Look out for the Assizes," said Lisbeth, who flattered herself that she should see Hulot there some day.

"Oh! it's Rue de Charonne," said Hulot, "a neighborhood where there's no noise made about anything that happens. No one will ever find me there. I'll disguise myself as Père Thorec, Lisbeth, and people will take me for an old cabinet-maker; the little one is fond of me, and I shall not have to eat the clothes off my back."

"No, that's already done!" said Lisbeth with a glance at his overcoat. "Suppose I drive you there, cousin?"

Baron Hulot jumped into the carriage, abandoning Mademoiselle Élodie without saying adieu to her, as one tosses aside a novel when it is read.

After a drive of half an hour, during which the baron talked of nothing but little Atala Judici, for he had arrived by degrees at the horrible passions which sap the lives of old men, his cousin deposited him, with two thousand francs in his pocket, on Rue Charonne, Faubourg Saint-Antoine, at the door of a house of very suspicious and ominous appearance.

"Adieu, cousin; now you will be *Père Thorec*, is that it? Don't send anybody to me but regular messengers, and never engage them twice in the same place."

"All right. Oh! I'm a lucky man!" exclaimed

the baron, whose face lighted up in joyful anticipation of the happiness in a new form which awaited him.

"She'll not find him there," said Lisbeth to herself, as she dismissed her cab on Boulevard Beaumarchais, whence she returned to Rue Louis-le-Grand in an omnibus.

*

The next morning Crevel was announced at his children's home, just as the whole family had assembled in the salon after breakfast. Célestine ran and threw herself on her father's neck, and ushered him into the room as if he had been there the day before, although it was his first visit in two years.

"Good-morning, father!" said Victorin, offering him his hand.

"Good-morning, my children!" said the consequential Crevel.—"Madame la Baronne, I offer you my profoundest respect. Heavens! how these children grow! they drive us about! they say: 'Grandpapa, I want my place in the sunlight!'—Madame la Comtesse, you are still wonderfully lovely!" he added, looking at Hortense.—"Ah! there's the balance of our crowns Cousin Bette, the wise virgin. Why, how comfortable you all are here,"—he continued, after this individual distribution of greetings, accompanied by roars of laughter which with difficulty moved the repose of the ruddy masses of his immense cheeks.

He glanced around his daughter's salon with something like disdain.

"My dear Célestine, I give you all the furniture on Rue des Saussayes; it will do very well here. Your salon needs to be furbished up.—Ah! there's

that little rascal of a Wenceslas! Well, do we be-
have ourselves, my little dears? you must look after
your morals."

"For those who haven't any," said Lisbeth.

"That sarcasm, my dear Lisbeth, doesn't concern
me now. I am going to put an end, my children,
to the false position I have occupied so long; and
like a good paterfamilias I have come to-day to announce my approaching marriage, without any ifs
or buts."

"You have the right to marry," said Victorin,
"and so far as I am concerned I give you back the
promise you made me when you consented to give
me my dear Célestine's hand."

"What promise?" demanded Crevel.

"That you would not marry again," replied the
advocate. "You will do me the justice to admit
that I asked for no such promise, that you gave it
voluntarily despite my remonstrances, for I urged
upon you at the time that you ought not to bind
yourself so."

"Yes, I remember, my dear boy," said Crevel
shamefacedly. "And on my word,—ah! my children, if you choose to live on good terms with
Madame Crevel you shall have no reason to repent
it.—Your delicacy touches me, Victorin.—No man
can be generous to me with impunity. *Sapristi!*
come, receive your mother-in-law kindly, come to
my wedding"

"You don't tell us who your *fiancée* is, father,"
said Célestine.

"Why, that's the secret of the play," said Crevel. "Let's not play at hide-and-seek! Lisbeth must have told you—"

"My dear Monsieur Crevel," retorted the Lorrainer, "there are names one can not pronounce here."

"Well, then, it's Madame Marneffe!"

"Monsieur Crevel," rejoined the advocate sternly, "neither my wife nor myself will attend your wedding, not from any interested motives, for I spoke to you just now with perfect sincerity. Yes, I should be very happy to know that you have found happiness in this union; but I am guided by motives of honor and delicacy which you must understand, and which I can not express, for I should reopen wounds which are still bleeding here."

The baroness made a sign to the countess, who took her child in her arms and said:

"Come, Wenceslas, come and have your bath!— Adieu, Monsieur Crevel."

The baroness bowed to Crevel without a word, and that worthy could not repress a smile as he saw the child's amazement at being threatened with this unexpected bath.

"You propose to marry, monsieur," cried the advocate when he was alone with Lisbeth, his wife and his father-in-law, "a woman who is laden with my father's spoils, and who with utter unconcern led him into his present plight; a woman who is living with the son-in-law, after ruining the father-in-law; a woman who is the cause of my sister's mortal suffering.—And you fancy that I will sanction your madness by my presence? I sincerely pity you, my dear Monsieur Crevel! you have no idea of the family, you do not understand the powerful bond of honor which binds its different members together. One can't reason with the passions —unfortunately I have had too much experience in that direction. Men who are ruled by their passions are as deaf as they are blind. Your daughter Célestine is too fully sensible of her duty to utter a single word of reproach.''

''That would be a fine thing for her to do!'' said Crevel, trying to cut short this lecture.

''Célestine would not be my wife if she said one word to you on the subject,'' rejoined the advocate; ''but I can try to stop you before you put your foot over the precipice, especially after I have proved my disinterestedness. It certainly is not your fortune, but you yourself, that I am concerned about. —And, to leave you in no doubt as to my feelings, I may add, were it only to set your mind at rest concerning your marriage-contract, that my pecuniary situation is such that we have nothing to wish for.''

''Thanks to me!'' cried Crevel, whose face had become purple.

''Thanks to Célestine's fortune,'' retorted the advocate; ''and if you regret having given your daughter, as a marriage-portion coming from yourself, a sum which does not represent the half of what her mother left her, we are all ready to return it to you.''

"Do you know, my good son-in-law," said Crevel, striking his attitude, "that, when I give Madame Marneffe the protection of my name, she will not be answerable to the world for her conduct, except as Madame Crevel?"

"That may be very noble," said the advocate; "it's very generous so far as affairs of the heart and the errors due to passion are concerned; but I know no name, no laws, no title which can cover up the theft of the three hundred thousand francs vilely extorted from my father!—I tell you plainly, my dear father-in-law, that your intended wife is unworthy of you, that she is deceiving you, that she is madly in love with my brother-in-law Steinbock, whose debts she has paid—"

"It was I who paid them!"

"Very good," retorted the advocate; "I am very glad for Comte Steinbock, who may be able to pay you some day; but she loves him, she loves him very dearly, and loves him often—"

"She loves him!" said Crevel, whose face bore witness to his great agitation. "It's a cowardly, dirty, mean, vulgar thing to slander a woman!—When one makes such statements as that, monsieur, one must prove them."

"I'll give you your proofs."

"I await them!"

"Day after to-morrow, my dear Monsieur Crevel, I will tell you the day, hour and moment when I shall be prepared to lay bare the shocking depravity of your future wife."

"Very well, I shall be charmed," said Crevel, recovering his self-possession.—"Adieu, my children, au revoir.—Adieu, Lisbeth."

"Pray go with him, Lisbeth," said Célestine in Cousin Bette's ear.

"Well, well, how you go on!" cried Lisbeth to Crevel.

"Ah!" said Crevel, "he's become a very great man, has my son-in-law; he's presumptuous. The Palais, the Chamber, the wiles of the law and the wiles of politics are making a very pretty fellow of him. Ah! he knows that I'm to be married next Wednesday, and on Sunday my gentleman proposes to tell me, three days after, the time when he will prove that my wife's unworthy of me. That's very clever. I am going back to sign the contract. Come, Lisbeth, come with me! They'll know nothing about it! I intended to leave Célestine forty thousand francs a year, but Hulot has acted in a way to alienate my heart forever."

"Give me ten minutes, Père Crevel; wait ten minutes for me in your carriage at the door, while I invent an excuse for going out."

"Very well, I'll do it."

"My dears," said Lisbeth returning to the family in the salon, "I am going with Crevel; the contract's to be signed to-night, and I may be able to tell you its provisions. It will probably be my last visit to that woman. Your father's in a furious rage. He means to disinherit you."

"His vanity will prevent him from doing it,"

replied the advocate. "He was anxious to own the Presles estate, and he'll keep it; I know him. Even if he should have children, Célestine will get half of what he leaves; the law forbids him bequeathing his whole fortune away from her.—But those questions have no weight with me; I am thinking solely of our honor.—Go, cousin," he said, pressing Lisbeth's hand, "and listen closely to the contract."

Some twenty minutes later Lisbeth and Crevel entered the house on Rue Barbet, where Madame Marneffe was awaiting in mild impatience the result of the step she had ordered to be taken. Valérie had, in the end, conceived a violent passion for Wenceslas, of the sort which assails a woman's heart but once in a lifetime. In her hands the unsuccessful artist had become so perfect a lover, that he was to her what she had been to Baron Hulot. Valérie had her slippers in one hand, and the other was in Steinbock's, against whose shoulder her head was resting. It might well be said of the disconnected conversation in which they had been engaged since Crevel's departure, as of the bulky literary productions of our day, which bear the legend on their title-pages: *Reproduction prohibited.* This delicious hour of poetic privacy naturally brought to the artist's lips a regret, which he expressed not without bitterness.

"Ah! how unfortunate it is that I married!" he said; "for, if I had waited, as Lisbeth advised, I might marry you now.'

"One must be a Pole to long to make one's de-voted mistress his wife!" cried Valérie. "To exchange love for duty! pleasure for ennui!"

"I know you to be so fickle!" Steinbock replied. "Haven't I heard you talking with Lisbeth about Baron Montès, that Brazilian?"

"Do you want to rid me of him?" said Valérie.

"That would be the only way of preventing you from seeing him," replied the ex-sculptor.

"Understand, my darling," said Valérie, "that I was playing him to make a husband of him, for I tell you everything—the promises I made this Brazilian,—oh! long before I knew you, she said in reply to a gesture from Wenceslas—"those prom-ises, which he is using now as weapons to torment me with, force me to marry almost in secret; for if he learns that I am to marry Crevel he is just the man to—to kill me!"

"Oh! as for any fear of that!—" exclaimed Steinbock, with a disdainful gesture which signified that that danger was quite insignificant for a woman who was beloved by a Pole.

Take notice that in the matter of personal cour-age the Poles are not to be accused of bravado, they are so truly and unequivocally brave.

"And that idiot of a Crevel, who insists upon giving a party, and is displaying his taste for mag-nificence—economical magnificence—in connection with our wedding, places me in an embarrassing position that I can't see my way out of!"

Could Valérie confess to the man she adored that

Baron Henri Montès, after Baron Hulot's dismissal, had inherited the privilege of visiting her at all hours of the night, and that, notwithstanding her address, she was still in imminent danger of a dispute in which the Brazilian would believe that she was entirely in the wrong? She was too well acquainted with the baron's quasi-savage disposition, which closely resembled Lisbeth's, not to tremble as she thought of her Moor from Rio-de-Janeiro. When they heard the carriage-wheels, Steinbock, whose arm was about Valérie's waist, moved away from her, and took up a newspaper in which he seemed to be deeply absorbed. Valérie was embroidering, with painstaking attention, a pair of slippers for her intended spouse.

"How they slander *her!*" said Lisbeth in Crevel's ear, pointing to the picture before them as they stood in the doorway.—"Look at her hair! is it tumbled? To hear Victorin talk, you might have expected to surprise a pair of turtle-doves in their nest."

"My dear Lisbeth," replied Crevel, in his favorite pose, "to make a Lucretia of an Aspasia, you see, all you need do is to inspire her with a real passion!"

"Didn't I always tell you," retorted Lisbeth, "that women love fat old libertines like you?"

"She'd be mighty ungrateful if she didn't," said Crevel; "for how much money have I laid out here? Nobody knows but Grindot and myself!"

And he went up stairs.

In the renovation of this mansion, which Crevel

looked upon as his own, Grindot had tried to measure
his strength with Cleretti, the architect then in
vogue, to whom the Duc d'Hérouville had entrusted
the decoration of Josépha's house. But Crevel, who
was utterly unable to understand art, determined,
like all men of his class, to spend a fixed sum, decided upon in advance. Restricted as he was by
an iron-clad estimate, it was impossible for Grindot
to realize his architectural dream. The principal
difference between Josépha's mansion and the one
on Rue Barbet was the same difference that exists
between any object that has an individuality of its
own and one that is utterly commonplace. The
things that one admired in Josépha's rooms one
saw nowhere else; the glittering ornaments of Crevel's salons could be bought anywhere. These two
different varieties of luxury are separated from each
other by the broad stream of the million. A mirror
of which there is no duplicate is worth six thousand
francs, the mirror invented by a manufacturer who
sells as many as he can of the same pattern, costs
five hundred. An authentic Boulle chandelier sells
as high as three thousand francs at public auction;
the same chandelier remoulded can be made for a
thousand or twelve hundred; one is in archæology
what a genuine Raphaël is in painting, the other is
its copy. What value do you attach to a copy of a
Raphaël? The Crevel mansion therefore was a
magnificent specimen of the splendor of fools, as
Josépha's was the most beautiful type of an artistic
habitation.

"The war is on," said Crevel, walking toward his fiancée.

Madame Marneffe rang.

"Go for Monsieur Berthier," she said to the footman, "and do not come back without him.—If you had succeeded," said she, winding her arms about Crevel, "we would have postponed my happiness, my little father, and we would have given a feast to make people open their eyes; but when a whole family opposes a marriage, my dear, decency requires that it should be celebrated quietly, especially when the bride is a widow."

"On the contrary I propose to have it celebrated on a scale of magnificence worthy of Louis XIV.," said Crevel, who had long since concluded that the eighteenth century was beneath contempt. "I have ordered new carriages: there's monsieur's carriage and madame's, two pretty little coupés, a calèche, and a state berlin, with a magnificent box which shakes like Madame Hulot."

"Aha! *I propose!*—So you won't be my lamb any longer? No, no, my buck, you'll do as I wish. We will sign our contract here, between ourselves, to-night. Then, on Wednesday, we'll be married formally, a genuine marriage, on the sly, as my poor mother used to say. We will go on foot, dressed very simply, to the church, where we will hear low mass. Our witnesses are Steinbock, Stidmann, Vignon and Massol, all clever fellows who will be at the mayor's office as if by chance, and who will make the sacrifice of listening to mass for our sake. Your colleague will make an exception in our case and marry us at nine o'clock in the morning. Mass is at ten o'clock and we shall be back here to breakfast at half-past eleven. I have promised our guests that we would not leave the table till evening. We shall have Bixiou, your former comrade Du Tillet, Lousteau, Vernisset, Léon de Lora, Vernou, the élite of the entertaining men of the day, none of whom need know that we are married; we will mystify them, we will get just a shade tipsy, and Lisbeth will be on hand; I want her to know of the marriage, Bixiou is to make some proposals to her, and teach her—a little something.''

For two hours Madame Marneffe poured forth a flood of playful talk, which suggested to Crevel's mind this sage reflection:

"How can a woman so light of heart be depraved? Frolicsome, if you please! but wicked—nonsense!''

"What did your children say about me?'' Valérie asked Crevel at a moment when she drew him close to her on her sofa; "horrible things, I suppose!''

"They declare,'' Crevel replied, "that you have a criminal passion for Wenceslas; you, virtue itself!''

"I should say that I do love my little Wenceslas!'' cried Valérie, calling the artist to her side, taking his head in her hands, and kissing him on the brow. "Poor boy, without friends or fortune! thrown aside in disdain by a carrot-colored giraffe! What do you expect, Crevel? Wenceslas is my poet, and I love him in broad daylight as if he were my

child! These virtuous women see evil everywhere
and in everything. Ah well! so they couldn't be
content without trying to injure me about a man?
I am like a spoiled child who has never been refused
anything; bonbons no longer cause me any emotion.
Poor women, I pity them!—Who was it, pray, who
maligned me like that?''

"Victorin," said Crevel.

"Well, why didn't you close his beak, the mag-
isterial parroquet, with his *mamma's* two hundred
thousand francs?''

"Ah! the baroness ran away,'' said Lisbeth.

"Let them beware, Lisbeth!'' exclaimed Madame
Marneffe with a frown; "either they will receive
me under their roof, and civilly, too, and will call
on their step-mother, every one of them! or I'll
sink them lower than the baron is now; tell them
so from me.—I propose to become wicked at last!
On my word, I believe evil is the reaping-hook
with which men gather in this world's goods.''

At three o'clock Monsieur Berthier, successor to
Cardot, read the marriage-contract, after a brief
conference with Crevel, for certain articles depended upon the decision of Monsieur and Madame
Hulot junior. Crevel made over to his future wife
a fortune consisting of:

1. Forty thousand francs a year, to be derived
from securities which were named;

2. The house on Rue Barbet and everything
contained therein; and

3. Three millions in cash.

12

Over and above this he gave his future wife all that the law allowed him to give; he provided that she need furnish no inventory; and in the event that there should be no children of the marriage, they agreed that the one who should die first should give to the other the whole of his or her property, real and personal. This contract reduced Crevel's fortune to two millions. If he had children by his new wife, it would cut down Célestine's share to five hundred thousand francs, because of the income provided for Valérie. That sum represented about one-ninth part of his present fortune.

Lisbeth returned to Rue Louis-le-Grand to dinner, with despair depicted on her countenance. She explained and dilated upon the marriage-contract, and found Célestine no less indifferent to the disastrous news than Victorin.

"You have angered your father, my children! Madame Marneffe has sworn that you shall receive Monsieur Crevel's wife, and that you shall call upon her," she said.

"Never!" said Hulot.

"Never!" said Célestine.

"Never!" cried Hortense.

Lisbeth was seized with an ardent longing to put down the haughty pride of all the Hulots.

"She seems to have some weapon to use against you!" she replied. "I don't know what it is, but I will know.—She spoke vaguely of some story about two hundred thousand francs, which has some connection with Adeline."

Madame Hulot quietly fell over on the couch where she was sitting, and a frightful attack of convulsions followed.

"Go to her, my children!—" cried she. "Receive the woman here! Monsieur Crevel is an infamous man! he deserves the greatest of all punishments. —Obey that woman.—Ah! she's a monster! *She knows all!*"

After she had uttered these words, mingled with tears and sobs, she summoned sufficient strength to go up to her own room, leaning on her daughter's arm and Célestine's.

"What does all this mean?" cried Lisbeth, when she was left alone with Victorin.

The advocate, rooted to the spot, in a state of stupefaction that can readily be conceived, did not hear Lisbeth.

"What's the matter, dear Victorin?"

"I am terrified!" said the advocate, whose face assumed a threatening expression. "Woe to her who injures my mother; my scruples have vanished! If I could do it, I would crush that woman as one would crush a viper.—Ah! she aims a blow at my mother's life and honor!"

"She said, but don't repeat this, my dear Victorin, she said that she would sink you all lower than your father.—She reproached Crevel roundly for not having closed your mouth with this secret which seems to frighten Adeline so."

A physician was sent for, for the baroness's condition grew worse. He ordered a draught containing a large amount of opium, and Adeline fell into a deep sleep as soon as she had taken it; but the whole family was alarmed beyond measure. The next day, the advocate started at an early hour for the Palais; he called at the prefecture of police on his way, and besought Vautrin, the chief of the secret service, to send Madame de Saint-Estève to him.

"We are forbidden, monsieur, to take any part in your affair, but Madame de Saint-Estève is in business on her own account, and she's at your service," replied the famous officer.

On his return the poor fellow learned that his mother's reason was in danger. Doctor Bianchon, Doctor Larabit and Professor Angard, in consultation, had decided to resort to heroic methods to check the flow of blood to the brain. While Victorin was listening to Doctor Bianchon giving his reasons for hoping that the crisis would end favorably, although his associates despaired of any such result, the footman announced Madame de Saint-Estève. Victorin left Bianchon in the middle of a sentence, and ran down stairs like a madman.

"Can there be a germ of contagious insanity in the family?" said Bianchon turning to Larabit.

The physicians went away, leaving an assistant to watch Madame Hulot.

"A whole lifetime of virtue!" were the only words the invalid had pronounced since her seizure.

Lisbeth did not leave Adeline's bedside; she had sat up all night with her and was looked upon with admiration by the two younger women.

"Well, my dear Madame Saint-Estève!" said
the advocate, showing the horrible old woman into
his study, and carefully closing the doors, "how
far have we got?"

"Well, my dear friend," she replied, looking at
Victorin with a coldly ironical eye, "have you reflected on what I said?"

"Have you done anything?"

"Will you give fifty thousand francs?"

"Yes," replied Hulot, "for we must go ahead.
Do you know that that woman has endangered my
mother's life and reason with a single sentence?
So, go on!"

"We have gone on!" said the old woman.

"Well?—" said Victorin convulsively.

"Well, do you stick at any expense?"

"On the contrary."

"The expenses already mount up to twenty-three
thousand francs."

Hulot stared at the Saint-Estève with an idiotic
expression.

"Well, well! can you be such a gull, you, one of
the shining lights of the Palais?" said the old woman. "For that sum we have procured a lady's
maid's conscience and a picture by Raphaël; that's
not a high price.—"

Hulot still stood stupidly by with his eyes opened
to their fullest extent.

"Well," continued La Saint-Estève, "we have
purchased Mademoiselle Reine Tousard, a young
lady from whom Madame Marneffe has no secrets."

"I understand."

"But if you're going to be stingy, say so!"

"I will pay you and trust to you," he replied; "go on! My mother told me that these people deserved the most severe of all punishments."

"They don't break people on the wheel any more," said the old woman.

"You will answer for the success of your plan?"

"Let me alone," said La Saint-Estève. "Your vengeance is simmering."

She looked at the clock; it was just six.

"Your vengeance is dressing, the ovens at the *Rocher de Cancale* are lighted, the horses in the carriages are stamping, my irons are being heated. Ah! I know your Madame Marneffe by heart. Everything is ready! There is bait in the trap, and I'll tell you to-morrow if the mouse will be poisoned. I think so! Adieu, my son."

"Adieu, madame."

"Do you know English?"

"Yes."

"Did you ever see the play of Macbeth, in English?"

"Yes."

"Well, my son, you shall be king! that is to say, you shall inherit!" said the frightful hag, whom Shakespeare imagined, and who seemed familiar with Shakespeare.

She left Hulot dumfounded on the threshold of his study.

"Don't forget that the case is on for to-morrow,"

said she graciously with the air of an experienced litigant.

She saw two people coming and was anxious to pass in their eyes for a *Comtesse de Pimbèche.*

"What assurance!" muttered Hulot, as he bowed to his pretended client.

*

Baron Montès de Montejanos was a lion, but a lion shrouded in mystery. Fashionable Paris, the Paris of the turf and the lorettes, admired the foreign nobleman's ineffable waistcoats, the irreproachable polish of his boots, his matchless canes, his much admired fine horses, his carriage, driven by perfectly trained and well-controlled negroes. The amount of his fortune was known; he had a credit of seven hundred thousand francs with Du Tillet the famous banker; but he was always alone. If he went to a first performance, he sat in an orchestra stall. He frequented no salon. He had never offered his arm to a lorette! It was impossible to connect his name with that of any charming woman in society. For pastime, he played whist at the Jockey Club. People were reduced to the necessity of attacking his manners, or, what seemed infinitely more amusing, his personal appearance; they called him Combabus!—Bixiou, Léon de Lora, Lousteau, Florine, Mademoiselle Héloïse Brisetout and Nathan, when supping one evening with the illustrious Carabine, with lions and lionesses galore, invented this most absurd appellation. Massol, in his capacity of Councilor of State, and Claude Vignon, who had once been a professor of Greek, had told the ignorant lorettes the famous anecdote, related in Rollin's Ancient History, concerning

Combabus, that voluntary Abelard to whom was entrusted the custody of the wife of a king of Assyria, Persia, Bactriana, Mesopotamia, and other divisions of the private geography of old Professor Du Bocage, who completed the work begun by D'Anville, the creator of the ancient Orient. This nickname, which furnished food for laughter to Carabine's guests for a quarter of an hour, was the subject of a multitude of decidedly broad jests in a work to which the Academy could not award the Montyon prize, but among them was noticed the name which clung to the bushy mane of the handsome baron, whom Josépha called a *magnificent Brazilian*, as one speaks of a magnificent *catoxantha!* Carabine, most illustrious of lorettes, whose refined beauty and witty sallies had wrested the sceptre of the thirteenth arrondissement from the hands of Mademoiselle Turquet, better known by the name of *Malaga*,—Carabine, or Mademoiselle Séraphine Sinet—such was her real name—was to the banker Du Tillet what Josépha Mirah was to the Duc d'Hérouville.

Now, on the morning of the very day when La Saint-Estève predicted success to Victorin, Carabine had said to Du Tillet about seven o'clock:

"If you were a good fellow, you'd give me a dinner at the *Rocher de Cancale,* and bring Combabus; we mean to find out whether he has a mistress.— I've bet on — and I want to win."

"He's always at the Hôtel des *Princes,* and I'll drop in and see him," replied Du Tillet; "we'll have

some sport. Have all the boys there : Bixiou,
Lora, the whole gang in fact!''

At half-past seven in the evening, the table was
laid for dinner in the finest salon of the establishment
where all Europe has dined; upon the table shone a
magnificent service of silver-plate made expressly
for use at dinner-parties where vanity liquidated
the bill in bank-notes. Torrents of light caused
cascades of brilliancy to play along the edges of the
chasing. Waiters, whom a provincial would have
mistaken for diplomatists, barring their age, moved
sedately about like men who knew that they would
be handsomely tipped.

Five persons had arrived and were awaiting the
arrival of nine others. First of all there was
Bixiou, the salt of every intellectual feast, still
on his feet in 1843, with a whole armor of jokes,
always new,—a phenomenon as rare in Paris as
virtue itself. Then there was Léon de Lora, the
greatest landscape and marine painter living, who
had the advantage over all his rivals of never
having fallen below the level of his first work. The
lorettes could not do without these kings of witti-
cism. No supper, no dinner, no party of any sort
was complete without them. Séraphine Sinet, alias
Carabine, as titular mistress of the Amphitryon of
the feast, had been one of the first to arrive, and
was exhibiting beneath the waves of light in all
their glory a pair of shoulders unrivaled in Paris, a
neck as faultless in outline as if turned on a lathe,
and without a wrinkle! a saucy face, and a dress

of figured satin, blue upon blue, trimmed with English lace in sufficient quantity to support a whole village for a month.   Pretty Jenny Cadine, who was not acting at her theatre and whose portrait is too well known to make any description necessary, arrived in a costume of fabulous splendor. To these ladies a party is always a Longchamp in the matter of toilettes, where each seeks to win the prize for her particular millionaire, saying, as it were, to her rivals:

"See how much I am worth!"

A third woman, doubtless just at the beginning of her career, was looking on, almost shamefacedly, at the magnificence of her two wealthy and established companions.   She was simply dressed, in white cashmere trimmed with blue lace; her hair had been dressed with flowers by a hairdresser of the *merlan* type, whose unskilful hand had, unwittingly, imparted the charm of simplicity to her lovely blonde locks.   Embarrassed as she still was by her costume, *she had the shyness inseparable from a first appearance*, according to the time-worn phrase. She came from Valognes to find employment in Paris for a despairingly-blooming freshness, innocence calculated to arouse the passions of a dying man, and beauty worthy to take rank with all those that Normandy has already furnished to the different theatres of the capital.   The perfect lines of her face fulfilled one's ideal of angelic purity. The milky whiteness of her skin reflected the light so perfectly that you would have said you were looking in a mirror. The delicate colors were laid upon her cheeks as with an artist's pencil. She was called Cydalise. She was, as we shall presently see, a necessary pawn in the game *Mame* Nourrisson was playing against Madame Marneffe.

"You haven't an arm in keeping with your name, my dear," said Jenny Cadine, to whom Carabine had introduced this sixteen-year chef-d'œuvre, and who had brought her to the dinner.

In truth Cydalise presented for public admiration a pair of lovely arms, compact and of fine texture, but reddened by the vigorous current of blood that flowed beneath.

"How much is she worth?" Jenny Cadine asked Carabine in an undertone.

"A fortune."

"What do you propose to make of her?"

"Madame Combabus of course!"

"And for that transaction you are to have—?"

"Guess!"

"A handsome service of plate?"

"I have three!"

"Diamonds?"

"I sell them."

"A green monkey?"

"No, a Raphaël!"

"What rat has got into your brain?"

"Josépha puts my nose out of joint with her pictures," replied Carabine, "and I propose to have finer ones than hers."

Du Tillet brought with him the hero of the

dinner, the Brazilian; the Duc d'Hérouville followed them with Josépha.   The cantatrice wore a simple velvet dress; but about her neck gleamed a necklace worth a hundred and twenty thousand francs, of pearls which could hardly be distinguished from her white camelia-like skin.   She had thrust among the black tresses of her hair a single red camelia—a *patch!*—with stunning effect, and she had amused herself by piling up eleven pearl bracelets on each arm.   As she pressed Jenny Cadine's hand, the latter said to her:

"Pray lend me your mittens, will you?"

Josépha removed her bracelets and offered them to her friend upon a plate.

"What style!" said Carabine; "she must be a duchess! Pearls, too! You've stripped the sea to adorn your girl, eh, Monsieur le Duc?" she added, turning to the little Duc d'Hérouville.

The actress took but two bracelets and replaced the other twenty on the singer's arms, on which she deposited a kiss.

Lousteau, the literary parasite, La Palférine and Malaga, Massol and Vauvinet, and Théodore Gaillard, part-proprietor of one of the leading political journals, completed the number of guests.   The Duc d'Hérouville, courteous, as a great nobleman always is, to everybody, exchanged with the Comte de la Palférine that special form of salutation which, without suggesting esteem or intimacy, says to all the world: "We are of the same family, of the same race, we know each other's worth."

That salutation, the *shibboleth* of the aristocracy, was invented to carry despair to the wits of the upper middle-class.

Carabine seated Combabus at her left and the Duc d'Hérouville at her right. Cydalise flanked the Brazilian and Bixiou was placed on the other side of the young Norman. Malaga was next the duke.

At seven they attacked the oysters. At eight, between two courses, they discussed frozen punch. Everybody knows the menu of such banquets. At nine o'clock they were chattering away as people will chatter after forty-two bottles of different kinds of wine have been emptied by fourteen persons. The dessert, the horrible dessert of the month of April, was served. The heady atmosphere had intoxicated none but the Norman girl, who was singing a Christmas carol. With the exception of that poor creature no one had lost his wits, for the drinkers, men and women, were the élite of supping Paris. Spirits were gay, eyes, although brilliant were still full of intelligence, but lips were tending to satire, anecdote and indiscretion. The conversation, which had thus far been confined within the vicious circle of racing and horses, Bourse operations, the different merits of the reigning lions compared with one another, and well-known scandalous anecdotes, threatened to become more private, and to be divided among groups of two hearts.

At this juncture, in obedience to divers meaning

glances bestowed by Carabine upon Léon de Lora,
Bixiou, La Palférine and Du Tillet, the subject of
love was brought forward.

"The best doctors never talk about medicine, real
noblemen never talk about their ancestors, talented
people never talk about their works," said Josépha;
"why should we talk about our profession?—I made
them close the doors at the opera so that I could
come, and it certainly wasn't for the purpose of
working here.   So let's not *pose*, my dear friends."

"They're talking about real love, my dear!"
said Malaga, "the love that makes a man throw
himself overboard, and his father and mother, sell
his wife and children and go to Clichy—"

"Talk away, then!" rejoined the singer.   "Not
up to it!"

"Not up to it."   This phrase, adopted into the
lorette's vocabulary from the slang of the Paris
gamin, becomes with the assistance of their eyes
and expression, a whole poem upon their lips.

"Don't I love you, Josépha?" said the duke in
a low voice.

"You may love me truly," the cantatrice whispered in his ear, with a smile; "but as for myself,
I don't love you with the kind of love they're talking about, the love that makes the world all black
without the man one loves.   You are very agreeable
to me, and useful, but you're not indispensable;
and if you should desert me to-morrow, I should
have three dukes for one—"

"Does love really exist in Paris?" said Léon de

Lora. "No one here has the time to make his fortune, and how can one yield to the true love which takes possession of a man as water does of sugar? One must be enormously rich to love, for love nullifies a man, as it has our dear Brazilian baron here. I have said for a long time that *extremes stop each other up.* A true lover resembles a eunuch, for women no longer exist on earth so far as he is concerned! He's a mysterious creature, he's like the true Christian, alone in his desert! Just look at our gallant Brazilian yonder!''

The whole table turned to look at Henri Montès de Montejanos, who was abashed to find himself the cynosure of every eye.

"He's been feeding there an hour without any more idea than an ox would have, that he's sitting beside the—I won't say in this presence the loveliest, but the freshest young woman in Paris.''

"Everything is fresh here, even the fish; that's the reputation of the house,'' said Carabine.

Baron Montès de Montejanos looked across at the landscape-painter with an affable expression, and said:

"Very good! I drink to you!''

And he nodded to Léon de Lora, put his full glass of port to his mouth and drank with great dignity.

"So you are in love?'' said Carabine to her neighbor, putting this interpretation upon the toast.

The baron ordered his glass refilled, bowed to Carabine and repeated the toast.

13

"To madame's health!'' then said the lorette, in so waggish a tone that the painter, Bixiou and Du Tillet roared with laughter.

The Brazilian maintained the gravity of a bronze statue. His indifference vexed Carabine. She was perfectly well aware that Montès was in love with Madame Marneffe; but she did not look for this uncompromising fidelity, the obstinate silence of a man whose mind is made up. We so often judge a woman by the attitude of her lover that we are accustomed to judge a lover by the bearing of his mistress. Proud of his love for Valérie and of being beloved by her, there was a tinge of irony in the smile the baron bestowed upon these accomplished connoisseurs; moreover he was superb to look upon; the wine had not changed his color, and his eyes, bright with the brilliancy peculiar to burnished gold, kept the secrets of his heart.

"What a woman!'' said Carabine to herself; "how she has sealed up that heart!''

"He's a stone!'' said Bixiou half-aloud, looking upon it all as a bit of fooling, and without a suspicion of the importance attached by Carabine to the demolition of this fortress.

While this discussion, apparently trivial, was going on at Carabine's right, the discussion concerning love was continued at her left by the Duc d'Hérouville, Lousteau, Josépha, Jenny Cadine and Massol. They were trying to decide whether these infrequent phenomena were produced by passion, by obstinacy, or by true love. Josépha, bored to death by their theories, tried to change the subject of conversation.

"You're talking about something of which you are absolutely ignorant! Is there any one of you who ever loved a woman enough, and a woman unworthy of him, to throw away his fortune and his children's, sell his future, besmirch his past, run the risk of the galleys by stealing from the State, kill his brother and uncle, and allow his eyes to be blindfolded so completely that he never thought it was being done to prevent him from seeing the pit, into which he was pushed, as a final jest? Du Tillet has a strong-box under his left breast, Léon de Lora has his wits there, Bixiou would laugh at himself if he loved anybody but himself, Massol has a minister's portfolio in place of a heart; Lousteau has nothing but a muscle there, for he allowed Madame de la Baudraye to leave him; Monsieur le Duc is too rich to be able to prove his love by ruining himself; Vauvinet doesn't count; I draw the line at the discounter of mankind. So you have never loved, any of you, nor have I, nor Jenny, nor Carabine.—For my own part I never have seen the phenomenon I have just described but once. That was our poor Baron Hulot," she said to Jenny Cadine, "whom I'm going to advertise for like a lost dog, for I want to find him."

"Oho!" said Carabine to herself with a meaning glance at Josépha; "has Madame Nourrisson two

of Raphaël's pictures, that I find Josépha playing
my game?"

"Poor man!" said Vauvinet, "he was very tall
and stately.   What style! what a figure!   He had
the carriage of François I.   What a volcano he was!
and what cleverness, what downright genius he displayed in raising money!   Wherever he is he's on
the look out for it, and he ought to be able to get
some out of the walls built of bones that you see
in the suburbs of Paris, near the gates, where he's
in hiding, no doubt—"

"And all for that little Madame Marneffe!" said
Bixiou.   "There's a female roué for you!"

"She's going to marry my friend Crevel!"
observed Du Tillet.

"And she's mad over my friend Steinbock!"
said Léon de Lora.

These three remarks were like three pistol shots
received by Montès full in the chest.   He turned
pale as death, and was in such agony that it was
difficult for him to rise.

"You're *canaille!*" he exclaimed.   "You've no
right to mingle a virtuous woman's name with the
names of all your abandoned creatures! nor, above
all things, to make her a target for your low jokes!"

Montès was interrupted by bravos and unanimous
applause.   Bixiou, Léon de Lora, Vauvinet, Du
Tillet and Massol gave the signal.   It was a grand
chorus.

"Vive l'Empereur!" said Bixiou.

"Crown him!" cried Vauvinet.

"A *groan* for Médor! *hurrah* for Brazil!" cried Lousteau.

"Aha! my copper-colored baron, you love our Valérie, do you?" said Léon de Lora; "you're not easily disgusted!"

"What he said wasn't parliamentary, but it was magnificent!" observed Massol.

"But, my love of a client, you have recommended me, I am your banker, your innocence will be a bad thing for me."

"Ah! you're a serious-minded man, do you tell me—" said the Brazilian to Du Tillet.

"Thanks for us all," said Bixiou, bowing.

"Tell me something positive," continued Montès, disregarding Bixiou's interruption.

"Well, my boy," replied Du Tillet, "I have the honor to tell you that I am invited to Crevel's wedding."

"Aha! Combabus assumes the defense of Madame Marneffe!" exclaimed Josépha rising solemnly from her chair.

She walked up to Montès with a tragic air, gave him a friendly little tap on the head, looked at him for a moment with an expression of amused admiration in her face, and shook her head.

"Hulot is the first example of love *in spite of all*, and here's the second," she said; "but he ought not to count, for he comes from the tropics."

As Josépha dealt Montès the above gentle tap upon the forehead, he fell back upon his chair, and appealed with a look to Du Tillet.

"I am the victim of one of your Parisian jokes," he said; "if your object was to wrest my secret from me—"

He enveloped the whole table with a circle of fire, embracing all the guests in a glance in which blazed the Brazilian sun.

"In God's name, tell me so," he went on in a supplicating, almost childlike tone; "but do not slander a woman whom I love."

"Ah!" said Carabine in his ear, "but suppose you were shamefully betrayed, deceived, played with by Valérie, and I should prove it to you within an hour at my house, what would you do?"

"I can't tell you before all these Iagos," said the Brazilian baron.

Carabine understood him to say *magots*—coxcombs—

"Well, keep quiet!" she replied with a smile; "don't give the brightest men in Paris a chance to laugh at you, but come to my house; we will talk—"

Montès was completely crushed.

"Proofs!—" he faltered; "reflect—"

"You shall have only too many," said Carabine, "and since the mere suspicion goes to your head so, I'm afraid for your reason."

"What an obstinate creature it is, he's worse than the late King of Holland!—I say, Lousteau, Bixiou, Massol, ohé! and you others! aren't you all invited to breakfast by Madame Marneffe for day after to-morrow?" asked Léon de Lora.

"*Ya.*" replied Du Tillet. "I have the honor to

tell you once more, baron, that if by any chance you intended to marry Madame Marneffe, you are rejected like the draft of a law by a ball in the name of Crevel. My friend, my old comrade Crevel, has eighty thousand a year, and you probably haven't exhibited as much as that or you'd have had the preference, I fancy."

Montès listened with a half-dreamy, half-smiling expression, which had a terrifying effect upon everybody present. The head waiter at this juncture approached Carabine and whispered that a relation of hers desired to speak with her in the salon. The lorette rose, left the room, and found Madame Nourrisson veiled in black lace.

"Well, am I to go to your house, my child? Has he bitten?"

"Yes, little mother, the pistol is so heavily loaded that I'm afraid it will go off," Carabine replied.

An hour later Montès, Cydalise and Carabine had returned from the *Rocher de Cancale* to Rue Saint-Georges, and entered Carabine's little salon. The lorette espied Madame Nourrisson ensconced in an easy-chair by the corner of the hearth.

"Ah! there's my good aunt!" said she.

"Yes, my child, I have come myself for my little allowance. You might forget me, although you have such a kind heart, and I have notes to pay to-morrow. A dealer in ladies' wardrobes is always hard up. Who's that you're dragging after you?— The gentleman seems to have had something to annoy him.—"

The repulsive Madame Nourrisson, who was completely metamorphosed and had the appearance of a
respectable old lady, rose to kiss Carabine, who
was one of the hundred and odd lorettes she had
launched in their horrible career of vice.

"He's an Othello who makes no mistakes, and
whom I have the honor to present to you: Monsieur
le Baron Montès de Montejanos—"

"Oh! I know monsieur, I've heard so much said
about him; they call you Combabus because you
love only one woman; in Paris that's the same
thing as having none at all. Well, does it happen
by any chance that something's wrong with your
beloved? with Madame Marneffe, Crevel's wife?—
My dear monsieur, you should bless your fate,
'stead of cursing it.—She's a nobody, that little
woman. I know her tricks!"

"Nonsense!" said Carabine, into whose hands
Madame Nourrisson had slipped a letter when she
kissed her; "you don't know the Brazilians.
They're a quarrelsome lot, and believe in stabbing
to the heart!—The more jealous they are, the more
they want to be. *Môsieur* talks about massacring
everybody, and he won't massacre anybody because
he's in love. By the way, I've brought Monsieur
le Baron here to furnish him with the proofs of his
hard luck, which I got from little Steinbock."

Montès was drunk, and listened as if he were not
himself concerned in what was going on. Carabine
went to throw off her velvet cape, and read the following letter in fac-simile:

" My pet, *he* is going to dine at Popinot's to-night, and will come to the opera for me at eleven.　I will leave the house about half-past five, and shall expect to find you at our paradise, where you will have a dinner sent from the *Maison d'Or*.　Dress yourself as though you were going to take me to the Opera.　We shall have four hours to ourselves.　You must return this little note to me, not that your Valérie distrusts you, for I would give you my life, my fortune, my honor, but I am afraid of the tricks chance may play us."

"There, baron, there's the love-letter sent to Comte Steinbock this morning; read the address! The original has been burned."

Montès turned the paper over and over in his hand, recognized the hand-writing, and was struck with a shrewd idea, which goes to prove how far his mind was disturbed.

"Tell me," said he, "what interest you have in tearing my heart to pieces, for you must have paid a high price to get this note into your hands long enough to have it lithographed?" said he, looking at Carabine.

"You great idiot!" said Carabine at a sign from Madame Nourrisson; "don't you see poor Cydalise here—a child of sixteen who's loved you so for three months that it's taken away her appetite, and who's in despair because she hasn't yet been honored even with one of your most absent-minded glances?"

Cydalise put a handkerchief to her eyes, and seemed to be weeping.

"She's furious, for all her demure looks, to see that the man she's mad over is the dupe of a villain," continued Carabine, "and she would kill Valérie—"

"No, no," said the Brazilian, "that's my business!"

"Kill her!—you, my dear?" said the Nourrisson. "That sort of thing isn't done any more here."

"Ah!" retorted Montès, "I'm not of this country! I live in a jurisdiction where I laugh at your laws; and if you give me proofs—"

"Proofs! is this note of no account?"

"No," said the Brazilian. "I don't believe in the handwriting, I want to see."

"Oh! to see!" said Carabine, marvelously quick to understand a second gesture on the part of her pretended aunt; "well, we will let you see everything, my dear tiger, on one condition.—"

"What is that?"

"Look at Cydalise."

At a signal from Madame Nourrisson Cydalise gazed affectionately at the Brazilian.

"Will you love her? will you set her up in life? A woman as beautiful as that is well worth a house and a carriage! It would be a crying shame to leave her to go on foot. And she has—debts.—How much do you owe?" said Carabine, pinching Cydalise's arm.

"She's worth what she's worth," said the Nourrisson. "It's enough that there's someone to buy!"

"Listen!" cried Montès, becoming conscious at last of the existence of this glorious chef-d'œuvre of womankind; "you will show me Valérie—"

"And Comte Steinbock, *parbleu!*" said Madame Nourrisson.

For ten minutes past the old lady had been watching the Brazilian closely, and she saw in him the instrument that she needed, tuned to the pitch of murder; most important of all she saw that he was so far blinded by passion that he would no longer care by whom he was guided, and so she interposed.

"Cydalise is my niece, my dear Brazilian, so I am somewhat interested. This whole business can be cleared up in ten minutes; for it's one of my friends who lets Comte Steinbock the furnished room where your Valérie is at this moment taking her coffee—a queer kind of coffee, but that's what she calls it. So, let us understand each other, Brazil! I love Brazil, it's a hot country. What will you do about my niece?"

"Old ostrich!" said Montès, whose attention was attracted by the feathers on the Nourrisson's hat, "you interrupted me. If you show me—show me Valérie and this artist together—"

"As you'd like to be with her," said Carabine, "that's understood."

"Well then, I will take this young Norman and carry her—"

"Where?—" queried Carabine.

"To Brazil!" the baron replied; "I'll make her my wife. My uncle left me ten square leagues of unsalable land; that's why I still own the estate; I have a hundred negroes there, nothing but negroes, negresses, and little negroes bought by my uncle—"

"A slave-dealer's nephew!—" exclaimed Carabine with a wry face, "that's to be considered.— Cydalise, my child, are you a negrophile?"

"Come, come, let's have no more *blaguing*, Carabine," said La Nourrisson. "What the devil! Monsieur and I are talking business now."

"If I take another Frenchwoman, I propose that she shall be all mine," continued the Brazilian. "I give you fair warning, mademoiselle, I'm a king, but not a constitutional king; I am a czar, I have bought all my subjects, and no one can leave my kingdom, which is a hundred leagues from any human habitation; it is bounded by a country of savages on the interior, and separated from the coast by a desert as great as the whole of France.—"

"I prefer an attic here!" said Carabine.

"That's what I thought," rejoined the Brazilian, "as I sold all my estates and everything I owned at Rio-de-Janeiro, to come over and join Madame Marneffe."

"One doesn't take such voyages for nothing," said Madame Nourrisson. "You are entitled to be loved on your own account, especially as you are so handsome.—Oh! he is handsome," she said to Carabine.

"Very handsome! handsomer than Longjumeau's postilion," retorted the lorette.

Cydalise took the Brazilian's hand, but he disengaged it as politely as possible.

"I returned to carry off Madame Marneffe!" he said, resuming his argument, "and do you know why I didn't return for three years?"

"No, savage," said Carabine.

"Well, she had told me so many times that she longed to live with me, alone, in a desert—"

"He's not a savage any longer," said Carabine, with a great burst of laughter, "he belongs to the tribe of civilized gulls."

"She had told me that so many times," continued the baron, insensible to the lorette's raillery, "that I prepared a delightful home for her in the centre of that vast property. I returned to France in quest of Valérie, and the night I inspected her for the first time,—"

"Inspected is a good word," said Carabine; "I'll remember it!"

"She told me to wait for that vile Marneffe's death, and I consented, at the same time forgiving her for receiving attentions from Hulot. I don't know whether the devil caught her skirts, but from that moment the woman has gratified all my whims, all my demands; in fact she has not given me reason to suspect her for a single moment!"

"That's very clever!" said Carabine to Madame Nourrisson.

Madame Nourrisson nodded her head assentingly.

"My faith in that woman," said Montès allowing his tears to flow freely, "equals my love. I was within an ace of fighting the whole party at table just now."

"So I saw!" said Carabine.

"If I am deceived, if she is to be married, if she is at this moment in Steinbock's arms, that woman deserves a thousand deaths, and I will kill her as one crushes a fly.—"

"And the gendarmes, my dear?" said Madame Nourrisson with the smile of an old hag trying to make her hearer's flesh creep.

"And the commissioner of police, and the magistrates, and the Assizes, and all the rest of the horrors?" said Carabine.

"You are a fool, my dear boy!" continued Madame Nourrisson, who was determined to know the Brazilian's plan of vengeance.

"I will kill her!" repeated Montès coldly. "Ah! you called me a savage. Do you suppose I will copy the idiocy of your compatriots who go and buy poison at a druggist's?—I thought, while we were driving to your house, of my vengeance in case your charges against Valérie were just. One of my negroes carries about him the most deadly of animal poisons; a terrible malady which works much better than a vegetable poison, and can be cured only in Brazil. I will give it to Cydalise to take, and she will give it to me; then, when death is planted in the veins of Crevel and his wife, I shall be beyond the Azores with your cousin, whom I will cause to be cured, and will make my wife. We savages have our way of doing things!—Cydalise," said he with a glance at the Norman, "is the creature I need. What does she owe?"

"A hundred thousand francs!" said Cydalise.

"She talks little, but well," said Carabine under her breath to Madame Nourrisson.

"I shall go mad!" cried the Brazilian in a hollow voice, falling back upon a sofa. "It will kill me! But I must see, for it's impossible! A lithographed note!—who says that it isn't the work of a forger? —Baron Hulot love Valérie!" he exclaimed recalling Josépha's harangue; "why the bare fact that she still lives proves that he didn't love her!—I won't allow her to live for anybody else, if she's not all mine!"

Montès was frightful to look at and more frightful to hear! He roared and writhed; everything he touched was broken; the violet-wood seemed as fragile as glass.

"How he is smashing things!" said Carabine, looking at Madame Nourrisson.—"My dear," she continued, touching the Brazilian on the arm, "Roland in a rage was very well in a poem, but in a room he's very prosaic and costly."

"My son," said the Nourrisson, rising and taking her stand in front of the crushed Brazilian; "I am of your religion! When one loves in a certain way, when one is *hooked till death,* the life is answerable for the love. The one who goes away tears up everything by the roots! its a general demolition. You have my esteem, my admiration, my consent, especially for the touch which makes me negrophile. But you're in love! perhaps you'll draw back?"

"Draw back!—if she's an infamous wretch, I—"

"Come, you talk too much after all!" rejoined
the Nourrisson, herself once more. "A man who
wants to be revenged, and who claims to be so fierce
in his dealings, is apt to act differently. In order
that you should see your charmer in her paradise,
you must take Cydalise, and enter the room as if
you had been shown in there with your partner,
through the mistake of a maid; but no commotion!
If you want to be revenged, you must cheat and pre-
tend to be in despair, and induce your mistress to
discard you.—Isn't that the way?" she said, noticing the Brazilian's surprise at so subtle a scheme.

"Go on, ostrich," he replied, "go on!—I understand."

"Adieu, my love," said Madame Nourrisson to
Carabine.

She motioned to Cydalise to go with Montès, and
remained a moment alone with Carabine.

"Now, my darling, I am afraid of one thing,
and that is that he'll strangle her. I should be in
a bad fix, for all our business must be done quietly,
I think that you've earned your Raphaël, but they
say it's a Mignard. Don't be alarmed, it's much
finer; they tell me that the Raphaëls are all black,
while this is as pretty as a Girodet."

"All I care about is to beat Josépha!" cried Carabine, "and it's all the same to me whether it's with
a Raphaël or a Mignard.—No, that thief wore pearls
to-night—pearls one would willingly be damned for!"

Cydalise, Montès and Madame Nourrisson entered

a fiacre which was waiting at Carabine's door. Madame Nourrisson gave the driver orders in a low voice to drive to a house in the Block des Italiens where they might have arrived in a few moments, for it is a drive of only seven or eight minutes from Rue Saint-Georges; but Madame Nourrisson ordered him to go by Rue Le Peletier, and to drive very slowly so as to pass in review the carriages stationed there.

"Brazilian!" said La Nourrisson, "see if you recognize your angel's servants and her carriage."

The baron pointed to Valérie's equipage just as the fiacre passed.

"She told her people to come at ten o'clock, and drove in a fiacre to the house where she now is with Comte Steinbock; she has dined there and will go to the opera in half an hour. It's very well done!" said Madame Nourrisson. "That explains how she succeeded in cheating you so long."

The Brazilian did not reply. Transformed into a tiger, he had resumed his imperturbable sang-froid, so much admired during the dinner. In short he was as calm as a bankrupt the day after making an assignment.

At the door of the fatal house a closed carriage with two horses was standing—one of those called *Compagnie Générale* from the name of the company that owns them.

"Stay where you are," said Madame Nourrisson to Montès. "You can't go in here as you'd enter a tavern; we'll come and call you."

14

*

The paradise of Madame Marneffe and Wenceslas could hardly be said to resemble Crevel's *petite maison*, which he had sold to Comte Maxime de Trailles, it having, in his opinion, become useless. This paradise, the paradise of a great many persons, consisted of a single room opening on the landing on the fourth floor of a house in the Block des Italiens. On each floor, opening upon each landing of the house in question, was a room originally intended to serve as a kitchen for the suite of which it formed a part. But as the house had become a sort of inn, in which rooms were let to clandestine lovers at exorbitant prices, the principal tenant, the real Madame Nourrisson, dealer in ladies' apparel on Rue Neuve-Saint-Marc, had conceived a just idea of the great value of these kitchens, and had converted each of them into a sort of dining-room. Each room, flanked on both sides by thick party-walls, was lighted from the street, and was totally isolated by means of very heavy folding-doors, which afforded a double protection on the landing. The occupants, therefore, could discuss important secrets at dinner, without running the risk of being overheard. For greater security the windows were provided with blinds without and shutters within. These rooms, because of the privacy thus afforded, cost three hundred francs a month. The house, pregnant with the mysteries of paradise, was let for twenty-four thousand francs to Madame Nourrisson I., who made twenty thousand out of it, taking good years and bad together, after paying her agent—Madame Nourrisson II.—for she did not manage the property herself.

The particular paradise let to Comte Steinbock had been furnished in chintz. The hard, cold, and mean red-tiled floor, could not be felt beneath a luxurious carpet. The furniture consisted of two dainty chairs and a bed in an alcove, at this time half hidden by a table laden with the remains of a choice dinner, on which two long-necked bottles, and an exhausted champagne bottle in its envelope of ice marked the bounds of the fields of Bacchus cultivated by Venus. One saw, sent without doubt by Valérie, a comfortable easy-chair beside a low fireside-chair, and a pretty rosewood commode with a mirror in a lovely Pompadour frame. A lamp hanging from the ceiling shed a sort of half-light, increased to some extent by the wax-candles on the table and those which adorned the mantel-piece.

This sketch will serve to depict, *urbi et orbi*, the pitiful surroundings in which clandestine love-affairs were carried on in the Paris of 1840. How immeasurably far removed, alas! from the unholy love symbolized by Vulcan's fillets, three thousand years ago!

As Cydalise and the baron ascended the stairs, Valérie was standing in front of the fireplace, where a few sticks were burning, while Wenceslas laced her corsets. It was the moment of all others, when the woman who is neither too stout nor too thin, like the slender and graceful Valérie, appears supernaturally lovely. The pink, moist flesh craves a glance from the sleepiest eyes. The lines of the body, so imperfectly concealed at such a time, are so plainly marked by the clinging folds of the skirt and the tight-fitting corset, that the woman is irresistible, like everything one is obliged to leave. The happy, smiling face reflected in the mirror, the foot tapping impatiently on the floor, the hand raised to arrange the disordered locks of the badly readjusted head-dress, the eyes overflowing with gratitude, and the flame of satisfied desire, which, like the rays of the setting sun, lights up every detail of the countenance,—everything, at that hour, makes an impression to be long remembered! —Certain it is that, whoever, as he looks back over the first errors of his life, recalls some of these delicious details, will understand perhaps, though he do not excuse, the follies of the Hulots and Crevels. Women are so well aware of their power at that moment, that they always gather then what we may call the aftermath of the assignation.

"Well, well! after two years, don't you know how to lace a woman yet? You're too much of a Pole! Here it is ten o'clock, my Wences—las!" laughed Valérie.

At that moment a mischievous maid, with the aid of a knife-blade, adroitly threw back the hook of the folding-door, which afforded Adam and Eve their only protection. She threw open the door without warning, for the tenants of these Edens have all too little time to themselves, and disclosed one of the charming *genre* paintings after Gavarni, so often exhibited at the salon.

"This way, madame!" said the girl. And Cydalise entered, followed by Baron Montès.

"Why there's somebody here!—Excuse me, madame," said the Norman in dismay.

"What's this! why, it's Valérie!" cried Montès, closing the door with violence.

Madame Marneffe, overcome by emotion too keen to be dissembled, fell back upon a low chair in the corner of the fireplace. Two tears glistened in her eyes, but immediately vanished. She looked at Montès, espied the Norman, and uttered a forced laugh. The dignity of the injured woman effaced all thought of the inelegance of her unfinished toilet; she went up to the Brazilian and looked him in the face so haughtily that her eyes gleamed like sword-blades.

"So this," said she, taking her stand in front of him, and pointing to Cydalise, "this is what you mean by fidelity, is it? You who have made me promises that would convince an atheist in love! you for whom I have done so much, even committed crime!—You are right, monsieur, I am nothing compared to a girl of her age and beauty!—I know what you are going to say," she continued, pointing to Wenceslas, whose disordered clothing was too convincing a proof to be denied. "That's my

business. If I could love you, after such infamous
treachery, for you have put spies on me, you have
bought every step of this staircase, and the mistress
of the house, and the maid, and perhaps Reine herself—Oh! how noble it all is!—if I had a spark of
affection left for such a dastard, I could give him
reasons of a nature to redouble his love!—But I
leave you, monsieur, with all your suspicions,
which will some day change to remorse.—Wenceslas, my dress!"

She took her dress and put it on, looked at herself
in the mirror, and tranquilly finished dressing
without looking at the Brazilian, precisely as if she
were alone.

"Wenceslas, are you ready? Go out first."

She had watched the Brazilian's face in the mirror and out of the corner of her eye, and she fancied
that she could detect in his pallor an indication of
the weakness which renders the strongest man the
slave of a woman's fascination; she took his hand,
standing so near him that he could inhale those
potent well-loved perfumes, which intoxicate lovers;
and, feeling his heart beat fast, she looked into his
face with a reproachful expression:

"I give you leave to go and tell Monsieur Crevel
of your expedition; he'll never believe you, so I
have a right to marry him; he will be my husband
day after to-morrow—and I shall make him very
happy!—Adieu! try to forget me—"

"Ah! Valérie," cried Montès throwing his arms
about her, "it's impossible!—Come to Brazil!"

Valérie glanced at him and recovered her slave.

"Ah! Henri, if you still loved me, in two years I would be your wife; but your face at this moment looks very sly—"

"I swear to you that they made me drunk, that false friends left this woman on my hands, and that it's all the work of chance!" said Montès.

"Might I still venture to forgive you then?" she asked with a smile.

"And you persist in being married?" demanded the baron in heartrending suspense.

"Eighty thousand francs a year!" she exclaimed with half-comic enthusiasm. "And Crevel loves me so dearly, that he will soon die of it."

"Ah! I undertsand you," said the Brazilian.

"All right, in a day or two, we'll have an understanding," said she.

And she went down stairs in triumph.

"I have no more scruples!" thought the baron, standing still for a moment. "What! the woman thinks of making use of her love to get rid of that old fool, just as she calculated on Marneffe's death! —I shall be the instrument of divine wrath!"

Two days later those of Du Tillet's guests who had torn Madame Marneffe to pieces most mercilessly, were sitting about her table an hour after she had donned a new skin by changing her name for the glorious name of a mayor of Paris. This tongue treachery is one of the most ordinary varieties of fickleness in Parisian life. Valérie had had the pleasure of seeing at the church the Brazilian nobleman,

whom Crevel, now a lawful husband, invited from
sheer bravado. Montès' presence at the breakfast surprised no one. All these men of genius had
long since become familiar with the cowardice of
passion and the bargaining of lust. The profound
melancholy of Steinbock, who was beginning to
despise her of whom he had made an angel, seemed
in the best of taste. It was as if the Pole took this
method of saying that all was at an end between
Valérie and himself. Lisbeth came in to embrace
her dear Madame Crevel, apologizing for not attending the breakfast, on the ground of Adeline's lament-
able condition.

"Have no fear," said she to Valérie as she took
her leave, "they will receive you there and you
will receive them here. The baroness is at death's
door simply from having heard the four words: *two
hundred thousand francs!* Oh! you have them all
in your power by that anecdote; but won't you tell
it to me?"

A month after her marriage Valérie had arrived
at her tenth quarrel with Steinbock, who insisted
upon an explanation from her respecting Henri
Montès; he reminded her of her remarks during
the scene in their paradise; and, not content
with withering Valérie with scornful epithets,
watched her so closely that she could not obtain a
single moment of liberty, so closely pressed was she
by Wenceslas' jealousy and Crevel's devotion.
As Lisbeth, whose advice was always most judi-
cious, was no longer with her, she lost her head so

far as to taunt Wenceslas bitterly about the money
she had loaned him. The Steinbock pride was
thereupon awakened and he came no more to the
Crevel mansion. Valérie's object was attained;
she wanted to keep Wenceslas away for a time in
order to recover her freedom of action. She awaited
the opportunity afforded by a visit Crevel paid to
Comte Popinot in the country to make arrangements for Madame Crevel's presentation, and was
thus enabled to make an appointment with the
baron, whom she desired to have to herself for a
whole day in order to supply him with explanations
calculated to redouble his love. On the morning of
the day in question, Reine, estimating the extent
of her crime by the magnitude of the sum she received, tried to warn her mistress, in whose welfare she was naturally more interested than in that
of strangers; but as they had threatened to make
her out a madwoman and send her to the Salpêtrière,
in case of any indiscretion, she was timid.

"Madame is so happy now," said she; "why
should she bother any more with this Brazilian?—
I don't trust him myself!"

"You are right, Reine," Valérie replied; "so I
mean to dismiss him."

"Oh! madame, I am so glad; he frightens me,
the black-a-moor! I believe he's capable of anything—"

"What a fool you are! He's the one to be
alarmed for, when he's with me."

At that moment Lisbeth appeared.

"My dear, sweet little kid, it's a long time since I saw you!" said Valérie—"I am very unhappy.— Crevel bores me to death, and I haven't any Wenceslas; we've had a row."

"I know it," replied Lisbeth, "and it's on his account that I've come here. Victorin met him about five in the evening just as he was going into a twenty-five-sous restaurant on Rue de Valois; he caught him fasting, worked on his feelings and brought him to Rue Louis-le-Grand.—When Hortense saw him, thin and sick and poorly-clothed, she gave him her hand.—That's the way you go back on me!"

"Monsieur Henri, madame!" said the footman in Valérie's ear.

"Leave me, Lisbeth; I'll explain it all to you to-morrow."

But, as we shall see, Valérie was soon to be in a condition in which she could explain nothing to anybody.

*

Toward the close of the month of May, Baron Hulot's pension was entirely freed from encumbrance by virtue of the successive payments made by Victorin to Baron de Nucingen. Everyone knows that the semi-annual payments of pensions are not made except upon presentation of a certificate of life, and as Baron Hulot's residence was unknown, the semi-annual payments assigned to Vauvinet had accumulated at the Treasury. Vauvinet having executed a release of his claim, it was indispensable to find the pensioner in order to collect the arrears. The baroness, thanks to the devoted care of Doctor Bianchon, had recovered her health. Kind-hearted Josépha contributed materially to her complete recovery by a letter, the orthography of which betrayed the collaboration of the Duc d'Hérouville. This is what the famous singer wrote the baroness after forty days of unremitting activity:

"MADAME LA BARONNE,

"Monsieur Hulot, two months ago, was living on Rue des Bernardins with Élodie Chardin, the lace-mender, who had stolen him from Mademoiselle Bijou; but he went away, leaving everything he owned behind him, without a word, and without a hint as to where he has gone. I am not discouraged, and I have put a man on his track, who thinks that he has seen him already on Boulevard Bourdon.

"The poor Jewess will keep her promise to the Christian.

May the angel pray for the devil! that must sometimes happen in Heaven.

"I am with profound respect, and forever, your humble servant,

"JOSÉPHA MIRAH."

Mâitre Hulot d'Ervy, hearing no more of the terrible Madame Nourrisson, seeing that his father-in-law was safely married, having induced his brother-in-law to return to the family fireside, finding that his new mother-in-law showed no disposition to attack him, and that his mother's health was improving from day to day, devoted himself to his legal and political labors, borne on by the swift current of Parisian life in which hours count for days. Having a report to prepare for the Chamber of Deputies, he was obliged, toward the close of the session, to work on it throughout the entire night. He was in his office about nine o'clock waiting for his servant to bring his shaded lamps, and was thinking of his father. He reproached himself for leaving the cantatrice to prosecute the search, and was thinking that he would see Monsieur Chapuzot on the subject the next day, when he saw at his window, in the fading twilight, a venerable bald head, fringed with white hair.

"My dear monsieur, tell them to let me come in; I am a poor hermit from the desert, seeking alms to assist in rebuilding a sacred place of shelter."

This apparition, which took to itself a voice, and suddenly recalled to the advocate's mind a prophecy of the horrible Nourrisson, made him shudder.

"Admit this old man," he said to his footman.

"He'll breed the plague in monsieur's office," the servant replied; "he has on a brown frock that he hasn't changed since he left Syria, and no shirt—"

"Admit this old man," the advocate repeated.

As he entered the room Victorin scrutinized with a suspicious eye this soi-disant hermit on a pilgrimage, and saw that he had before him a superb specimen of those Neapolitan monks whose frocks are true sisters to the rags of the lazzaroni, whose sandals are rags of leather, as the monk himself is a rag of humanity. His make-up was so complete, that, although his suspicions remained, the advocate reproached himself for having believed in Madame Nourrisson's sorcery.

"How much do you want?"

"Whatever you think you ought to give me."

Victorin took one hundred sous from a pile of change, and handed the coin to the stranger.

"That's very little on account of fifty thousand francs," said the beggar from the desert.

This remark banished all Victorin's uncertainty.

"Has Heaven kept its promises?" he said with a frown.

"Doubt is an insult, my son!" rejoined the recluse. "If you prefer not to pay me until the funeral is over, you are within your right; I will come again in a week."

"The funeral!" cried the advocate, rising.

"We have been at work," said the old man,

leaving the room, "and deaths come quickly in Paris!"

When Hulot, who hung his head at these words, attempted to reply, the old man had disappeared.

"I don't understand a word of it," said Hulot to himself. "But, a week hence, I will ask him about my father if we haven't found him. Where does Madame Nourrisson—yes, that's what she calls herself—find such actors?"

The next day Doctor Bianchon allowed the baroness to go down to the garden, after he had examined Lisbeth, who had been compelled, by a slight bronchial trouble, to keep her room for a month past. The learned doctor, who did not dare express his whole opinion concerning Lisbeth until he had detected some more decisive symptoms, accompanied the baroness to the garden in order to study the effect of the fresh air, after two months' confinement, upon the nervous trembling which he was seeking to overcome. The cure of this nervous disorder called forth all Bianchon's talent. When they saw the great and famous physician sitting beside them and giving them a few moments of his valuable time, the baroness and her children politely opened a conversation with him.

"Your life is very fully occupied, and very sadly!" said the baroness. "I know what it is to spend one's days looking constantly upon poverty or physical suffering."

"Madame," the physician replied, "I know something of the sights which your charitable work obliges you to witness; but you will get accustomed to them in time as we all do. It is the law of society. The confessor, the magistrate, the lawyer, would be impossible if the *good of the State* did not subdue the *heart of the man.* Could we live except for the happening of this phenomenon? The soldier, in time of war, is doomed, is he not, to witness sights even more cruel than ours? and all soldiers who have seen fire are kind-hearted. We have the pleasure of successfully effecting a cure, as you have the pleasure of rescuing a family from the horrors of hunger, depravity, misery, by providing them with work, and restoring them to social life; but what satisfaction have the magistrate, the commissioner of police and the lawyer, who pass their lives investigating the most villainous schemes of self-interest, that social monster which knows the regret of failure, but which will never know repentance? One-half of society passes its life watching the other half. I have long had for a friend a lawyer, now retired from practice, who told me that, for the last fifteen years, the notaries and lawyers were as suspicious of their clients as of their clients' adversaries. Your son, madame, is a lawyer—has he never been compromised by the man whose defence he undertook?''

"Oh! often,'' said Victorin with a smile.

"What is the source of this deep-seated evil,'' the baroness asked.

"Absence of religious feeling,'' replied the physician, "and the invasions of finance, which is nothing

15

else than selfishness solidified.   In the old days
money was not everything; other forms of superiority were admitted, which took precedence of it.
There were nobility, talent, and services rendered the State; but to-day the law makes money
the universal standard, and has adopted it as the
basis of political capacity!   Certain magistrates
are not eligible, Jean-Jacques Rousseau would not
be eligible!   The constant division of inheritances
compels everyone to think for himself as soon as he
is twenty years old.   Well, between the necessity
of making money and the depravity of the various
combinations effected there is no obstacle, for religious sentiment is lacking in France, notwithstanding the praiseworthy efforts of those who are striving
to bring about the restoration of the Catholic faith.
That is what everyone says, whose occupation, like
mine, gives him an insight into the very bowels of
society.''

"You have little relaxation?'' said Hortense.

"The true physician,'' replied Bianchon, "is
passionately devoted to science.   He is sustained
by that sentiment as well as by the certainty of his
usefulness to society.   For instance, at this moment
I am experiencing a sort of scientific joy, and yet
many superficial observers would take me for a
man without a heart.   I am going to announce a
new discovery to the Academy of Medicine to-morrow.   I am watching at the present time the progress of a long-lost disease; a fatal disease, too,
against which we are helpless in temperate climates,

although it is curable in the Indies—a disease
which was prevalent in the Middle Ages. It's a
noble struggle—the struggle of the physician with
such a malady. For ten days past I have thought
of little but my patients, for there are two of them,
the husband and wife! By the way are they not
kinsfolk of yours? I believe you are Monsieur
Crevel's daughter, madame?" he added, addressing
Célestine.

"What! can it be that this patient of yours is
my father?" exclaimed Célestine. "Does he live
on Rue Barbet-de-Jouy?"

"He does, indeed," replied Bianchon.

"And the disease is fatal?" said Victorin in
dismay.

"I am going to my father!" cried Célestine, rising.

"I positively forbid you to do it, madame," said
Bianchon tranquilly. "The disease is contagious."

"But you go there, monsieur," retorted the
young woman. "Don't you think that a daughter's
duty is more imperative than a physician's?"

"Madame, a physician knows how to protect
himself from contagion, and your unreflecting devotion is sufficient proof to my mind, that you could
not have my prudence."

Célestine returned to her room and dressed to go
out.

"Monsieur," Victorin asked Bianchon, "do you
hope to save Monsieur and Madame Crevel?"

"I hope to, but hardly expect to," replied Bianchon. "It's a most inexplicable case to me.—The

disease is one peculiar to the negroes in the American colonies, whose cutaneous system differs from that of the white races. Now, I am unable to establish any connection between the negroes, the Indians or the half-breeds and Monsieur or Madame Crevel. Although it is a very interesting disease from our point of view, it's a most frightful one to everybody else. The poor creature, who, they tell me, was very pretty, is well punished in the same direction in which she sinned, for to-day she is shockingly ugly, if indeed she can be said to be anything!—Her teeth and her hair are falling out, she looks like a leper, and her aspect is horrifying to herself; her hands are a fearful sight, they are badly swollen and covered with greenish pustules; her nails are loosened and remain in the sores that she scratches; in fact, all her extremities are being destroyed by the sanies which is consuming them."

"But what is the cause of it all?" queried the advocate.

"Oh!" said Bianchon, "the cause is the rapid degeneration of the blood; it is decomposing with frightful rapidity. I hope to attack the blood; I have had it analyzed, and I am now going home to learn the result of the labors of my friend Professor Duval, the renowned chemist, preparatory to undertaking one of those desperate strokes we sometimes play against death."

"The finger of God is in it!" said the baroness in a tone of deep feeling. "Although that woman has been the cause of all my misery, which has led me in moments of madness, to invoke divine justice against her, I most earnestly hope, God knows! that you may succeed, Monsieur le Docteur."

Victorin's head swam, he looked alternately at his mother, his sister and the doctor, trembling lest they should divine his thoughts. He considered himself a murderer. Hortense, for her part, deemed God most just. Célestine reappeared to beg her husband to accompany her.

"If you go there, madame, and you, monsieur, remain a foot away from the sick-bed; that is the only precaution you need take. Neither your wife nor yourself must entertain the thought of kissing the dying man! You had better go with your wife, Monsieur Hulot, to see that she doesn't disobey this order."

Adeline and Hortense, being left to themselves, went up to sit with Lisbeth. Hortense's hatred of Valérie was so bitter that she could not refrain from an explosion.

"Cousin, my mother and I are avenged!—" she cried. "That poisonous creature must have bitten herself, she's in a state of decomposition!"

"Hortense," said the baroness, "you are not a true Christian now. You ought to pray God that he will deign to bring the wretched woman to repentance."

"What are you saying?" cried Bette, rising from her chair, "are you talking about Valérie?"

"Yes," Adeline replied, "she is doomed; she is

dying of a horrible disease, the mere description of which is enough to make one shudder."

Cousin Bette's teeth chattered, the cold sweat stood upon her forehead, she experienced a terrible shock, which disclosed the depth of her passionate affection for Valérie.

"I am going there!" she said.

"But the doctor forbade your going out."

"No matter! I am going!—Poor Crevel! what a state he must be in, for he loves his wife!"

"He is dying too!" rejoined Countess Steinbock. "Ah! all our enemies are in the devil's hands—"

"In God's hands, my child."

Lisbeth put on her famous yellow cashmere, her black velvet cape, and her boots; and in defiance of the remonstrances of Adeline and Hortense started off as if she were impelled by a power not to be resisted. She reached Rue Barbet a few moments after Monsieur and Madame Hulot, and found seven physicians there whom Bianchon had summoned to watch this unique case; he himself had just joined them. The doctors stood in the salon discussing the case, and sometimes one of them, sometimes another entered Valérie's room or Crevel's, and returned with an argument based upon the results of his rapid observation.

These princes of science were divided between two opinions. One of them stood alone in the belief that it was a case of poisoning, and talked about private vengeance, denying that it was a reappearance of the disease known in the Middle

Ages. Three others insisted that it was a case of decomposition of the lymph, and humors in the blood. The second party, which included Bianchon, maintained that the disease was caused by degeneration of the blood which was poisoned by some unknown noxious principle. Bianchon brought the result of the analysis of the blood made by Professor Duval. The curative methods, although desperate and altogether experimental, depended upon the solution of this medical problem.

Lisbeth stood as if turned to stone three feet from the bed on which Valérie was dying, for she saw the vicar of Saint-Thomas d'Aquin at her friend's pillow, and a sister of charity in attendance upon her. Religion found a soul to save in a putrefying mass which retained, of the five senses of the human being, that of sight alone. The sister of charity,—nobody else could be found to undertake the task of attending Valérie,—stood at a distance. Thus the Catholic Church, that divine body, always animated by the spirit of self-sacrifice in everything, came to the assistance, in its double essence of spirit and flesh, of this infamous, tainted dying woman, pouring out upon her its infinite gentleness and its inexhaustible treasures of pity.

The terrified domestics refused to enter monsieur's room or madame's; they thought only of themselves and considered that their masters were justly smitten. The decomposition was so rapid that, although the windows were wide open, and the most powerful perfumes were scattered broadcast, none could remain long in Valérie's room. Religion alone kept constant watch there. How could a woman of so superior an intellect as Valérie's have failed to ask herself what interest those two representatives of the Church could have in remaining by her side? So it was that the dying woman had listened to the voice of the priest. Repentance had laid hold of that perverse heart with an ardor proportioned to the inroads the malignant disease had made upon her beauty. The delicate Valérie had offered less resistance to the disease than Crevel, and she was likely to be the first to die,—indeed she was attacked first.

"If I hadn't been sick I would have come and nursed you," said Lisbeth at last, after exchanging a glance with her friend's mournful eyes. "I have kept my room for fifteen or twenty days; but as soon as I learned of your condition from the doctor I hurried to you."

"Poor Lisbeth, you still love me, I see that," said Valérie. "Listen to me! I have but a day or two more to think, for I can't say *to live*. As you see I haven't any body, I am a mass of filth.—They don't let me look at myself in the mirror.—I have no more than I deserve. Ah! I would like to undo all the harm I have done, so that I might be admitted to pardon."

"Oho!" said Lisbeth, "if you talk that way, you must be as good as dead!"

"Don't interfere with this woman's repentance; leave her to her Christian thoughts," said the priest.

"Nothing left!" said Lisbeth to herself in dire dismay. "I don't recognize her eyes or her mouth! Not a single one of her features remains! And her mind is unhinged! Oh! it's horrible!—"

"You don't know," rejoined Valérie, "what death is, what it is to be compelled to think of the day after one's last day, and of what one will find in the grave; worms for the body, but what for the soul?—Ah! Lisbeth I feel that there is another life! —and I am in the grasp of a deadly terror which prevents me from feeling the torture of my decomposing flesh!—I who said laughingly to Crevel, while making sport of a saint, that God's vengeance assumed the shape of all varieties of misfortune! Oh! well, I was a prophet!—Don't joke about sacred things, Lisbeth! If you love me, follow my example. Repent!"

"I repent!" said the Lorrainer; "I have seen vengeance everywhere in nature, insects die to satisfy the thirst for vengeance when they are attacked! And don't these gentlemen," she added, pointing to the priest, "tell us that God wreaks vengeance, and that his vengeance is eternal!"—

The priest cast a glance overflowing with gentleness at Lisbeth and said to her:

"You are an atheist, madame."

"But consider what has come to me then?" said Valérie.

"Where did you get all this corruption?" asked the old maid, persisting in her peasant-like incredulity.

"Oh! I received a note from Henri which left me in no doubt as to my fate.—He has killed me. To think of dying just when I had made up my mind to live an honest life, and to die an object of horror!—Lisbeth give up all idea of vengeance! Be kind to your family, to whom I have already, in my will, bequeathed all that the law allows me to dispose of! Go, my child, although you are the only being to-day who doesn't shrink from me in horror—go, I beg you, leave me; I have no time to do anything more than give myself up to God!—"

"She has lost her wits!" said Lisbeth to herself on the threshold.

The most violent sentiment known to mankind, a woman's love for a woman, had not the heroic constancy of the Church. Lisbeth, suffocated by the noisome fumes, left the room. She saw the doctors still discussing. But Bianchon's opinion carried the day, and they were simply considering the method of performing the experiment.

"It will be a magnificent autopsy at all events," said one of the dissentients, "and we shall have two subjects for purposes of comparison."

Lisbeth went back with Bianchon, who approached the sick-bed without seeming to notice the fetid exhalations.

"Madame," said he, "we propose to try the effect of a powerful preparation upon you, which may save your life."

"If you save my life," she said, "shall I be as beautiful as I was?"

"Perhaps," said the eminent physician.

"I understand your *perhaps!*" said Valérie; "I shall look like a woman who has fallen into the fire! Leave me entirely to the Church! I can please nobody but God now! I am going to try and reconcile myself with him; that will be my last flirtation! Yes, I must take the sacrament.

"There's my poor Valérie's last word, I recognize her there!" said Lisbeth, weeping.

The Lorrainer thought it her duty to go on to Crevel's bedroom, where she found Victorin and his wife sitting three feet away from the plague-stricken man's bed.

"Lisbeth," said he, "they are concealing my wife's condition from me; you have just seen her— how is she?"

"She is better, she says that she is saved," replied Lisbeth, permitting herself this pun in order to set his mind at rest.

"Ah! that is well," said the mayor, "for I was afraid that I was the cause of her illness. I haven't been a druggist's traveling salesman for nothing. I have been reproaching myself. If I should lose her what would become of me? On my word of honor, my children, I adore that woman."

Crevel sat up in bed and tried to strike his attitude.

"Oh! papa," said Célestine, "if you could only get well, I would receive my step-mother. I make that vow!"

"Poor little Celestine!" said Crevel, "come and kiss me!"

Victorin restrained his wife, who was darting to the bed.

"You are not aware, monsieur," said the advocate gently, "that your disease is contagious."

"True," replied Crevel; "the doctors are congratulating themselves that they have discovered in me some pest or other of the Middle Ages which they thought lost for ever, and they're making a great noise about it in their Faculties.—It's very amusing!"

"Papa," said Célestine, "have courage, and you will triumph over the disease."

"Never fear, my children; death looks twice before striking down a mayor of Paris!" he said with comical sang-froid. "And even if my arrondissement is so unfortunate as to be deprived of the man whom it has twice honored with its suffrages —Hem! see how gracefully I express myself!— why I shall know how to pack my trunks. I'm an old commercial traveler and I'm used to breaking camp. Ah! my children, I'm an atheist."

"Papa, promise me to let the Church come to your bedside."

"Never!" replied Crevel. "What would you have? I have sucked the milk of the Revolution; I haven't the mind of Baron d'Holbach, but I have his strong heart. I am the Regent, Gray Guardsman, Abbé Dubois, and Maréchal de Richelieu more than ever! *Sacrebleu!* my poor wife, who's out of her mind, just sent a man in a frock to me— to me, the admirer of Béranger, the friend of

Lisette, the child of Voltaire and Rousseau.—The
doctor said to me, to try me, to find whether the
disease was abating; 'Did you see Monsieur
l'Abbé?'—And I followed the example of the great
Montesquieu. Yes, I looked at the doctor, see, like
this," he exclaimed, turning three-quarters round
as in his portrait, and putting forth his hand mag-
isterially, "and I said:

> " 'The slave arrived,
> His order showed, but naught derived.'

"*His order* is a pretty play upon words which
proves that in his death agony Monsieur le President de Montesquieu preserved all the charm of his
genius, for they had sent him a Jesuit!—I love that
passage—one cannot say of his life, but of his death.
Ah! the passage! another pun! the passage—or passing—of Montesquieu!"

Hulot gazed sadly at his father-in-law, wondering
if folly and vanity do not possess a power equal to
that of true grandeur of soul. The causes which
put in motion the mechanism of the soul seem to be
entirely foreign to the results. Can it be that the
courage displayed by a great criminal is of the
same nature as that which enables a Champcenetz
to walk proudly to the scaffold?

At the end of the week Madame Crevel was
buried after suffering untold torture, and Crevel
followed his wife two days later. Thus the disastrous effects of the marriage-contract were averted,
and Crevel inherited from Valérie.

On the day following the burial the advocate saw
the old monk once more, and received him without
a word. The monk silently put out his hand, and
Master Victorin Hulot silently handed him eighty
bank-notes of one thousand francs each, taken from
the money found in Crevel's secretary. Madame
Hulot the younger inherited the estate of Presles
and thirty thousand francs a year. Madame Crevel had bequeathed three hundred thousand francs
to Baron Hulot. The scrofulous Stanislas was to
have, at his majority, the Crevel mansion on Rue
Barbet and twenty-four thousand francs a year.

*

Among the numerous and praiseworthy associations founded by the charitable Catholics of Paris, there is one, founded by Madame de la Chanterie, the purpose of which is to bring about the marriage, civil and religious, of couples who are living together in good faith. Our legislators, who are much interested in swelling the proceeds of registration, and the reigning bourgeoisie, who covet notarial honors, feign to be ignorant of the fact that three-fourths of the common people are unable to pay fifteen francs for their marriage-contract. In this respect the Chamber of Notaries stands on a lower plane than the Chamber of Advocates. The advocates of Paris, a much slandered body, undertake gratuitously the conduct of causes for those who are unable to pay, while the notaries have not yet decided to draw contracts of marriage for the poor without charge. As for the Treasury the whole governmental machine must be set in motion in order to obtain any relaxation of its rigor in that direction. The registrar's office is deaf and dumb. The Church, too, levies taxes upon marriages. The Church in France is excessively mercenary; it lowers itself so far as to countenance in the very house of God, a despicable traffic in little benches and chairs, at which strangers wax wroth, although it can not have forgotten the Saviour's wrath when

(239)

he drove the money-changers forth from the Temple.
If the Church is so loath to abandon its fees we
must conclude that its fees,—called property—
constitute to-day one of its main sources of revenue, and the fault of the churches would then become the fault of the State. The combination of
these various circumstances, at a time when people
are busying themselves far too much with negroes
and petty police court offenders to pay any heed to
the sufferings of honest men, leads to this result,—
that a great number of well-meaning couples go on
living in concubinage, for lack of thirty francs, the
lowest price at which the notary, the registrar, the
mayor and the Church can make two Parisians one.
Madame de la Chanterie's society, instituted for
the purpose of giving such needy couples a fair
start upon a legal and religious path, is constantly
seeking them out, and unearths them the more easily
in that it relieves their poverty, before it interferes
to regulate their unlawful mode of life.

When Madame Hulot was fully restored to health,
she resumed her former occupations. Then it was
that the estimable Madame de la Chanterie urged
her to add the legalizing of natural marriages to the
other charitable undertakings in which she acted
as agent.

One of the baroness's first essays in this direction took place in the unsavory quarter, formerly
called *Little Poland,* bounded by Rue du Rocher,
Rue de la Pépinière and Rue de Miroménil. It is a
sort of branch of Faubourg Saint-Marceau. To

describe the neighborhood it will suffice to say that the owners of certain houses occupied by mechanics without work, by dangerous ruffians, by beggars engaged in nefarious trades, dare not demand their rents and can find no bailiffs who will undertake to expel their insolvent tenants. At the present moment, speculation, which is bent upon changing the aspect of this corner of Paris, and upon building up the unoccupied space which lies between Rue d'Amsterdam and Rue du Faubourg-du-Roule, is almost certain to change the character of its population, for the trowel is more of a civilizing instrument in Paris than one would imagine. By building handsome, stylish houses, with concierges, laying sidewalks in front of them, and arranging shops on the street-floor, the speculator places rents at so high a figure as to exclude vagabonds, families without belongings and undesirable tenants generally. Thus the quarters in question are gradually ridding themselves of their unsavory inhabitants, and of the dens in which the police never set foot except by special orders from the powers above.

In June, 1844, the aspect of Place de Laborde and its neighborhood was still by no means reassuring. The fashionable lounger, who happened to stray from Rue de la Pépinière into one of those disreputable streets, was amazed to see that aristocracy was jostled there by the dregs of Bohemia. In these districts, where ignorant indigence and want vegetate in the last stages of wretchedness, the lowest public writers to be found in Paris live and flourish.

16

Wherever you see the two words: *Public writer,*
in coarse running hand, upon a white paper pasted
on the window of the entresol or ground-floor of some
disreputable looking den, you may safely conclude
that the quarter contains many illiterate people,
and consequently much misery and vice and crime.
Ignorance is the mother of all crimes.   A crime is,
first of all, a lack of reasoning power.

Now, during the baroness's illness, this quarter,
to which she was a second providence, had made
an acquisition in the shape of a public writer, who
had established himself on the Passage du Soleil;
the name being one of those antitheses familiar to
Parisians, for that "Sun" passage was more than
ordinarily dark.   This writer, suspected of being
a German, was named Vyder, and was living in
concubinage with a girl, of whom he was so jealous that he would allow her to visit nowhere
except at the house of certain honest flue-builders
on Rue Saint-Lazare, Italians like all flue-builders,
and for many years settled in Paris.   These people
had been saved from inevitable failure, which
would have reduced them to want, by Baronne
Hulot, acting for Madame de la Chanterie.   In a
few months comparative ease had succeeded poverty,
and religion had entered the hearts, which formerly
cursed Providence, with the ardor peculiar to Italian
flue-builders.   So it was that one of the baroness's
first visits was paid to this family.   She was over-
joyed by the spectacle which met her eyes in the
house occupied by these good people on Rue Saint-

Lazare near Rue du Rocher. Above the workshop, now well-furnished and swarming with journeymen and apprentices, all Italians from the valley of Domo d'Ossola, the family occupied a small suite of rooms to which sufficient work had brought material abundance. The baroness was welcomed as if she were the Blessed Virgin returned to earth. After a quarter of an hour passed in looking about, Adeline, who was obliged to await the husband's return, in order to ascertain how his business was prospering, took advantage of the interval to carry on her blessed work by inquiring as to any people needing help whom the flue-builder's family might know.

"Ah! my kind lady, who would save the damned from hell," said the woman, "there's a young girl close by to be saved from perdition."

"Do you know her well?" inquired the baroness.

"She's the grand-daughter of a former employer of my husband named Judici, who came to France at the time of the Revolution, in 1798. Père Judici was one of the first flue-builders in Paris, under the Emperor Napoleon; he died in 1819 leaving his son a handsome fortune. But young Judici has squandered it all on bad women, and ended by marrying one of them, cleverer than the others, who bore him this poor little daughter, who's just past fifteen."

"What has happened to her?" asked the baroness, deeply impressed by the resemblance between this Judici's character and her husband's.

"Well, madame, the little creature—her name is

Atala—left her father and mother to come and live
near by with an old German, at least eighty years
old, named Vyder, who attends to everything for
folks who can't read or write. If the old libertine,
who, they say, bought the little one from her
mother for fifteen hundred francs, would only marry
her, as he undoubtedly hasn't long to live and as
they say he's likely to have a few thousand francs,
why the poor child, who's a little angel, would come
to no harm, and would escape poverty, which will
be her ruin."

"I thank you for having told me of this opportunity to do a good deed," said Adeline; "but we
must act with prudence. Who is this old man?"

"Oh! madame, he's a good man; he makes the
little one happy, and he doesn't lack good sense;
for he left the quarter where the Judicis live, to
save the child from her mother's claws, I suppose.
The mother was jealous of her daughter, and she
may have had an idea of making the most of her
beauty, of making the child a *mademoiselle!*—Atala
thought of us and advised *her gentleman* to set up in
business near our house; and as the good man saw
what sort of people we are he lets her come here;
but marry them, madame, and you will do a deed
worthy of you.—Once married, the little one will
be free, in that way she will escape from her
mother, who keeps an eye on her, and would like
to see her go on the stage, or make a success in the
horrible career she started her in, so that she could
make something out of her."

"Why hasn't the old man married her?"

"It wasn't necessary," said the Italian, "and although goodman Vyder is not downright wicked, I think he's crafty enough to prefer to be the little one's master, whereas if he marries her, lady! he dreads, poor old fellow, what constantly threatens all old men."

"Can you send for the girl?" said the baroness; "I will see her here and find out if there's any way."

The woman made a sign to her eldest daughter, who at once left the room. Ten minutes later she returned, holding by the hand a girl of some fifteen years and a half, beautiful after the Italian style of beauty.

Mademoiselle Judici inherited from her father the complexion, which sallow by daylight, at night, by artificial light, becomes as white as the lily, eyes whose size and shape and brilliancy were worthy of the Orient, thick, drooping eyelids which resembled little black feathers, hair as black as ebony, and that majestic bearing, innate in the Lombard, which leads the foreigner who walks through the streets of Milan on Sunday, to imagine that the porter's daughters are so many queens. Atala, informed by the flue-builder's daughter of the presence of the great lady of whom she had often heard, had hastily donned a pretty silk dress, a stylish cape and laced boots. A cap with cherry colored ribbons increased ten-fold the effect of her shapely head. The little creature stood in an attitude of artless curiosity, looking askance at the

baroness, whose nervous trembling astonished her
much.   The baroness heaved a deep sigh to see
such a masterpiece of female loveliness wallowing
in the slough of prostitution, and she swore to lead
her back into the paths of virtue.

"What is your name, my child?"

"Atala, madame."

"Do you know how to read or write?"

"No, madame; but that makes no difference,
since *monsieur* knows."

"Did your parents ever take you to church?
Have you had your first communion? Do you know
your catechism?"

"Madame, papa tried to make me do things like
what you say, but mamma wouldn't have it."

"Your mother!" cried the baroness.   "Tell me
is your mother very cruel?"

"She was always whipping me! I don't know
why, but my father and mother were continually
quarreling about me."

"Did they never talk to you about God?" cried
the baroness.

The child opened her eyes to their fullest extent.

"Oh! mamma and papa often said: 'Holy name
of God! God's thunder! God damn!—'" she
replied with refreshing innocence.

"Have you never seen any churches? did it
never occur to you to go into one?"

"Churches?—Oh! yes, Notre-Dame and the
Pantheon,—I saw them in the distance when papa

took me into Paris, but that didn't happen often. There are no churches like that in the faubourg.''

"In what faubourg were you?''

"In the faubourg.''

"What faubourg?''

"Why, Rue de Charonne, madame.''

The denizens of Faubourg Saint-Antoine never call that celebrated quarter anything but the faubourg. To them it is *the* faubourg *par excellence,* the king of faubourgs, and the manufacturers understand by that word when used alone, the Faubourg Saint-Antoine.

"Did they never tell you what was good and what was bad?''

"Mamma beat me when I didn't do things according to her idea.''

"But didn't you know you were doing a wrong thing when you left your mother and father to go and live with an old man?''

Atala Judici looked at the baroness with a haughty air and did not reply.

"She's a totally uncivilized child!'' said Adeline to herself.

"There are many like her in the faubourg, madame,'' said the flue-builder's wife.

"But she knows nothing at all, not even what wrong is, *mon Dieu!*—Why don't you answer me?'' the baroness asked trying to take Atala by the hand.

But Atala was angry and drew back.

"You're an old fool!'' said she. "My father

and mother had been fasting for a week! Mother
wanted to make something very bad of me, because
father beat her and called her a thief. Then Monsieur Vyder paid all father's and mother's debts,
and gave them money—oh! a whole bagful!—
And he took me away, and my poor papa wept.
But we had to part!—There, is that wicked?'' she
demanded.

"And do you love this Monsieur Vyder dearly?''
"Do I love him?—'' said she. "I should think
so, madame! He tells me fine stories every evening!—and he has given me lovely dresses and linen
and a shawl. Why, I'm rigged out like a princess,
and I don't wear wooden shoes any more! For two
months I haven't known what it is to be hungry.
I don't eat potatoes now! he brings me bonbons and
sugared almonds! Oh! how good almond-chocolate
is! I do everything he wishes for a bag of choco-
late. And then, my old Père Vyder is very kind;
he takes care of me so nicely and neatly that
I can see what mother should have done.—He's
going to get a good old woman to help me, for he
doesn't want me to soil my hands cooking. A
month ago about, he began to earn money pretty
fast; he brings me three francs every night and I
put them in a money-box. Only he won't let me go
out except to come here.—That's a man's love! so
he does what he pleases with me. He calls me his
little darling, and my mother never called me anything but little b—, f— p— or thief, or vermin, or
I don't know what!''

"Well, then, my child, why don't you make Père Vyder your husband?"

"Why, it's all done, madame!" said the girl looking proudly into the baroness's face, without a blush, calm-eyed and with unclouded brow. "He told me I was his little wife; but it's very tiresome to be a man's wife!—That is, without the almonds, I mean!"

"My God!" murmured the baroness, "who is the monster who could take advantage of such perfect, holy innocence? Might one not atone for many sins by leading this child into the straight path?—I knew what I was doing!" she said to herself thinking of her scene with Crevel; "but she knows nothing at all!"

"Do you know Monsieur Samanon?—" asked Atala coaxingly.

"No, my dear; but why do you ask me that?"

"Honor bright?" said the innocent creature.

"Don't be afraid of madame, Atala," said the flue-builder's wife, "she's an angel!"

"You see my old pet is afraid of being found by this Samanon; he's in hiding, and I would like very much to have him free."

"Why?"

"Damme! he'd take me to Bobino! perhaps to the Ambigu!"

"What a fascinating creature!" said the baroness, throwing her arms about the child.

"Are you rich?" asked Atala, playing with the baroness's lace ruffles.

"Yes and no," she replied. "I am rich for good little girls like you, when they are willing to allow a priest to teach them the duties of a Christian, and to walk in the right road."

"In what road?" said Atala. "I'm a good one on my legs."

"The road of virtue!"

Atala glanced at the baroness with a sly, mocking expression.

"Look at madame," said the baroness pointing to the flue-builder's wife; "see how happy she is since she was received into the bosom of the Church. Your marriage is like the pairing of animals!"

"Marriage?" replied Atala; "why, if you choose to give me what Père Vyder gives me, I should be satisfied not to be married. He's a nuisance! do you know what that means?"

"When one has once been united to a man, as you are," observed the baroness, "virtue demands that you should remain faithful to him."

"Till he dies?—" said Atala cunningly. "I shan't have him long. If you knew how Père Vyder coughs and how he blows!—Peuh! peuh!" she exclaimed, imitating the old man.

"Virtue and good morals require that the Church, which represents God, and the mayor, who represents the law, shall legalize your marriage," rejoined the baroness. "See madame, she is lawfully married."

"Will that be more fun?" queried the child.

"You will be happier," said the baroness, "for

none can blame you for that marriage. You will please God! Ask madame if she was married without receiving the sacrament of marriage."

Atala looked at the flue-builder's wife.

"What has she got that I haven't?" she asked. "I'm prettier than she is."

"Yes, but I'm an honest woman," interposed the Italian, "and anyone can call you a vile name."

"How can you expect God to protect you if you trample divine and human laws under foot?" said the baroness. "Do you know that God holds paradise in reserve for those who obey the commands of His church?"

"What is there in paradise? theatres?" queried Atala.

"Oh! paradise contains all the delights you can imagine," said the baroness. "It is full of angels, with snow-white wings. There we shall see God in His glory, we shall share His power, and be happy always and forever!"

Atala Judici listened to the baroness as she would have listened to music; and Adeline, realizing that she had gone beyond her powers of comprehension, concluded that she must adopt a different plan and appeal to the old man.

"Return home, my dear, and I will come and talk with Monsieur Vyder. Is he a Frenchman?"

"He's an Alsatian, madame; but he'll be rich by-and-by! If you would only pay what he owes that villain Samanon, he would pay you back! for in a few months, he says he shall have six thousand francs a year, and then we're going to live ever so far away in the country, in the Vosges."

The word *Vosges* caused the baroness to fall into a deep reverie. She seemed to see her native village once more. She was aroused from her sorrowful abstraction by the greetings of the flue-builder himself, who was anxious to exhibit the evidence of his prosperity.

"In a year, madame, I shall be able to return the money you loaned us, for it belongs to the merciful Lord, to the poor and unfortunate! If I prosper, some day you shall draw upon our purse, and I will repay to others by your hands the assistance you brought to us."

"Just now," said the baroness, "I do not ask you for money, but for your co-operation in a work of charity. I have just seen little Judici, who is living with an old man, and I want to have them married in accordance with law and religion."

"Ah! Père Vyder is a very worthy and excellent man, and his advice is always good. The poor old man has made friends in the quarter already in the two months he's been here. He makes out my bills in fine shape. He's a gallant colonel, I think, who served the Emperor faithfully—Ah! how he loves Napoléon! He is decorated, but he never wears any decoration. He is waiting till he's square again, for he has debts, poor dear man!—Indeed I think he's in hiding, and the bailiffs are after him."

"Tell him that I'll pay his debts, if he chooses to marry the girl."

"Ah! that will be soon done!—Come, madame, let us go there; it's only a step away, in the Passage du Soleil."

The baroness and the flue-builder set out together for the Passage du Soleil.

"This way, madame," said the Italian, turning into Rue de la Pépinière.

The Passage du Soleil begins at Rue de la Pépinière and runs into Rue du Rocher. About half-way along the passage, which is of recent creation, the shops therein being rented at a very modest figure, the baroness espied, above a window screened with green taffeta to a sufficient height to prevent passers-by from casting inquisitive glances within: PUBLIC SCRIVENER, and upon the door:

BUSINESS OFFICE.

Petitions drawn up here, Accounts
adjusted, etc.
Secrecy and Dispatch.

The interior resembled the waiting-rooms provided by the omnibus companies of Paris for the convenience of their patrons. An interior stairway led doubtless to the apartments on the entresol, lighted from the gallery, and which were let in connection with the shop. The baroness noticed a desk of blackened whitewood, some cards, and a shabby second-hand easy-chair. A cap with a vizor, and a shade of green taffeta strung on an iron wire, both filthy, indicated precautions taken for disguise or else an infirmity of the eyes not to be wondered at in an old man.

"He is upstairs," said the flue-builder; "I'll go up and tell him and send him down."

The baroness lowered her veil and sat down. A heavy step shook the little wooden staircase, and Adeline could not restrain a piercing cry as she recognized her husband, Baron Hulot, in a gray knitted vest, gray swanskin trowsers much worn, and slippers.

"What can I do for you, madame?" said Hulot courteously.

Adeline rose, seized Hulot's arm, and exclaimed in a voice trembling with emotion:

"At last I have found you!"

"Adeline!" cried the stupefied baron, securing the shop-door.—"Joseph!" he cried to the Italian, "go out into the hall."

"My dear," said she, forgetting everything else in her exuberant joy, "you can come back to your family, for we are rich! your son has a hundred and sixty thousand francs a year! your pension is free, and there are arrears to the amount of fifteen thousand francs simply awaiting a certificate that you are living! Valérie is dead and has left you three hundred thousand francs. Your name is forgotten, you can return to the world, and you will find a fortune awaiting you beneath your son's roof. Come, our happiness will be complete. For nearly three years I have been looking for you, and I was so hopeful of falling in with you, that I have a room all ready to receive you. Oh! come away, come away from this horrible place I find you in!''

"I am very willing to go," said the bewildered baron; *"but can I take the little one?"*

"O Hector, give her up! do this for your Adeline, who has never asked the slightest sacrifice from you! I promise to find a good husband for the child, to provide a suitable *dot* for her, and to have her educated. Let it be said that one of those who have made you happy is happy herself, and do not fall-back again into vice, into the mire!''

"So it was you who wanted me to marry?" rejoined the baron with a smile.—"Stay here a moment," he added, "I will go and dress upstairs, where I have some decent clothes in a trunk."

When Adeline was alone, and looked once more about the horrible place, she burst into tears.

"He has been living here," she said, "and we are living in opulence!—Poor man! how he has been punished, he who was always refinement itself!''

The flue-builder returned to say adieu to his benefactress, who told him to call a carriage. When he returned the baroness begged him to take little Atala Judici home with him, to take her away at once.

"You may say to her," she added, "that if she chooses to put herself under the direction of the curé of the Madeleine, on the day when she goes to communion for the first time, I will give her a *dot* of thirty thousand francs, and a good husband, some clever young man!''

"My eldest son, madame.   He is twenty-two, and he worships the child."

The baron came down at this moment, his eyes wet with tears.

"You are taking me away," he said in his wife's ear, "from the only creature who ever approached your love for me!   The little creature is crying her heart out and I can't leave her so.—"

"Never fear, Hector! she will be taken into a virtuous family, and I will answer for her morals."

"Ah! then I can go with you," said the baron, escorting his wife to the carriage.

Hector, become Baron Hulot d'Ervy once more, had donned a blue cloth frock coat and trowsers, white waistcoat, black cravat and gloves.   When the baroness had taken her seat in the carriage Atala glided in with a snake-like movement.

"Oh! madame," said she, "let me go with you. See, I will be polite and obedient, I will do whatever you want me to; but don't part me from Père Vyder, my benefactor, who gives me such nice things.   I shall be thrashed!"

"Come, come, Atala," said the baron, "this lady is my wife, and we must part."

"Your wife! as old as that!" replied the child; "why she trembles like a leaf!   Oh! what a head!"

And she mischievously imitated the baroness's trembling.   The flue-builder, who was looking for her, came to the carriage door.

"Take her away!" said the baroness.

He took Atala in his arms and carried her home with him by force.

"Thanks for this sacrifice, my dear," said Adeline, taking her husband's hand and pressing it with delirious joy. "How changed you are! How you must have suffered! Think what a surprise for your daughter and for your son!"

Adeline talked, as lovers talk when they meet after a long separation, of a thousand things at once. In ten minutes the baron and his wife reached Rue Louis-le-Grand, where Adeline found the following letter:

"MADAME LA BARONNE,

"Monsieur la Baron d'Ervy remained a month on Rue de Charonne, under the name of Thorec, an anagram of Hector. He is now on the Passage du Soleil under the name of Vyder. He calls himself an Alsatian, is a writer and lives with a young girl named Atala Judici. Be wary, madame, for active search is being made for the baron, I don't know in whose interest.

"The actress has kept her word, and subscribes herself, as always,

"Madame la Baronne,
"Your humble servant,
"J. M."

17

*

The baron's return aroused transports of joy which made him a convert to the delights of family-life. He forgot little Atala Judici, for the excessive indulgence of his passions had brought him to a point where his emotions were as fickle as those of a child. The happiness of the family was somewhat clouded by the change that had taken place in the baron. When he left his children he was still strong and well, and he returned almost a centenarian in appearance, bent and broken, his features bearing the stamp of vice. A splendid dinner improvised by Célestine recalled to the old man's mind the dinners given by Josépha; he was fairly dazzled by the family splendor.

"You are celebrating the return of the Prodigal Father!" he said in Adeline's ear.

"Hush!—everything is forgotten," she replied.

"And what of Lisbeth?" queried the baron, noticing that the old maid was not present.

"Alas!" Hortense replied, "she is in bed; she will never leave it again, and we shall soon have to endure the grief of losing her. She expects to see you after dinner."

The next morning at sunrise Victorin Hulot was informed by his concierge that his house was entirely surrounded by soldiers of the Municipal Guard. The officers of the law were in quest of Baron Hulot.

The bailiff, who followed close upon the concierge's heels, presented judgments in proper form to the advocate, and inquired if he proposed to pay, for his father, the amount due thereon. It was a matter of ten thousand francs in notes of hand, discounted by a usurer named Samanon, who had probably given the baron some two or three thousand francs. Victorin requested the bailiff to send his people away, and paid the amount of the judgment.

"Will this be the last?" he said to himself with some anxiety.

Lisbeth, who was wretched enough over the good fortune which was shining upon the family, could not endure this last happy event. She grew worse so rapidly that Doctor Bianchon announced that she would die within a week; vanquished at last after a long struggle marked by so many victories for her. She kept the secret of her hate amid the horrible agony of the last stages of phthisis. Moreover she had the supreme satisfaction of seeing Adeline, Hortense, Hulot, Victorin, Steinbock, Célestine and their children all in tears around her bed, weeping for her as the good angel of the family.

Baron Hulot, having his fill of substantial and nourishing food, a thing unknown to him for almost three years, recovered his strength, and eventually almost resembled his old self. This change for the better made Adeline so happy that her nervous trembling decreased sensibly in intensity.

"She will end by being perfectly happy!" said Lisbeth to herself on the day before her death,

noticing the sort of veneration in which the baron
held his wife, whose sufferings had been described
to him by Hortense and Victorin.

This feeling hastened Cousin Bette's end, and
her funeral was attended by a whole family in
tears.

Baron and Baronne Hulot, having reached the
age when absolute repose is most desirable, gave
up the magnificent apartments on the first floor to
Comte and Comtesse Steinbock, and took up their
own quarters on the second floor. The baron,
through the efforts of his son, obtained a place on a
railroad in the early part of 1845, with a salary of
six thousand francs, which, added to his retiring
pension of six thousand and the fortune bequeathed
to him by Madame Crevel, gave him an income of
twenty-four thousand francs. Hortense having had
a separate estate from that of her husband during
the three months of their estrangement, Victorin
no longer hesitated to transfer to his sister the two
hundred thousand francs held by him in trust, and
he gave Hortense an allowance of twelve thousand.
Wenceslas, finding himself the husband of a rich
wife, was guilty of no further infidelity; but he idled
his time away, unable to make up his mind to undertake any work, however trifling. An artist *in par-
tibus* once more, he had much success in salons and
was consulted by many amateurs; in short, he became a critic, as all incapables do whose beginnings
give promise that is not fulfilled. Each of these
various households therefore possessed its own

private fortune, although they lived together as one family. Learning wisdom from her many misfortunes the baroness left the care of the whole property in her son's hands, and thus restricted the baron to his salary, hoping that the slender proportions of that source of revenue would prevent him from falling back into his former errors. But, by a strange stroke of good fortune, upon which neither the mother nor the son had calculated, the baron seemed to have renounced the fair sex. His quiescence in this respect, which was credited to the account of nature, so reassured the family that at last they could enjoy, unreservedly, the restored amiability and charming qualities of Baron d'Ervy. He was unflagging in his attentions to his wife and children, accompanied them to the theatre, reappeared in society with them, and did the honors of his son's salon with exquisite grace. In short, this prodigal father, restored, afforded the liveliest satisfaction to his family. He was an agreeable old man, completely broken down physically, but clever and witty, and had retained of his vice only those elements which tended to make it a social virtue. Naturally, they felt at last perfectly secure. The baroness and her children held the head of the family in great regard, forgetting the death of the two uncles. Life cannot go on without examples of noble forgetfulness!

Madame Victorin, who managed this enormous household and displayed great talents as a housekeeper, due to the teaching of Lisbeth, had been

compelled to hire a male cook.   The cook made it
necessary to have a scullery-maid.   Scullery-maids
are in these days ambitious creatures, intent upon
prying into the chef's secrets, and they become
cooks as soon as they know how to stir gravies.
Therefore, they changed scullery-maids very frequently.   Early in December, 1845, Célestine
hired in that capacity a stout Norman girl from
Isigny, short, with fine red arms and a very ordinary face, and as stupid as an impromptu play; so
stupid that she could hardly be induced to lay aside
the classic cotton cap which is the ordinary head-
dress of the damsels of Lower Normandy.   This
damsel, endowed with the figure of a wet-nurse,
seemed as if she were always on the point of burst-
ing the cotton goods in which her waist was enveloped.   One would have said that her ruddy face
was cut out of flint, so immovable were its yellow
outlines.   Naturally no heed was paid to the addition to the household of this Agathe, the genuine
sophisticated girl sent daily to Paris from the provinces.   Agathe tempted the cook but very little,
her language was so vulgar, for she had been waiting upon wagoners, she came from a suburban
tavern, and instead of making a conquest of her
superior and inducing him to instruct her in the
great art of cooking, she became the object of his
contempt.   The cook was courting Louise, Countess
Steinbock's maid.   So it was that the Norman,
finding that he treated her badly, complained of
her lot; she was always sent outside upon one

pretext or another when the chief was preparing some new dish, or putting the finishing touches to a sauce.

"It's certain that I have no chance here," she said, "I'll go to some other house."

Nevertheless she remained, although she had already asked twice to go.

One night Adeline, awakened by a strange sound, found that Hector was not in the bed he occupied beside hers, for they slept in twin beds, as it becomes old people to do. She waited an hour, but the baron did not return. Seized with terror, dreading some horrible catastrophe, apoplexy or the like, she went first of all to the upper floor, to the attics where the servants slept, and was attracted to Agathe's room as much by the bright light that streamed out through the half-open door as by the murmur of voices. She paused in dismay as she recognized the baron's voice; fascinated by Agathe's charms, he had been led on so far by the shameless coarse woman's premeditated resistance as to say these odious words:

"My wife hasn't long to live, and, if you choose, you shall be a baroness."

Adeline shrieked, dropped her candle and fled.

Three days later the baroness, who had received the last sacraments the night before, was at the point of death, surrounded by her family, all in tears. A moment before she died she took her husband's hand, pressed it, and whispered to him:

"My dear, I had nothing else but my life to give

BARON HULOT AND AGATHE PIQUETARD

———

"My wife hasn't long to live, and, if you choose, you shall be a baroness."

Adeline shrieked, dropped her candle and fled.

G.Cain del. Gaujean sc.

you; in a moment you will be free, and you can make a Baroness Hulot."

And they saw, what must indeed be rare, tears starting from the eyes of a corpse. The ferocity of vice had conquered the patience of the angel, from whose lips, on the brink of eternity, escaped the only reproachful word she had uttered in her whole life.

Baron Hulot left Paris three days after the burial of his wife. Eleven months later Victorin learned indirectly of his father's marriage to Mademoiselle Agathe Piquetard, which was celebrated at Isigny, on the first of February, 1846.

"Parents may oppose the marriage of their children, but children can not prevent the follies of their parents in their dotage," said Master Hulot to Master Popinot, the second son of the former Minister of Commerce, who mentioned this marriage to him.

END OF FIRST EPISODE

PIERRE GRASSOU

TO THE

LIEUTENANT-COLONEL OF ARTILLERY, PÉRIOLLAS,

As a testimony of the affectionate esteem of the author

DE BALZAC.

PIERRE GRASSOU

*

Every time that you have been seriously to see the Exposition of works of sculpture and painting, arranged as it has been since the Revolution of 1830, have you not been conscious of a feeling of uneasiness, of weariness, of sadness, at the view of the long and encumbered galleries? Since 1830, the Salon has no longer existed. For the second time the Louvre has been taken by assault by the crowd of artists who are supported by it. Formerly, when it offered the choicest works of art, the Salon conferred the greatest honor upon the creations which were exposed in it. Among the two hundred pictures selected, the public made a still further selection; a crown was awarded to the masterpiece by unknown hands. There were passionate discussions over certain canvases. The insults offered to Delacroix, to Ingres, served to increase their fame no less than the eulogiums and the fanaticism of their admirers. To-day, neither the public nor the critics feel any enthusiasm for the products of this bazaar. Obliged to make the choice which formerly fell to the jury of examination, their interest wearies in this work; and when it is finished, the exhibition closes. Before 1817, the pictures admitted never extended farther along the wall than the first two columns of the long gallery in which are the works of the old masters, and this year they fill the whole of this space, to the great astonishment of the public. The historical genre, the *genre* properly so called, the easel pictures, the landscapes, the flowers, the animal subjects and the water-colors, these eight specialties offered to the public no more than twenty pictures worthy of their attention, and a greater number of works cannot awaken their interest. The greater the increase in the number of artists, the more exacting should be the jury of admission. Everything is lost when the Salon is continued into the gallery. The Salon should have remained a determined and restricted locality, of inflexible dimensions, in which each genre should expose its masterpieces. An experience of ten years has proved the wisdom of the ancient institution. In place of a tournament, you have a mob; instead of a glorious exhibition, you have a tumultuous bazaar; instead of a selection, you have the totality. What happens? The great artist loses by it. The *Turkish Café*, the *Children at the Fountain*, the *Punishment of Hooks*, and the *Joseph*, of Decamps would have contributed more to his glory, exhibited all four of them in the grand salon with the hundred good pictures of that year, than do his twenty canvases lost among the three thousand works confounded in the six galleries. By a strange contrariness, since the doors have been opened to all the world, there is much talk of unknown geniuses. When, twelve years ago, the *Courtesan* of Ingres and those of Sigalon, the *Medusa* of Géricault, the *Massacre of Scio* of Delacroix, the *Baptism of Henri IV.* by Eugène Devéria, admitted by celebrities who were accused of jealousy, made known to the public, despite the denials of the critics, the existence of young and glowing palettes, no complaints were heard. Now-a-days, when the worst dauber of canvases may send his work, there is nothing to be heard but concerning uncomprehended geniuses. Where there is no longer any judgment, there is no longer anything to be judged. Whatever the artists may do, they will return to the investigation of that which will recommend their work to the admiration of the crowd to whom they appeal. Without the selection of the Academy, there would be no longer any Salon, and without the Salon, art would perish.

Since the catalogue has become a great volume there appear in it many names which remain in their obscurity, notwithstanding the list of ten or twelve pictures each which accompany them. Among these names, the most unknown, perhaps, is that of an artist named Pierre Grassou, a native of Fougères, better known as Fougères in the artistic world, who occupies to-day a conspicuous place in the eyes of the public, and who suggests the bitter reflections with which the sketch of

18

his life commences, reflections which are applicable
to several other individuals of the tribe of artists.

In 1832, Fougères lived in the Rue de Navarin,
on the fourth floor of one of those narrow and high
houses which resemble the obelisk of Luxor, which
have a passage-way, a dark little stairway with
dangerous turnings, that show only three windows in each story and in the interior of which
may be found a court-yard, or, to speak more exactly, a square pit.   Above the three or four rooms
of the apartment occupied by Grassou of Fougères
was his atelier, which looked out over Montmartre.
The atelier painted brick color, the floor carefully
stained of a brown color and polished, each chair
furnished with a little fringed stuff, the sofa very
simple but clean as that of the bed-chamber of a
grocer's wife, everything here denoted the petty
life of a small mind and the economies of an indigent
man.   There was a closet to hold the various
atelier utensils, a table for breakfast, a buffet, a
secretary, in fact all the furniture necessary for a
painter, everything in order and very clean.   The
stove even shared in the benefits of this system of
Dutch carefulness, all the more visible that the
pure and almost unchanging north light inundated
with its clear and cold illumination this immense
room.   Fougères, a simple painter of genre, had
no need of those enormous machines which ruin
the historical painters, he had never found in himself
sufficiently complete faculties to enable him to undertake ambitious painting, he still held to his easel.

At the commencement of the month of December of this year, a period at which the bourgeois of Paris conceive periodically the burlesque idea of having their faces perpetuated—as though they were not sufficiently superfluous in themselves—Pierre Grassou, having risen at an early hour, prepared his palette, lit a fire in his stove, ate a roll of bread dipped in milk, and waited to commence his work till the thawing of the ice on his window panes admitted sufficient daylight. The weather was clear and cold. At this moment, the artist, who was eating with that patient and resigned air which reveals so much, recognized the step of a man who had exercised upon his life that influence which this species of person has on those of most artists, —Élias Magus, a picture-dealer, the usurer of canvases. In fact, Élias Magus surprised the painter at the moment when, in this atelier, so very clean, he was about to go to work.

"How are you, old shark?" said the artist to him.

Fougères had received the Cross, Élias bought his pictures for two or three hundred francs, he gave himself very artistic airs.

"Business is bad," replied Élias. "You put on so many airs, you talk of two hundred francs as soon as you have put six sous worth of color on a canvas. —But you are a good fellow, you are! You are an orderly man, and I have got you a good thing."

"*Timeo Danaos et dona ferentes*," said Fougères.

"Do you know Latin?"

"No."

"Well, that means that the Greeks never propose any good things to the Trojans without gaining something for themselves. Formerly, they said: 'Take my horse.' To-day we say: 'Take my bear.' What would you have! Ulysse-Lagingeole-Élias Magus?"

These words will serve to give the measure of the mildness and the spirit with which Fougères employed that which the painters call studio charges.

"I do not say that you will not make me two pictures for nothing."

"Oh! Oh!"

"I leave you free about it, I do not ask them. You are an honest artist."

"Well, what is it?"

"Well, I bring you a father, a mother and an only daughter."

"All of them onlies?"

"Certainly, yes!—and whose portraits are to be painted. These bourgeois, crazy for art, have never dared to venture into an artist's atelier. The daughter has a dot of one hundred thousand francs. You can very well paint these people. They will be perhaps your family portraits."

This old stick of a German, which passed for a man and which called itself Élias Magus, interrupted itself to laugh with a dry laugh whose loud explosions scared the painter. He thought he heard Mephistopheles preaching marriage.

"The portraits will be five hundred francs apiece, you can make me three pictures."

"Well, yes," said Fougères gaily.

"And if you marry the daughter you will not forget me."

"I get married, I!" cried Pierre Grassou, "I who have the habit of going to bed alone, of getting up very early, who have my life all planned."

"A hundred thousand francs," said Magus, "and a nice girl, full of golden tones like a real Titian!"

"What sort of people are these?"

"Formerly traders, at present, lovers of the arts, having a country house at Ville-d'Avray, and ten or twelve thousand francs of income."

"What business were they in?"

"Bottles."

"Do not say that word, it makes me think I hear them cutting corks, and it sets my teeth on edge.—"

"Shall I bring them up?"

"Three portraits, I will send them to the Salon, I can go into portrait painting,—well, yes."

The ancient Élias descended to fetch up the Vervelle family.

In order to understand to what extent this proposition would affect the painter, and what effect the Sieur Vervelle and his wife adorned by their only daughter, would be likely to produce upon him, it will be necessary to take a glance at the previous life of Pierre Grassou of Fougères.

As a pupil, Fougères had studied design under Servin, who passed in the academic world for a great designer. Afterwards, he had gone to Schinner to glean there the secrets of that powerful and magnificent color which distinguished that master. The master, the pupils, had all been very discreet, Pierre had gleaned nothing. From there, Fougères had passed into the atelier of Sommervieux, in order to familiarize himself with that branch of art which is known as composition, but composition was intractable and forbidding to him. Then he had undertaken to wrest from Granet, from Drolling, the mystery of their interior effects. These two masters had not allowed him to carry off anything from them. Finally, Fougères had finished his education under Duval-Lecamus. During these studies and these different transformations, Fougères has possessed tranquil and orderly manners which furnished the material for raillery in the different ateliers in which he sojourned, but everywhere he disarmed his comrades by his modesty, by the patience and the gentleness of a lamb. The masters had not the slightest sympathy for this good youth; the masters love brilliant subjects, the spirits which are eccentric, whimsical, fiery, or sombre and profoundly reflective, which denote a future talent. Everything in Fougères proclaimed mediocrity. His surname of Fougères, that of the painter in the piece of Fabre d'Églantine, furnished material for a thousand slurs; but through force of circumstances he accepted the name of the city in which he had *first seen the day*.

Grassou of Fougères resembled his name. Plump —*grassouillet*—and of a medium figure, he had a faded complexion, brown eyes, black hair, a trumpet-like nose, a sufficiently-large mouth and long ears. His peaceful, passive and resigned air, enlivened but little these principal features of his physiognomy, full of health but without any expression. He would never be likely to be tormented neither by that abundance of blood, nor by that violence of thought, nor by that comic enthusiasm by which the great artists may be recognized. This young man, born to be a virtuous bourgeois, who had come from his native place to be a clerk in the shop of a color merchant, originally of Mayenne and a distant relative of the d'Orgemonts, had ordained himself painter through that obstinacy which constitutes the Breton character. What he had suffered, how he had lived during the period of his studies, God alone knows. He suffered as much as do the great men when they are pursued by poverty and hunted like wild beasts by the pack of the mediocrities and by the crowd of vanities thirsty for vengeance. As soon as he thought himself of sufficient strength to fly with his own wings, Fougères took an atelier in the upper part of the Rue des Martyrs, where he had commenced to make his own way. He made his debut in 1819. The first picture which he presented to the jury for the Exposition of the Louvre represented a village wedding, painfully enough copied from the picture by Greuze. This picture was refused. When Fougères heard the fatal decision, he did not fall into one of those furies, or into one of those epileptic accessions of self-love, to which the superb spirits

are given, and which terminates sometimes by
challenges sent to the director or to the secretary
of the Musée, by menaces of assassination. Fougères received back his canvas tranquilly, wrapped
it up in his handkerchief, carried it back into his
atelier, swearing to himself that he would become
a great painter. He placed his canvas upon his
easel, and went to see his former master, Schinner,
a man of immense talent, an artist mild and patient,
whose success had been complete at the last
Salon; he entreated him to come and criticize the
rejected work. The great painter dropped everything and went. When the poor Fougères had set
him in front of the picture, Schinner, at the first
glance, grasped Fougères hand.

"You are an honest youth, you have a heart of
gold, it is not necessary to deceive you. Listen,
you are fulfilling all the promises which you
made at the atelier. When one finds such things
as those at the end of his brush, my good Fougères,
it is better to leave his colors in Brullon's shop,
and not steal the canvas from others. Come home
early, put on a cotton night-cap, go to bed at nine
o'clock; go to-morrow morning at ten o'clock to
some office where you will apply for a situation,
and leave the arts."

"My friend," said Fougères, "my picture has
already been condemned, and it is not the decision
that I ask for, but the reasons."

"Well, your painting is gray and dull, you see
nature through a veil; your design is heavy and

overloaded; the composition is an imitation of Greuze, who only redeemed his own defects by qualities which you lack."

As he detailed the faults of the picture, Schinner saw on the face of Fougères so profound an expression of sadness that he carried him off to dinner and endeavored to console him. The next day, at seven o'clock in the morning, Fougères, at his easel, was working on the condemned picture; he warmed up the color, he made the corrections indicated by Schinner, he repainted his figures. Then, disgusted with his working-over, he carried it off to Élias Magus. Élias Magus, a species of Dutch-Belgian-Fleming, had three reasons for being that which he had become, avaricious and rich. Originally from Bordeaux, he had commenced in Paris bargaining in pictures and living on the Boulevard Bonne-Nouvelle. Fougères, who relied upon his palette to enable him to go to the baker's, ate with the greatest intrepidity bread and nuts, or bread and milk, or bread and cherries, or bread and cheese, according to the season. Élias Magus, to whom Pierre offered his first picture, peered at it a long time, and finally gave him fifteen francs for it.

"With fifteen francs of income a year, and a thousand francs of expenses," said Fougères smiling, "one would go fast and far—"

Élias Magus made a gesture, he gnawed his thumbs in thinking that he might have had the picture for a hundred sous. For several days afterwards every morning Fougères went down the Rue des Martyrs, concealed himself in the crowd on the boulevard opposite to that in which was situated the shop of Magus, and his eye searched out his picture, which did not seem in the least to attract the attention of the passers-by. Toward the end of the week the picture disappeared. Fougères ascended the boulevard again, he directed his steps toward the shop of the dealer, with the air of a lounger. The Jew was standing in his doorway.

"Well, you have sold my picture?"

"Here it is," said Magus, "I have put a frame upon it to be able to offer it to some one who thinks he knows about pictures."

Fougères no longer dared to return to the boulevard. He undertook a new picture; he occupied himself for two months in licking it into shape, while eating like a mouse and enjoying the comforts of a galley-slave.

One evening he went as far as the boulevard, his feet carried him like a fatality to the shop of Magus, he did not see his picture any where.

"I have sold your painting," said the merchant to the artist.

"And for how much?"

"I got my money back with a little interest. Make me some Flemish interiors, an anatomy lesson, a landscape, I will pay you for them," said Élias.

Fougères would have clasped Magus in his arms, he regarded him as a father. He returned home with a joyful heart; the great painter, Schinner, was then mistaken! In this immense city of Paris there were then hearts which beat in unison with that of Grassou, his talent was comprehended and appreciated. The poor youth, at twenty-seven years of age, had the innocence of a youth of sixteen. Another, one of those suspicious and ferocious artists, would have remarked the diabolical air of Élias Magus, he would have observed the bristling of the hairs of his beard, the irony of his moustache, the movement of his shoulders, which betrayed the satisfaction of Sir Walter Scott's Jew cheating a Christian. Fougères walked along the boulevards in a state of joy which gave a proud expression to his countenance. He was like a pupil of the Lycée who has taken a woman under his protection. He met Joseph Bridau, one of his comrades, one of those eccentric talents destined to glory and to unhappiness. Joseph Bridau, who had some sous in his pocket, according to his own expression, carried Fougères off to the opera. Fougères did not see the ballet, he did not hear the music; he was conceiving pictures, and painting. He left Joseph in the middle of the performance, he hastened home to make sketches by lamp-light, he invented thirty pictures full of reminiscences, he thought himself a genius. The next morning, he bought some colors, some canvases of various dimensions; he made a provision of bread and cheese on his table, he filled his pitcher with water, he procured a stock of wood for his stove; then, to use the expression of the ateliers, he began to "dig" at his pictures; he had some models, and Magus lent him some draperies.   After two months of seclusion, the Breton had finished four pictures. He requested again the advice of Schinner, to whom he added Joseph Bridau.   The two painters saw in these canvases a servile imitation of Holland landscapes, of the interiors of Metzu, and in the fourth a copy of the Anatomy Lesson of Rembrandt.

"Ever pastiches," said Schinner.   "Ah! Fougères, take the trouble to be original."

"You should do something else than painting," said Bridau.

"What?" asked Fougères.

"Throw yourself into literature."

Fougères lowered his head after the manner of the sheep when it rains.   Then he requested, he obtained again some useful advice and retouched his pictures before carrying them to Élias.   Élias paid for each canvas twenty-five francs.   At this price Fougères gained nothing, but he lost nothing, owing to his temperate living.   He took several walks to see what had become of his pictures, and experienced a singular hallucination.   His pictures, so finished, so sharply cut, which had the hardness of sheet-iron and the brilliancy of paintings upon porcelain, seemed as if covered with a fog, they resembled old paintings.   Élias had gone out, Fougères was not able to obtain any information concerning this phenomenon.   He thought he had experienced

an optical illusion. The painter returned to his
atelier, there to make some new ancient paintings.
After seven years of continuous labor, Fougères
succeeded in becoming able to compose and to execute passable pictures. He did as well as do all
the artists of the second rank. Élias bought and
sold all the pictures of the poor Breton, who gained
with difficulty a hundred louis a year, and did not
spend more than twelve hundred francs a year.

At the exposition of 1829, Léon de Lora, Schinner and Bridau, all three occupying high positions and finding themselves at the head of the
movement in the direction of the arts, were taken
with pity for the persistence, for the poverty, of
their old comrade; and they caused to be admitted
to the Exposition, in the grand salon, a painting by
Fougères. This picture, powerful in interest,
which recalled Vigneron by the sentiment, and the
first manner of Dubufe by the execution, represented a young man who in the interior of a prison
was having his hair cut off at the nape of his neck.
On one side a priest; on the other, an old and a
young woman in tears. An official of the court
read a stamped paper. On a wretched table might
be seen a repast which no one had touched. The
daylight entered through the bars of a high window. There was in it something to make the
bourgeois shudder, and the bourgeois shuddered.
Fougères had drawn his inspiration quite completely
from the masterpiece of Gérard Dow; he had
turned the group of *The Dropsical Woman*

toward the window, instead of presenting the figures in full face.   He had replaced the dying woman by the condemned man; the same pallor, the
same regard, the same appeal to God.   In the place
of the Flemish physician he had painted the cold
and official figure of the functionary clothed in
black; but he had added an old woman near the
young girl of Gérard Dow.   And, finally, the cruelly
good-natured face of the headsman dominated this
group.   This plagiarism, very skilfully disguised,
was not perceived.

The catalogue contained this title:

"510. GRASSOU DE FOUGÈRES (PIERRE),
"Rue de Navarin, 2.
"The Toilet of a Chouan, condemned to death in 1809."

Mediocre as it was, this picture had a prodigious
success, for it recalled the affair of the robbers
of Mortagne.   A crowd collected every day before
this canvas à la mode, and Charles X. stopped
before it.   MADAME, informed of the patient life
of this poor Breton, conceived an enthusiasm for
him.   The Duc d'Orleans bargained for the picture.
The ecclesiastics said to Madame la Dauphine that
the subject was full of righteous thoughts; there
pervaded it, in fact, a religious air very satisfying.
Monseigneur the Dauphin admired the dust on the
flag-stones, a great, heavy error, for Fougères had
smeared them with greenish tints which proclaimed
the dampness of the base of the walls.   MADAME

bought the painting for a thousand francs, the Dauphin ordered another. Charles X. gave the cross to the son of the peasant who had formerly fought for the royal cause in 1799. Joseph Bridau the great painter was not decorated. The Minister of the Interior ordered two church pictures of Fougères. This Salon was for Pierre Grassou his whole fortune, his glory, his future, his life. To invent, in anything, is to wish to die by inches; to copy, is to live. After having finally discovered a vein full of gold, Grassou de Fougères practised the precepts of that cruel maxim to which society owes these infamous mediocrities charged with the task to-day of electing the superiors in every social class, but which, naturally, elect themselves, and wage a bitter war against the real talents. The principle of election, applied to everything, is false; France will yet abandon it. Nevertheless, the modesty, the simplicity, the surprise of the good and mild Fougères, silenced the recriminations and the envy. Moreover, he had for him all the successful Grassous, sponsors for the Grassous to come. Some persons, struck with the energy of a man whom nothing had discouraged, spoke of Domenichino, and said: "It is necessary to reward the exercise of will in the arts! Grassou has not stolen his success! here are ten years that he has been digging, poor fellow!"

This exclamation of *poor fellow* counted for at least half in the support and congratulations which the painter received. Pity lifts as many mediocrities, as envy pulls down of great artists.

The daily journals had not spared their criticism,
the Chevalier Fougères digested them as he
digested the advice of his friends, with an angelic
patience. Wealthy now, with some fifteen thous-
and francs very painfully acquired, he furnished
his apartment and his atelier in the Rue de Navarin,
he completed the picture ordered by Monseigneur
le Dauphin and the two church paintings ordered
by the Minister by the appointed day, with a
promptness very embarrassing for the funds of the
Minister, accustomed to very different methods.
But admire the happiness of those who have a talent
for order! If he had delayed, Grassou, surprised
by the Revolution of July, would never have been
paid. At thirty-seven years of age, Fougères had
manufactured for Élias Magus about two hundred
paintings, completely unknown, but by the aid of
which he had attained to that satisfying manner,
to that degree of execution which makes the artist
shrug his shoulders, and which the bourgeoisie
cherish. Fougères was dear to his friends because
of a rectitude of ideas, because of a security of feelings, a perfect good nature, a great loyalty; if they
had no opinion of his palette, they loved the man
who held it.

"How unfortunate it is that Fougères should
have the vice of being a painter," said his comrades to each other.

Nevertheless, Grassou gave excellent advice,
quite in the manner of those pamphleteers who
are quite incapable of writing a book themselves

and who know, perfectly, just where all books sin, but there was between the literary critics and Fougères a difference,—he was eminently sensible to beauty, he recognized it, and his counsel was actuated by a sentiment which made the justness of his remarks acceptable. After the Revolution of July, Fougères sent to each Exposition some ten pictures, among which the jury accepted four or five. He lived with the most rigid economy, and his entire household consisted of a female housekeeper. For his only amusement, he visited his friends, he went to see objects of art, he allowed himself certain short journeys in France, he proposed to go and seek inspiration in Switzerland. This detestable artist was an excellent citizen; he mounted guard, attended all the reviews, paid his rent and his bills with the exactitude of the most strict bourgeois. Having lived in hard work and in poverty, he had never had time to love. Up to this period a bachelor and poor, he did not in the least think of complicating his so simple existence. Incapable of inventing any manner of increasing his fortune, he carried at the end of every three months to his notary, Cardot, his savings and his quarterly receipts. When the notary had a thousand crowns of these economies in hand he invested them in first mortgages with succession in the name of the wife, if the borrower were married, or succession in the name of the seller, if the borrower had a sum to pay. The notary collected the interest and added it to the sums delivered by

19

Grassou of Fougères. The painter waited for the
fortunate moment when his funds should arrive at
the imposing figure of two thousand francs of income to give himself the *otium cum dignitate* of the
artist and to paint pictures, oh! but such pictures,
in fact, real pictures, finished, *tip-top, brilliant,
nobby ones!* His future, his dreams of happiness,
the superlative of his hopes, would you wish to
know them? they were to enter the Institute and
to have the rosette of the officer of the Legion of
Honor! to seat himself at the side of Schinner and
of Léon de Lora! to arrive at the Academy before
Bridau! to have a rosette in his buttonhole! What
a dream! It is only the mediocrities who think of
everything.

Hearing the noise of several steps on the stairway, Fougères pushed up his fore-lock, buttoned
up his vest of bottle-green velvet, and was only
moderately surprised to see entering, a figure that
is vulgarly called "a melon" in the ateliers. This
fruit surmounted a pumpkin, draped in blue cloth
ornamented with a jingling bunch of seals. The
melon was blowing like a porpoise, the pumpkin
traveled on two roots, improperly called legs. A
real painter would have thus taken stock of the
little bottle-merchant, and shown him immediately
to the door, saying to him that he did not paint
vegetables. Fougères looked at the customer without laughing, for Monsieur Vervelle wore a diamond
worth a thousand crowns in his shirt front.

Fougères glanced at Magus and said, "There is

fat," employing a slang word, then in fashion in the ateliers.

On hearing this word, Monsieur Vervelle knit his brows. This bourgeois had drawn to himself another complication of vegetables in the persons of his wife and his daughter. The wife presented a face of a mahogany complexion, she resembled a cocoanut surmounted by a head and girdled by a waistband. She pivoted on her feet; her dress was yellow with black stripes. She displayed proudly, upon swollen hands, extravagant mittens like the gloves of a standard-bearer. The feathers of a hearse of the first-class floated over an exceptional bonnet. Falls of lace adorned shoulders which were as round behind as before; thus the spherical form of the cocoanut was perfectly maintained. Her feet, of that kind which the painters call *abatis*, were ornamented with a puffed-up cushion half an inch above the varnished leather of the shoes. How had the feet ever been made to enter them? No one knows.

Then there followed a young asparagus, with a green and yellow dress, and who showed a little head crowned with a growth of hair, in fillets, of a carroty-yellow which a Roman would have adored; stringy arms, spots of red upon a sufficiently white complexion, large, innocent eyes, with white eye-lashes, very faint eyebrows; her hat was made of Leghorn straw with two modest bows of satin ribbon bordered with an edging of white satin, the hands virtuously red and feet like her mother's.

These three beings had, in looking around the atelier, an air of happiness which announced in them a respectable enthusiasm for the arts.

"And it is you, monsieur, who are going to make our likenesses," said the father, assuming a little swaggering air.

"Yes, monsieur," replied Grassou.

"Vervelle, *he* has the Cross," whispered the wife to the husband while the painter had his back turned.

"Would I have been likely to have had our portraits done by an artist who was not decorated?—" replied the former dealer in corks.

Élias Magus bowed to the Vervelle family and went out, Grassou accompanied him to the landing of the stairway.

"It takes you to fish up such dumplings."

"A hundred thousand francs of dot."

"Yes, but what a family!"

"Three hundred thousand francs of expectations, a house in the Rue Boucherat, and country house at Ville d'Avray."

"Boucherat, bottles, bottle corks, bottles corked, bottles uncorked," said the painter.

"You will be beyond the reach of want for the rest of your days," said Élias.

This idea penetrated the head of Pierre Grassou, as the morning light penetrated into his garret. In arranging the father of the young person, he somehow found him to be of good appearance and he admired this face full of strong tones. The mother

and the daughter hovered around the painter filled
with surprise at all his preparations, he appeared
to them as a god. This visible admiration pleased
Fougères. The golden calf threw upon this family
its fantastic reflection.

"You must gain a perfectly crazy sum of money,
but you spend it as easily as you gain it?" said
the mother.

"No, madame," replied the painter. "I do not
spend it, I have not the means to amuse myself.
My notary invests my money, he keeps my accounts, once my money is in his hands I no longer
think of it."

"I have heard, I have," cried the père Vervelle,
"that the artists are all sieves."

"Who is your notary, if it is not indiscreet to
ask?" said Madame Vervelle.

"An honest fellow, perfectly square, Cardot."

"Well, well, isn't that funny!" said Vervelle,
"Cardot is ours."

"Do not disarrange yourself," said the painter.

"You must not move, Anténor," said the wife,
"you will bother monsieur, and if you could see
him working, you would understand."

"Mon Dieu, why have you not taught me the
arts?" said Mademoiselle Vervelle to her parents.

"Virginie," cried the mother, "a young person
should not learn certain things. When you are
married,—good, but, until that time, keep thyself
quiet."

During this first sitting, the Vervelle family

became almost familiar with the honest artist.
They were to return two days later. As they
departed the father and the mother told Virginie to
go before them; but, notwithstanding the distance,
she heard these words which were calculated to
arouse her curiosity:

"A man with a decoration,—thirty-seven years
old,—an artist that has commissions, who invests
his money with our notary. We will consult Cardot.—Hein! to be called Madame de Fougères!—
He doesn't look like a wicked man.—You say to
me, a merchant?—but a merchant, unless he has
retired, you never know what may become of your
daughter, whilst an economical artist.—And then
we love the arts.—Well!—"

While the Vervelle family discussed him, Pierre
Grassou discussed the Vervelle family. It was
impossible for him to remain quietly in his atelier,
he went out to walk on the boulevard, he looked at
the reddish haired women who passed him! He
gave himself up to the strangest reasoning;—gold
is the most beautiful of all the metals, the yellow
color represents gold, the Romans admired red-
headed women, and he would become a Roman, etc.
After two years of married life, what man concerns
himself with the color of his wife? Beauty goes,
—but ugliness remains. Money is the half of happiness. That night, when he went to bed, the
painter already found Virginie Vervelle charming.

When the three Vervelles entered, the day of the
second sitting, the artist welcomed them with an

amiable smile. The scoundrel had trimmed his beard, he had put on white linen; he had arranged his hair in a very agreeable manner, he had chosen a pair of very becoming pantaloons and red slippers, à *la poulaine*, that is, with long, curved points. The family replied by a smile as flattering as that of the artist, Virginie became the color of her hair, lowered her eyes and turned her head while looking at the various studies. Pierre Grassou found these little affected airs ravishing. Virginie was graceful, she did not take after, luckily, either her father or her mother; but whom did she take after?

"Ah! I know," said he continually to himself, "the mother has had a friend in her business."

During the sitting, there were various skirmishes between the family and the painter, who had the audacity even to find the père Vervelle sprightly. This flattery enabled the family to enter the heart of the painter at double-quick step, he gave one of his drawings to Virginie and a sketch to her mother.

"For nothing?" said they.

Pierre Grassou could not keep himself from smiling.

"You ought not to give away your pictures in this manner, they are money," said Vervelle to him.

At the third sitting, the père Vervelle spoke of the fine gallery of paintings which he had at his country-place at Ville-d'Avray,—Rubens, Gérard Dows, Mieris, Terburgs, Rembrandts, a Titian, Paul Potters, etc.

"Monsieur Vervelle has manifested extravagances," said Madame Vervelle pompously, "he has as much as a hundred thousand francs' worth of pictures."

"I love the arts," said the former bottle-merchant.

When the portrait of Madame Vervelle was commenced, that of the husband was almost finished. Then the enthusiasm of the family no longer knew any bounds. The notary had given the painter the highest eulogiums,—Pierre Grassou was in his eyes one of the best youths in the world, one of the best established artists, who, moreover, had saved up thirty-six thousand francs; his days of poverty were over, he made about ten thousand francs each year, he capitalized the income; finally, he was incapable of making a woman unhappy. This last phrase threw an enormous weight in the scales. The friends of the Vervelles no longer heard of anything but the celebrated Fougères. The day on which Fougères commenced the portrait of Virginie, he was already *in petto* the son-in-law of the family Vervelle. The three members of this family flowered out in this atelier, which they had come to consider as one of their residences; there was for them an inexplicable attraction in this interior so clean, cared for, genteel, artistic. *Abyssus abyssum*, the bourgeois attracts the bourgeois. Toward the end of the sitting, the staircase outside was shaken, the door was brutally flung open, and Joseph Bridau entered; he was in an overmastering rage, his hair was disheveled, his big face was excited, he threw around the room his flashing glance, made the tour of the atelier and came up to Grassou abruptly, drawing his frock coat over his gastric region and endeavoring, but in vain, to button it, the button having escaped from its cloth covering.

"Wood is dear," said he to Grassou.

"Ah."

"The English are after me—What, you painting such things as that?"

"Shut up."

"Ah! yes.—"

The Vervelle family, superlatively shocked by this strange apparition, passed from its ordinary red to the cherry-red of intense fire.

"That fetches!" resumed Joseph. "Is there any *aubert en fouillouse*—(tin in the pocket)?"

"Do you want much?"

"A bill for five hundred.—I have after me one of those sharpers who are like bull-dogs, who, when once they have taken hold, never let go till they take the piece with them. What a race!"

"I will write you a word to my notary.—"

"You have a notary, then?"

"Yes."

"That explains to me, then, why you still make the cheeks with such pink tones, which would be excellent for a perfumer's sign."

Grassou could not keep from blushing, Virginie was posing.

"Take nature as it is!" said the great painter

continuing. "Mademoiselle is reddish. Well, is
that a mortal sin? everything is magnificent in
painting.   Put some cinnabar on your palette,
warm me up those cheeks there, put in their little
brown spots, butter me up all that! Do you want
to have more wit than nature herself?"

"Wait," said Fougères, "take my place while I
write a line."

Vervelle rolled himself over to the table and
whispered in the ear of Grassou:

"But that *scrub there* will spoil everything,"
said the merchant.

"If he would do the portrait of your Virginie, it
would be a thousand times better than mine," replied Fougères, indignantly.

On hearing this the bourgeois retreated softly
towards his wife, who was stupefied at the invasion
of this ferocious beast, and very little reassured to
see him co-operating in the portrait of her daughter.

"There, follow those indications," said Bridau
returning the palette and receiving the note. "I do
not thank you.—I can return to the chateau of
d'Arthez for whom I am painting a dining room and
where Léon de Lora is doing panels to go over
doors, master-pieces. Come and see us."

He went out without any salutation, so much had
he had enough of them in looking at Virginie.

"Who is that man?" asked Madame Vervelle.

"A great artist," replied Grassou.

There was a moment of silence.

"Are you quite sure," said Virginie, "that he

has not done harm to my portrait?—he frightened me."

"He has only done good to it," replied Grassou.

"If that is a great artist, I like better a great artist who resembles you," said Madame Vervelle.

"Ah! Mamma, monsieur is a much greater painter, he will do me altogether," observed Virginie.

The aspect of the genius had thrown into consternation these bourgeois so orderly.

It was now the beginning of that autumnal period so pleasantly called *St. Martin's Summer*. It was with the timidity of the neophyte in the presence of a man of genius, that Vervelle risked an invitation to visit his country place on the following Sunday; he knew how little attraction a bourgeois family could offer an artist.

"You others," said he, "you require emotions, great spectacles and spiritual companions.—But there are some good wines, and I count on my picture gallery to compensate you for the ennui that an artist like you can find among traders."

This idolatry, which pampered exclusively his self-love, charmed the poor Pierre Grassou, so little accustomed to receive such compliments. The honest artist, this ignominious mediocrity, this heart of gold, this loyal life, this stupid designer, this honest youth decorated with the royal order of the Legion of Honor, put himself under arms to go and enjoy the last five days of the year, at Ville d'Avray. The painter went modestly by the public conveyance, and could not suppress his admiration

for the handsome pavilion of the bottle-merchant,
set down in the middle of a park five acres in
extent, on the summit of Ville d'Avray, on the
finest point of view.   To marry Virginie, that
would be to possess, some day, this beautiful villa!
He was received by the Vervelles with an enthusiasm, a joy, a happiness, a frank bourgeois stupidity
which confounded him.   It was a day of triumph.
The future son-in-law was conducted through the
shady walks of nankeen color, which had all been
raked over, as they should be for a great man.
The trees themselves had an air of having been
combed, the lawns were all mown.   The pure air
of the country brought to them the odors of cooking
infinitely comforting.   Everything in the house
said: "We have a great artist!"   The little père
Vervelle rolled around in his park like an apple, the
daughter undulated like an eel, and the mother followed with a noble and worthy step.   These three
did not leave Grassou during seven hours.   After
the dinner, the duration of which equaled its sump-
tuousness, Monsieur and Madame Vervelle arrived
at their grand *coup de theâtre*, at the opening of the
gallery   illuminated   by skilfully arranged lamp-
light.   Three neighbors, old merchants, an uncle
with an inheritance, bidden for the ovation to the
great artist, an old demoiselle Vervelle and the
guests followed Grassou into the gallery, sufficiently
curious to hear his opinion of the famous collection
of the little père Vervelle, who overwhelmed them
with the fabulous value of his paintings.   The

bottle-merchant seemed to have wished to have
contended with the king Louis-Philippe and the galleries of Versailles.   The paintings, magnificently
framed, all had tablets on which might be read, in
black letters on a gold ground :

"RUBENS.

" *Dance of Fauns and Nymphs.*'

"REMBRANDT.

"*Interior of a Dissecting-room.*

" *Dr. Tromp lecturing to his pupils.*"

There were a hundred and fifty paintings, all of
them varnished, dusted ; some of them were covered
with green curtains which were not drawn in the
presence of young people.   The artist stood with
limp arms, and mouth open, without a word on
his lips, on recognizing the half of his own pictures
in this gallery,—he was Rubens, Paul Potter,
Mieris, Metzu, Gérard Dow!—He was in himself
twenty great masters!

"What is the matter with you? you grow pale!"

"My daughter, a glass of water!" cried Madame
Vervelle.

The painter took the père Vervelle by the button
of his coat and drew him into a corner, under the
pretext of seeing a Murillo.   Spanish pictures were
at that time in fashion.

"You have bought your paintings from Élie
Magus?" said he to him.

"Yes—all of them originals."

"Between ourselves, for how much has he sold to you those which I will point out to you?"

Together they made a tour of the gallery. The guests marveled at the serious air with which the artist proceeded, in company with his host, to the examination of the masterpieces.

"Three thousand francs!" said Vervelle in a low voice when they came to the last; "but I say forty thousand francs!"

"Forty thousand francs for a Titian?" repeated the artist aloud, "but that is no price at all."

"As I said to you, I have paintings worth a hundred thousand crowns!" cried Vervelle.

"I made all of those pictures myself," said Pierre Grassou in his ear, "and I sold them altogether for not more than ten thousand francs.—"

"Prove it to me," replied the bottle-merchant, "and I will double my daughter's dot, for in that case you are Rubens, Rembrandt, Terburg, Titian!—"

"And Magus is a famous picture merchant," said the painter, who understood the ancient appearance of his paintings and the usefulness of the subjects which the dealer had required of him.

Far from falling in the estimation of his admirer, Monsieur de Fougères, as the family persisted in calling Pierre Grassou, increased so much in their esteem that he painted gratuitously the portraits of the family, and offered them quite naturally to his father-in-law, to his mother-in-law and to his wife.

To-day Pierre Grassou, who does not miss a

single Exposition, passes in the bourgeois world for a good portrait painter. He earns some twelve thousand francs a year, and spoils about five hundred francs' worth of canvas. His wife received six thousand francs of income as her dot; he lives with his father-in-law and his mother-in-law. The Vervelles and the Grassous, who get along marvelously well together, have a carriage and are the happiest people in the world. Pierre Grassou never issues from this bourgeois circle in which he is considered one of the greatest artists of the epoch. There is not a family portrait between the Barrière du Trône and the Rue du Temple which is not executed in the atelier of this great painter, which does not pay at least five hundred francs. The grand reason of the bourgeois for employing this artist is this: "Say what you please about him, he invests twenty thousand francs a year in the hands of his notary!" As Grassou behaved very well in the disturbances of the twelfth of May he has been appointed officer of the Legion of Honor. He is Chef de Bataillon in the National Guard. The Musée of Versailles has not been able to avoid ordering a Battle from so excellent a citizen, who promenaded himself all over Paris so that he might meet his former comrades and say to them with an easy air:

"The King has given me a Battle to execute."

Madame de Fougères adores her husband, to whom she has presented two children. This painter, good father and good husband, can not, however, rid himself of a fatal thought,—the artists scoff at him, his name is a term of derision in the ateliers, the feuilletons never méntion his works. But he labors still, and moves toward the Academy,—which he will enter. Then, vengeance which swells his heart! he will buy pictures by the celebrated painters when they are in need, and he will replace the daubs of the gallery of Ville d'Avray by real master-pieces—which are not by himself.

There are to be met with mediocrities more niggardly and more malicious than that of Pierre Grassou, who is moreover an anonymous benefactor and perfectly obliging.

Paris, December, 1839.

HISTORY OF THE THIRTEEN

THE GIRL WITH THE GOLDEN EYES

DEDICATED TO

EUGÈNE DELACROIX, PAINTER

Louis Edouard Fournier

R de Los Rios, sc.

IN THE RUE ———

She appeared then to Henri so marvelously beautiful that the old woman and all the horrid phantasmagoria of rags, antiquated, rusty, worn draperies, the green straw cushions of the arm-chairs, the red foot-stool much worn, all this miserable luxury vanished entirely.

THE GIRL WITH THE GOLDEN EYES

*

Certainly one of the most terrible spectacles one can witness is the general aspect of the Parisian people. Emaciated, wrinkled, sallow and dried up, they are horrible to look upon. Paris is but a vast field incessantly swept by a tempest of interests, ever whirling men here; whom Death harvests more frequently than elsewhere, only to be replaced in ranks as serried as before: men whose distorted, eager faces distil through every pore the thoughts, the desires, the poison that is seething in their brains; masks, we should call them, rather than faces,—masks of weakness and of strength, masks of suffering and of joy, masks of hypocrisy; but all wearing that same tired strained look; all bearing the ineffaceable marks of their overpowering eagerness. What is it they seek? Gold, or pleasure!

A few observations on the moods and idiosyncrasies of Paris may serve to explain the causes of its cadaverous physiognomy, which has but two ages, youth and senility: a pale and colorless youth, a painted old-age whose desire is to appear young.

Travelers,—who are not generally of a reflective turn,—on beholding this anæmic race are at first moved by a sensation of disgust for the great capital, laboratory of all delights, that holds them willing captives and where they remain to transform and pervert their natures. A few words will suffice to give a physiological explanation of the almost infernal complexion of the Parisians, for it is not merely in hyperbole that Paris is sometimes styled a hell.—It may be so regarded in truth. There everything smokes, burns, blazes, boils, flames, goes out, ignites again, crackles, sparkles, and is consumed. In no country was life ever more feverish or more intense. This social nature, always in a state of fusion, on the completion of each task seems to cry: "Another!" as nature herself does, and like it further, this social nature busies itself with insects, with the flowers of a day, with trifles and ephemera, and at the same time spouts fire and flame from its perpetual crater. Perhaps, before analyzing the special causes which give to each tribe of this intelligent and active nation a physiognomy of its own, it will be well to point out the general cause that decolorizes the race, giving to individuals a complexion more or less pale, gray, brown or bluish green.

Through interesting himself in everything, the Parisian in the end comes to feel interest in nothing. His face, rendered expressionless by all he sees and hears, becomes gray and blank, like housefronts that for years have received their daily coat of dust and smoke. Indifferent, in fact, to-day to that which, to-morrow, will excite him to frenzy, the Parisian, no matter what may be his age, lives always a child. He grumbles at everything, is consoled for everything, laughs at everything, forgets everything, wants everything, enjoys everything, seizes everything with eagerness, casts aside everything with indifference—his kings, his conquests, his glory, his idol, be it of bronze or glass— as he discards his old stockings, his hats, his fortune. At Paris, sentiment does not stand in the way, and in the course of the struggle the passions are blunted; love is but a desire, hate a mere velleity; one's truest relative a thousand-franc note, his best friend the pawnbroker. This general indifference bears its fruit, and in the salon as in the street, no one is *de trop*, no one is absolutely necessary nor entirely objectionable—blockheads and rogues, men of learning and probity alike; everything is tolerated, government and the guillotine, religion and the cholera. You will always find a place and a welcome in that society, you will never be missed by it. What is it then that reigns supreme in that community, devoid of morals, belief, and sentiment, but where all sentiment, all belief, all morality have their inception and their completion? Gold and pleasure! Take these two words as a light to your feet and explore the recesses of this cage of plaster, this human hive with its black and noisome gutters, follow the ramifications of that thought which moves and stirs it! See for

yourselves.   First look at the class which pos-
sesses nothing!

The working man, the proletarian, the man who
struggles with feet, hands, tongue, back, arms, and
fingers to earn a living, whose first duty indeed,
should be to husband his vital principle—well, he
abuses and wastes his strength, harnesses his wife
to a cart, perhaps, and assigns to his growing child
a task beyond its years.   The manufacturer, that
intermediate wire which, being pulled from above,
sets in motion all those puppets who with their
grimy hands turn and decorate china, sew coats and
gowns, hammer iron, plane boards, harden steel,
spin hemp and flax, polish bronzes, engrave the
crystal, make artificial flowers, embroider woolen
stuffs, break horses, make harness and lace, mould
brass, paint carriages, vaporize cotton, blow glass,
cut diamonds, burnish metals, give to marble the
forms of leaves and flowers, carve gems, clothe the
thought in fitting words, coloring, brightening and
shading all—the manufacturer, I say, that go-
between, appears upon the scene and,—whether in
the name of the caprices of the great city or of that
monster which we call Speculation,—promises untold wealth to that perspiring, willing, patient and
industrious world.   Thereon those quadrumana are
up and doing, waking when they should sleep, suffering, toiling, swearing, fasting, walking; all wear
themselves out, in order to possess the gold that
has such a fascination for them.   Careless of the
future, athirst for pleasure, relying on their strong

arms as the painter does on his palette, these fine
gentlemen of a day squander their money every
Monday in the taverns that surround the city with
a zone of uncleanness—girdle of the most impure of
Venuses, that is hourly being clasped and un-
clasped—where the weekly earnings of these people,
as uncontrollable in their pleasures as they are
quiet and patient in their laboring hours, are lost
as rapidly as at the gaming-table.   For five days,
then, no rest for these toilers of Paris! For five
days they abandon themselves to occupations to
break forth in a thousand streams of creative will,
the effect of which is visible in pallid faces, heavy
eyes, lean and stunted forms and ungraceful carriage.
Then, by way of recreation and response, follows a
debasing debauch—the dull skin, blackened by blows,
pale from drunkenness or sallow from indigestion—
which lasts only two days, but steals the future
bread and the soup for a week, the wife's gowns
and the clothing of the babe.   These men, undoubtedly born to be handsome, for every created being
has a form of relative beauty, enlisted while
they were yet children in the great army of workers,
under the standard of the hammer, the shears or
the pincers, and were promptly vulcanized. Vulcan,
with his ugliness and strength, should be the tute-
lary genius of this ugly and strong people,—sublime
in its mechanical ingenuity, patient when it is in
the mood to be so, terrible once in a century,
inflammable as gunpowder and primed with brandy
for revolutionary incendiarism—intelligent enough,

to take fire on the expression of a captious word, which, in its ears, always signifies: Gold and pleasure! Counting all those who extend their hand for alms, for fairly-earned wages, or for the five francs accorded to every species of Parisian prostitution—all those, in short, who receive a wage, whether honestly earned or otherwise—this class numbers three hundred thousand individuals. Would not the government be overturned every Tuesday were it not for the taverns and pot-houses? On Tuesday, luckily, these gentry are in a torpid state, are sleeping off the fumes of their potations, have not a sou to bless themselves with, and so go back peaceably to their tasks and to their dry bread, stimulated by a necessity of material procreation that has become to them a second nature. Nevertheless this race has its rare examples of virtue, its fully-equipped men, its unrecognized Napoléons, who are types of its strength raised to its highest expression, and represent its social aims and standards by an existence in which reflection and action are combined, not so much with the intention of infusing enjoyment into life as of modifying the various forms of suffering.

Chance has produced a frugal working man and endowed him with a modicum of sense; he has kept an eye on the future, has taken to himself a wife, and becomes a father. After enduring years of privation he hires a shop and sets up in business in a small way as a mercer. Provided he has prospered moderately, and neither sickness nor vice has

interfered to hinder his progress, the following will
be a pretty accurate sketch of his normal life.

But, first of all, salute this monarch of Parisian
activity, who has subjected to himself time and
space. Yes, salute this being, a compound of salt-
petre and gas, who during his laborious nights gives
children to France and by day is ubiquitous in the
service, and for the glory and pleasure of his fellow-
citizens. This man solves in his person the problem of serving acceptably at the same time many
masters: the wife of his bosom, his household, the
Constitutionnel, the National Guard, his shop, the
opera, and God; but with a view, be it understood,
of transforming shop, wife, *Constitutionnel*, National
Guard, opera and God into money. In other words,
salute an irreproachable accumulator. Up and stirring every morning at five o'clock, like a bird he
traverses the distance that lies between his domicile and the Rue Montmartre. Let it blow, thunder,
rain or snow, he will be found at the *Constitutionnel*
office, waiting for the regular number of papers
which he has contracted to distribute. He receives
his dole of political daily bread, hoists it on his
shoulder, and is off. At nine o'clock he is in the
bosom of his family, cracks jokes with his wife,
gives her a very loud kiss, swallows a cup of coffee
and lectures the children. At a quarter of ten he
appears at the mayor's office. There, stationed on
a high stool, like a parrot on his perch, warmed at
the expense of the City of Paris, he inscribes in a
big book until four, without ever according to

them a tear or a smile, the births, marriages and
deaths of an entire district. The joys and sorrows
of the quarter flow from the nib of his pen, as
earlier the wit and learning of the *Constitutionnel*
rode on his shoulders. Nothing is too heavy for
him! He always goes straight ahead, takes his
patriotism as he finds it, ready-made for him in the
newspaper, never contradicts anyone, shouts and
applauds with the multitude, and is as careless and
happy as a swallow. As his parish church is only
a few steps away, he can in case of an important
ceremony leave his place to a supernumerary and
step across to sing a *Requiem* in the choir, of which
on Sundays and holidays he is the finest ornament,
the most imposing voice, and where he energetically
twists his large mouth into impossible shapes as he
thunders out a joyful *Amen.* He is a lay-clerk.
Released at four o'clock from his official duties, he
presently appears in the most celebrated shop there
is in all the city, bringing with him mirth and jol-
lity. A happy woman is his wife, for he has not
time to be jealous; he is a man of action rather
than of sentiment. As soon as he puts his foot
inside the door he begins to harry and tease the
salesladies, whose bright eyes bring many a customer; he tumbles over the fichus, the finery, the
thousand articles of filmy muslin fashioned by the
girls' deft fingers; or, still oftener, before dinner is
served he waits on a purchaser, posts his books, or
takes to a court-officer some overdue bill. Six
o'clock, every other evening, is sure to find

him at his post. He has a permanent position
as bass in the chorus of the opera, where he
is ready to exchange his own proper *ego* for that of
a soldier, an Arab, a prisoner, a savage, a peasant,
a phantom, the foot of an elephant, a lion, a demon,
a hobgoblin, a slave, a eunuch, black or white, —
ever an expert in mirth or sorrow-making, pity or
surprise, always ready to fight or run away, to
shout or to be silent, to represent Rome or Egypt;
but always, *in petto*, the mercer. At midnight he
is a man once more, loving husband and tender
father; he slips into the conjugal bed, his passion
fired by the recollection of the voluptuous beauty
of the nymphs of the ballet and the seductive
curves of the Taglioni's leg. He falls asleep quickly
and despatches his slumbers as he has despatched
the business of the day. Is he not the embodiment
of the principle of activity, the conqueror of time
and space, the Proteus of civilization? He is a
compendium of everything: history, politics, literature, government, religion, military science. Is
he not a living encyclopædia, a grotesque Atlas, like
Paris unceasingly on the go and never at rest? He
is all legs. Among such labors no physiognomy
could preserve its purity. It may be that some
well-to-do philosophers will maintain that the
laborer who dies at thirty an old man, the lining of
his stomach destroyed by his progressive doses of
alcohol, is happier than the mercer. One is
stricken down suddenly without warning, the other
dies by degrees. The latter, from his various

sources of income: shoulders, voice, hands, wife
and trade, as from so many productive farms, can
show as profit his children, a few thousand francs,
and the most laboriously earned happiness that
ever lightened the heart of man. The little fortune
and the children, or rather the children, who are all
in all to him, are generally swallowed up by the
class next higher in the social scale, to which he
devotes his ducats and his daughter, or the college-
educated son, who, wiser in his generation than his
father, has higher aims and aspirations. The
younger son of a small retail merchant often aspires
to high position under the government.

This ambition brings us to the second of the
Parisian spheres. Ascend one story to the entresol, or descend from the garret and stop at the fourth
floor; in short, look in on the people who have something: you will arrive at the same results. Whole-
sale merchants and their bookkeepers and account-
ants, functionaries of government, bankers of small
means and great probity, rogues and rascals, spies,
pimps and suborners, clerks of high and low degree,
court officers, clerks in lawyers' and notaries'
offices—in a word, the members of that active, calculating and speculating small bourgeoisie which
watches the necessities of Paris with an eye to its
own profit, cornering the market for breadstuffs,
hoarding the manufactured product of the working-
people, packing the fruits of the South, the fish of
the sea, and the wine from every hillside warmed
by the sun; stretching out its hands to the East

and purchasing the shawls rejected by the Turks and Russians, extending its operations even to the Indies, and patiently awaiting the moment when it may turn its merchandise into cash and realize the longed-for profit; lending money on household goods, tucking away stocks and bonds in its trousers' pockets; laying all Paris under contribution, providing for its comfort and amusement; anticipating the fancies of the young, catering to the caprices and vices of those more advanced in years, doctoring the sick and burying the dead— all these, while they do not, like the working-man, bestialize themselves with brandy or wallow in the filth and slime of the *barrières*, do, like him, exhaust their strength, tax beyond endurance the powers of mind and body, acting reciprocally on each other, grow thin and wizened through inordinate desires, and by unnecessary hurry prepare for themselves an early grave. It is the whip of interests, and the spur of ambitions that, in this monstrous city, are constantly tormenting the more elevated classes, and to these are due that physical stress which, in the proletariat, is produced by the imperious *I will have it* of an aristocracy constantly and cruelly reiterating its demand for material progress. Here, too, in obedience to the universal tyranny of gold or pleasure, one must wear himself to the bone, kill himself, devour time, find a way of crowding more than twenty-four hours into a day and night, and purchase two years of sickly repose with thirty years of old age. Only, the laboring man dies in

the hospital when his days of penury are ended,
while the small bourgeois persists in living, and
lives—but in a state of semi-idiocy; you will meet
him dragging himself heavily along the boulevard,
the girdle of his Venus, of his loved city, with a
dull, worn, aged face, lustreless eyes and enfeebled
legs.   What was the bourgeois' ambition?   A com-
mission in the National Guard, a never-failing *pot-
au-feu,* a conspicuous plot in Père-Lachaise, and for
his old age a small fortune, honestly gained.   His
Monday is Sunday; his recreation is the outing in
a carriage from the livery-stable, the picnic in the
country when wife and children broil in the fierce
sunshine and joyously swallow clouds of dust; his
barrière is the restaurant famous for its indigestible
dinners, or the private family-ball where everyone
stifles and swelters until midnight.   Some dunces
are astonished at sight of the species of Saint Vitus
dance that affects the animalcules which the microscope shows us in a drop of water, but what would
Rabelais' Gargantua, a character incomprehensible
in its sublime audacity, what would the kindly old
giant, fallen from the celestial spheres, say on beholding the activities and employments of this
second stage of Parisian life, of which we have
been trying to give an imperfect sketch?   Have you
seen those little wooden booths, cold in summer
and in winter heated only by a small stove, placed
under the great copper dome which surmounts the
Corn Exchange?   Madame is there daily before the
sun has risen; she is a produce dealer, a *dame des*

Halles, and earns, it is said, twelve thousand francs
a year at her calling.   Monsieur, as soon as
madame has left the house, betakes himself to a
little dark office, where he lends out his money by
the week to the small tradesmen of his *quartier.*
At nine o'clock he is found at the passport office,
where he holds a position as assistant chief of
bureau.   Evening will find him in the box-office of
the Théâtre-Italien, or any other theatre you may
choose to mention.   The children are put out to
board with a nurse, whence they are brought home
when old enough to go to boarding-school or college.
Monsieur and madame occupy a third-floor apartment, have only a woman-servant to do their cooking, give little dances in a drawing-room twelve
feet by eight and lighted by oil lamps; but they
furnish a dowry of a hundred and fifty thousand
francs with their daughter and at fifty commence to
take life more easily, appearing in the third-tier
boxes at the opera, in a cab at Longchamp, or, on
sunny days, in antiquated faded costumes on the
boulevards, the espalier of the preceding fructifica-
tions.   Esteemed by their neighbors, favorably
regarded by the government, connected by marriage
with the higher bourgeoisie, monsieur at fifty-five
obtains the cross of the Legion of Honor, and the
father of his son-in-law, who is mayor of an arrondissement, invites him to his soirées.   It will be
seen, therefore, that those labors of a lifetime inure
to the benefit of the children, whose inevitable
tendency is to rise from the ranks of the lower to

21

those of the upper bourgeoisie. Each sphere thrusts
its spawn into the social sphere immediately above
it.   The son of the lumber dealer develops into a
full-fledged magistrate, the son of the well-to-do
grocer becomes a notary.   Not a cog fails to fill its
groove, and everything stimulates the upward course
of money.

We are now brought to the third sphere of our
hell, which will, perhaps, some day find its Dante.
In this third social sphere, which may be likened to
the belly of Paris, in which the interests of the
city are digested and compressed into that form
which we call *business*, the great multitude of doctors, lawyers, notaries, counselors, bankers, brokers,
attorneys, speculators, merchant-princes and magistrates stir and work with bitter and rancorous
intestinal disturbance.   There, more than anywhere
else, are to be found the causes of moral and physical deterioration.   These men nearly all pass their
days in close, unwholesome little offices, poisonous
court-rooms or small chambers, bending under the
pressure of their business ; they rise with the dawn
that they may not be caught napping, that no one
may steal a march on them, rob or cheat them, that
they may gain all and lose nothing, that they may
secure a man or his money, that they may make
or mar an enterprise, that they may take advantage
of passing circumstances to hang or acquit an
accused man.   They make even their poor horses
suffer, over-driving and often foundering them, so
that, like themselves, they grow old before their

time.   They are the slaves of Time; it fails them,
it vanishes, it cannot be extended or chained.
What soul can remain great, pure, moral and generous, and consequently what face can retain its
beauty, in the debasing exercise of a profession
that compels one day after day to bear the burden
of human sorrows, to analyze them, to weigh and
measure them, and file them away each in its
appropriate pigeon-hole?   Those men deposit their
hearts, where?—I do not know, but they must certainly, if they have them, leave them somewhere,
before they daily probe the innermost core of the
miseries which torment families.   For them there
are no mysteries; they see the dark side of the
society of which they are the confessors, and they
despise it.   In any event, of two things one is sure
to happen: either, through constant contact with
vice, they conceive a horror of it and become
gloomy pessimists; or, from sheer lassitude, and
by a secret compromise with conscience, they look
with too great indulgence on the wrong-doer; but
in either case all sentiment is deadened if not
destroyed in those whom the laws, men and society
require to chase their prey with the avidity of a
vulture settling on a still palpitating corpse.   Not
a moment passes but the man of wealth weighs the
living, the man of contracts weighs the dead, the
man of law weighs the conscience.   Constrained to
be continually talking, they make words serve for
ideas, phrases for sentiments, and their soul becomes a word-box.   They wear themselves out and

are demoralized. Neither the great merchant nor
the judge nor the lawyer retain their rectitude of
perception; they have ceased to feel, they apply
rules and maxims that wrong their species. Swept
away by the torrent of their existence they are
neither husbands, fathers nor lovers; they glide
over the affairs of life just like a sleigh over the
ground, unremittingly burdened with the affairs
of the great city. On returning to their homes
after their day's work they feel it incumbent on
them to attend the opera or show themselves at
some social entertainment, whither they resort to
make acquaintances, clients, and protectors. All
eat to excess, gamble, and keep late hours, and as
a consequence they become corpulent, red-faced and
dull, with expressionless features. They repair
their continued moral dwarfing, not by pleasure,
which is too insipid and does not afford sufficient
contrast, but by debauchery, a secret, horrible and
detestable debauchery, for society is at their disposal and they frame its code of morals. Their
specialty in science serves as a cloak to hide their
real stupidity. They have their profession at their
fingers' ends, but outside of it are ignorant of everything. To save their *amour-propre*, therefore, they
make a point of questioning everything, criticising
men and measures at random; posing as skeptics,
they are in reality without any definite opinions,
and are gullibly credulous, rising to the most transparent bait; they attest their intelligence by
interminable discussions. Almost to a man,

they conveniently adopt social, literary or political prejudices instead of forming individual judgments, just as they place their consciences under the ægis of the Code or the Tribunal of Commerce. Starting early in life with the intention of making their mark, they have developed into nobodies, crawling on the social summits. Hence the harsh pallor, the unnatural coloring of their faces, the dull, fishy eyes with their dark circles, the sensual, babbling mouth, which tell the observer of the debasement of thought and its revolution in a narrow and special circle which destroys both the creative force of the brain and the faculty of seeing things comprehensively, of generalizing, and drawing correct deductions. They become shriveled in the furnace of public affairs. There is no possibility of a man ever attaining greatness, who has once allowed himself to be involved in the whirl of this vast mechanism. If he is a doctor he has either had little practice or is an exception, a Bichat who dies young. If, being a great merchant, he continues to be a man of some account, he is almost a Jacques Cœur. How was it with Robespierre? Danton was an idler who waited on events. And who, moreover, ever envied the figures of Danton and Robespierre, superb as they may have been? Those men to whom business is the sole aim in life pre-eminently attract wealth to themselves and heap it up in order that they may ally themselves with aristocratic families. If the ambition of the working-man is the same as that of the small

bourgeois, here, too, the same passions rule. In Paris
vanity swallows up all the other passions. If you
would have a type of this class, whether the struggling, pushing bourgeois who, after a life of consuming anxiety and incessant planning, enters the
Council of State as an ant crawls through a crack
in the wall; or the editor of a newspaper thoroughly
seasoned in intrigue, whom the king constitutes a
peer of the realm, perhaps to spite the nobility; or
a notary who has been elected mayor of his arrondissement; all are men who have been flattened
out by the routine of business, and if they succeed in reaching the goal of their ambition, find
themselves dead to the enjoyment of it. In France
wig-worship is customary. Only men like Napoleon
and Louis XIV. had the sagacity to select young
men to be their lieutenants and second them in
their designs.

Above this last sphere dwells the artistic world.
Here again the faces bearing the stamp of originality are marred—not ignobly, it is true, but they
are not faultless and show the marks of fatigue and
dissipation. Exhausted by the demand of constant
production, kept poor by their expensive fancies,
their strength sapped by a consuming genius,
always athirst for pleasure, the artists of Paris all
try to make up by strained effort the time they
have lost in their fits of idleness, and vainly en-
deavor to conciliate glory and fashion, art and
money. In the beginning the artist is incessantly
harassed by creditors, his necessities engender

debts, and his debts demand from him his nights. After work, pleasure. The actor is on the stage until midnight, studies his part in the morning, and rehearses at noon; the sculptor stoops from his labor on his statue; the thoughts of the journalist are as inseparable from him as the knapsack from the soldier on a campaign; the painter with a name is overwhelmed with work, the painter without orders devours his heart if he feels that he has genius. Competition, rivalries, calumnies are the destroyers of talent. Some, in despair, wallow in the depths of vice, others die young and unknown, having too early discounted their future. Few of those faces, originally sublime, retain their beauty. Moreover, the flowing beauty of their features is not appreciated by the multitude. An artist's face is always abnormal, always either above or below the conventional standard called by idiots the beau ideal. What is the power that wrecks them? Passion! All passion at Paris is resolvable into two terms: Gold and pleasure.

Do you not breathe now freely? Don't you find the air and place purer and fresher? Here, neither work nor trouble. The upward course of gold has reached its summits. From the depths of the gutter where the rivulets started, from the inside of shops where it is held in coffers, from the counting-houses and great refineries where it is converted into bars, and sometimes in the shape of rich dowries brought by maidens fair, again as great fortunes bequeathed by those who have toilsomely

amassed them, the gold now rests with the aristocratic class where it sparkles, spreads itself and
trickles.   But, having explained the foundations
upon which the wealth and prosperity of patrician
Paris may be said to rest, and having recited the
moral causes of their deterioration, before leaving
the subject it is proper we should speak of the
physical causes that are constantly operating on
the lower classes, and point out a latent, subjacent
plague-spot; to describe a baneful influence whose
corruption is only equaled by that of the municipal
government that remains wilfully blind to its existence.

The air of the houses in which the bourgeois for
the most part live is contaminated, the atmosphere
of the street vomits its death-dealing miasma into
the tightly-closed back-shops, but that is not the
worst: in addition to that pestilential condition, the
foundations of the forty thousand houses of the
great city are bathed by liquid filth, which the
authorities have not seriously desired to confine
within walls of concrete that would prevent the
fetid mire from percolating through the soil, poisoning the wells and perpetuating underground, Lute-
tia's celebrated name.   One-half of Paris nightly
retires to rest breathing putrid exhalations from
streets, yards and places of necessity.   But let us
give a look at the airy and decorated salons, at the
mansions standing in their own gardens, at the
classes which have wealth and leisure.   The faces
you will see there are wasted and consumed by

vanity.   All is for show and display, nothing is
real.   To seek for pleasure is to find ennui.   The
leaders in the race of fashion early set a pace that
they could not keep up; they have broken down.
Their sole occupation being to minister to their
pleasures, they quickly misused their senses, as the
workingman misuses liquor.   Pleasure is like certain drugs : to obtain continuously the same effect
the doses must be doubled, and that means death or
impairment of the physical and moral nature.   All
the inferior classes crouch before the rich and
observe their inclinations in order to convert them
into vices and profit by them.   Who can avoid
the pleasantly seductive and artful snares that are
set for the unwary in this country?   You will find
Paris full of slaves to habit, whose opium is gaming, belly-worship or illicit love.   Hence, you will
soon see that those gentry know no passion, they
have but feeble likings, romantic fancies, lukewarm
loves.   It is the realm of feebleness; no more ideas
there; like masculine energy they have been absorbed in womanish affectation and the grimaces of
the boudoir.   There are greenhorns of forty, grave
old doctors of sixteen.   The rich find at Paris wit
ready-made, learning duly catalogued and indexed
for immediate application, opinions carefully form-
ulated up to date—which relieves them of the
necessity of having wit, learning or opinions of
their own.   The lack of common sense in the class
we are speaking of is as remarkable as its feebleness and licentiousness.   People become avaricious

of their time in proportion as they waste it. And do not look for affections there, any more than for ideas. A man will embrace you and be perfectly indifferent at heart; if he is polite it is a sign that he despises you. It is the fashion there never to love others. Shallow witticisms, a great deal of scandal, gossip and old wives' tales, and above all, futile commonplaces,—these form the staple of their conversation; but these *fortunate* unfortunates assert that they only meet to express and fashion maxims à la Rochefoucauld—as if the eighteenth century had not discovered a golden mean between plethora and absolute vacuity. Should a superior man gain entrance to the exclusive circle and attempt to enliven the conversation with a delicate and subtle wit he finds he is not understood, and after a little, weary of giving and not receiving, he remains at home and abandons the field to the fools and blockheads. This hollow life, this continual waiting for a pleasure that never comes, this eternal ennui, this emptiness of spirit, heart and brain, this weariness of the great Parisian round of fêtes, are reproduced on men's features, and cause those paste-board like faces, those premature wrinkles, that rich man's physiognomy, in which feebleness grins, gold is reflected and whence intelligence has fled.

This glimpse at Paris in its moral aspect proves that physical Paris cannot be other than it is. The crowned city is a queen who, always pregnant, suffers irresistibly-intense longings. Paris is the brain of the world, a brain teeming with genius and directing the movements of human civilization, a great man, an ever-creative artist, a far-sighted statesman, and must necessarily have the crotchets and vices of the great man, the fancies of the artist, the skepticism and cynicism of the politician. Her physiognomy implies the germination of good and evil, the battle and the victory—the moral conflict of '89, whose trumpets are still resounding in every quarter of the world, and also the ruin and defeat of 1814. As for expecting to find morality, sincere affection, or cleanliness in a city like this, you might as well look for them in the boilers of the great steamers that you admire as they cleave the waves. May we not call Paris a proud ship, deep-laden with a cargo of intelligence? Yes; the city arms is one of those oracles that fatality sometimes condescends to utter. LA VILLE DE PARIS has her tall mainmast, all of bronze and carved with glorious victories; Napoléon is at the helm. True, the staunch craft has her spells of rolling and pitching, but she ploughs the waters of the world, firing broadsides from the hundred mouths of her tribunes, rides the intellectual seas in full sail, hailing from her tops with words of cheer by the voice of her artists and savants: "Forward, onward! follow me!" She carries a numerous crew, whose delight it is to keep her decked with fresh-won pennants. There are 'prentices and cabin-boys frolicking in the rigging; her ballast is the heavy bourgeoisie; you recognize the workmen and sailors by their tarry apparel; the happy passengers are in the cabins; trim midshipmen lean indolently against the netting and smoke their cigarettes; while together on the forecastle the young and ardent soldiers peer forth expectantly, to discern the new shores they are approaching and to which they are bringing the torch of civilization, clamoring for glory, which is pleasure, and for love that demands gold.

Thus we see how the normal ugliness of the Parisian physiognomy is explained by the excessive activity of the proletariat, the depravity of the interests which crush the two classes of the bourgeoisie, the hardships of the artists' life, and the excesses of the pleasures incessantly demanded by the great. It is in the East alone that the human race can boast of real perfection of form and face; it is a result of the imperturbable calmness of those profound philosophers, with their long pipes, small legs and deep chests, who hold in holy horror and despise activity, in all its shapes; while at Paris all hands, great and small, are eternally running, jumping and capering under the lash of a pitiless goddess, Necessity: necessity of money, of glory, of amusement. Hence to see there a fresh, calm, pleasing, really young face is the most striking of exceptions; it is a spectacle that is rarely met with. Should you by chance see one, you may rest assured that it belongs to either a young and enthusiastic priest, or a good, honest, double-chinned abbé of forty; a pure-minded young girl, such as you will still find here and there in bourgeois families; a mother of twenty who has not yet parted with all her illusions and is nursing her first-born; a young man fresh from the provinces, entrusted to the mercies of a pious old dowager who leaves him without a sou; or some clerk in a store who goes to bed at midnight very tired after rolling and unrolling calico all day and rising at seven o'clock to sweep out the shop; or a poet, perhaps, or man of science with a noble thought who lives at his ease like a hermit, and is patient, chaste and temperate; or a fool, revelling in health, feasting on his meagre intelligence and well pleased with himself and his belongings; or the lazy and effeminate guild of idle loiterers, the only truly happy people in Paris, who find anew every hour, passing poems in the old city. Nevertheless there is at Paris a class of privileged beings who profit by this immense activity in the manufactures, arts, money and other interests. These beings are the women. Although they too have a thousand secret cares which tend, there more even than elsewhere, to destroy their beauty, there are to be found in the feminine world certain happy little tribes who live in the oriental manner and manage to preserve their good looks; but it is seldom that these women show themselves on foot in the streets; they live secluded, like rare plants that unfold their petals only at certain hours, and who constitute a truly exotic exception. Paris, however, is essentially the land of contrasts. If genuine sentiment is rare, instances of noble friendship and unbounded devotion are met with, there as elsewhere. Affections, sublime in their juxtaposition, once aroused reach their full development with more rapidity on that battle-field of the interests and passions, just as they do in those ambulatory associations that we call armies, where egotism triumphs and in which each man looks to his own right arm as his defender. And much the same conditions prevail in regard to faces. At Paris, sometimes, in the higher aristocracy, may be seen, few and far between, charming faces of young men, the result of exceptional training and education. To the fresh young beauty of the English race they add purity of contour, the Southerner's firmness of feature, the Frenchman's intelligence. The fire in their eyes, their delicious blood-red lips, the lustrous sheen of their soft black hair, their fair complexion, their clear-cut, distinguished features impart to them a beauty as of magnificent animated flowers, a delightful spectacle to look on after the great mass of other visages, old, wrinkled, dull as they are. The women admire these young men with the same keen delight that men experience in contemplating a pretty, modest and gracious maiden, adorned with all those virginal attributes with which our imagination loves to embellish the ideal woman. The main object of our story will have been attained if, in this cursory glance at the constituent elements of Parisian society, we have succeeded in making it clear to the reader how great a rarity is a Raphaelesque face and how profound the admiration it

excites when seen. *Quod erat demonstrandum,*
which was the question we desired to prove, if it be
permissible to apply a formula of logic to a study
of manners.

On one of those beautiful spring mornings when
the trees, whose leaves, though unfolded, are not
yet green, when roofs flash back the sunlight and
the sky is blue; when the good people of Paris
crawl forth from their hibernal retreats and, like a
huge, sinuous, many-colored serpent, lazily wind
their way along the Rue de la Paix in the direction
of the Tuileries, celebrating the renewal of the nup-
tials of Earth and Nature—on one of those jocund
mornings, we say, a young man, handsome as the
light of that bright day, neatly and tastefully
attired, of easy and elegant manners—we will let
the cat out of the bag and admit he was a child of
love, the natural son of Lord Dudley and the celebrated Marquise de Vordac—was walking in the
main alley of the Tuileries' gardens.   This Adonis,
Henri de Marsay by name, was born in France,
whither Lord Dudley had come to bestow the young
person, already Henri's mother, in marriage upon
an elderly gentleman known as Monsieur de Marsay.
This faded and almost dead old butterfly, consented
to assume the relations of paternity to the child in
consideration of an annuity of one hundred thousand
francs, which was to revert ultimately to his putative son—an extravagance that was not likely to
beggar Lord Dudley, French rentes being at that
time quoted at seventeen francs and fifty centimes.

The old gentleman died without having known his wife. Madame de Marsay afterward married the Marquis de Vordac; but in the interim before she became a marquise she did not concern herself much about her child and Lord Dudley. In the first place, the war between France and England had separated the two lovers, and fidelity in spite of obstacles was not, and never will be, the mode at Paris. Then the social successes of the pretty, attractive and universally-adored young woman smothered the Parisienne's maternal sentiment. Lord Dudley manifested as little solicitude for his progeny as did the mother. Perhaps the readiness with which a young girl whom he had fondly loved displayed her infidelity produced in him a sort of aversion for everything connected with her. Perhaps, too, fathers only love those children with whom they have had ample opportunity to make acquaintance; a social belief of the utmost importance to the peace and tranquility of families and that should be entertained by every bachelor, as demonstrating that paternity is a sentiment raised under glass and that the forcing process is conducted by woman, morality, and the laws.

Poor Henri de Marsay found a father only in that one of the twain who was under no obligation to assume that relationship. Naturally, Monsieur de Marsay's paternity was of an incomplete order. In the natural order of things it is only for a few moments that children have a father, and the gentleman imitated nature. The old fellow would not have sold his name if he had not had vices.   Without remorse, he ate, drank and was merry, distributing the semi-annual payments that the treasury of the nation makes to its creditors, among the gambling hells and other dubious resorts of the great capital.   Then he turned the child over to an aged sister, a Demoiselle de Marsay, who was devoted in her care of him and from the scanty allowance made her by her brother gave him a preceptor, a penniless abbé, who measured the young man's expectations and resolved to take his pay for the attentions given to his pupil, for whom he conceived an affection, from the latter's fortune.   This preceptor chanced to be a genuine priest, one of those ecclesiastics cut out to be cardinals in France or Borgias under the tiara.   In three years he taught the boy all he would have learned in ten at college.   This great man—who was called the Abbé de Maronis—completed his charge's education by introducing him to the study of civilization in all its forms: he fortified him with his own experience.   The churches, which at that time were nominally closed, he troubled very little, but he sometimes conducted the lad behind the scenes at the theatre, and still more frequently among the courtesans.   He dissected human nature as he would have taken apart the works of a watch, taught him politics in the salons where it was then a burning topic, disclosed to him the mysteries of the mechanism of government, and did his best, from a friendly feeling for a nature uncultivated but rich in promise, to be a

22

masculine substitute for a mother : is not the Church the mother of orphans? The pupil showed himself not unworthy of such attentions. The worthy man died a bishop in 1812, with the proud satisfaction that he left behind him a child whose mind and heart were so well trained at sixteen years of age that he need not fear contending on equal terms with a man of forty. Who would have looked to find a heart of brass, a subtle brain beneath an exterior as pleasing and seductive as ever the old painters, those artless artists, gave to the serpent in the terrestrial paradise? But that was not all; the worldly-wise ecclesiastic had placed the pupil of his predilection in touch with certain individuals high in place at Paris who, if properly used by the young man, might well produce him an additional hundred thousand francs of income. In a word, this versatile priest, depraved but far-sighted, skeptical but learned, perfidious but charming, feeble in appearance but equally vigorous in mind and body, was so really useful to his charge, so complaisant to his foibles, so good a calculator of strength of every kind, so deep in his diplomacy, so young at table, at Frascati, at—I do not know where, that in 1814 the grateful Henri de Marsay never knew a momentary impulse of tenderness save when he looked on the portrait of his loved bishop, the only memento bequeathed him by the prelate, an admirable type of the men whose genius will save the Catholic, Apostolic and Roman Church, at the present time endangered by the

weaknesses of her recruits and the senility of her
pontiffs; but such is the will of the Church! The
continental war prevented young de Marsay from
making the acquaintance of his real father, whose
name it may be doubted if he knew. Neither did
the disowned child have the advantage of Madame
de Marsay's acquaintance. Naturally his grief for
his putative father was slight. As for Mademoiselle
de Marsay, the only mother he ever knew, when
she died he erected to her memory a very handsome
little monument in the cemetery of Père-Lachaise.
Monseigneur de Maronis had assured the old maid
that she should have one of the choicest seats in
Heaven, so that Henri, seeing how gladly she welcomed death, shed for her a few selfish tears; he
wept for her on his own account. The Abbé,
observing this display of grief, dried his pupil's
tears by reminding him of the good spinster's disgusting habit of snuff-taking, and added that he
should be grateful to Death for removing her; so
repulsive, deaf and tiresome had she become. The
Bishop had relaxed his control over his charge in
1811. Then, when Monsieur de Marsay's mother
married again, the priest convoked a family council, selected an honest blockhead known to him
through the medium of the confessional, and entrusted to him the management of the young man's
fortune, of which, while applying the income to
their common needs, he wished the principal to
remain intact.

Toward the end of the year 1814, therefore,

Henri de Marsay had absolutely no earthly ties and
was as free as a bird without a mate.   Although he
was past twenty-two years old, he scarcely looked
seventeen.   He was generally considered, even by
the most hypercritical of his rivals, as the hand-
somest young man in Paris.   From his father, Lord
Dudley, he had inherited the most amorously alluring blue eyes; from his mother, his profusely
clustered black hair; from them both, a pure and
generous blood, the complexion of a young girl, a
gentle and unassuming air, a slender, aristocratic
figure, and surpassingly beautiful hands.   To see
him was, for a woman, to go wild over him; you
understand? to conceive one of those desires that
bite and sting the heart, but which are forgotten in
the impossibility of satisfying them, for women in
Paris are customarily not persistent.   There are
few of them who are capable, like men, of adopting
the motto: JE MAINTIENDRAI, of the house of Orange.
With this young, fresh life, and in spite of his
limpidly-liquid eyes, Henri had the courage of a
lion and the agility of a monkey.   He could split a
bullet at ten paces on the blade of a penknife, rode
a horse in a manner to realize the fable of the cen-
taur, drove four-in-hand with the perfection of easy
grace; he was as light as a cherub and gentle as a
lamb, but could beat an habitué of the Faubourg at
the terrible games of *savate* or single-stick; then he
fingered the keys of the piano in such a way that
he might have set up as a professor had he come to
want, and owned a voice for which Barbaja would

have gladly paid him fifty thousand francs a season.
But alas! all these fine qualities and engaging defects were overshadowed by a horrible obliquity:
he believed neither in man nor woman, in God nor
devil. Capricious nature commenced his endow-
ment, a priest finished it.

It is necessary here to add, in order to explain
the future developments of this history, that Lord
Dudley naturally found many women quite willing
to assist him in producing additional copies of so
charming a portrait. His second masterpiece in
this line was a young girl named Euphémie, the
offspring of a Spanish lady, who, having received
her early training in Havana, returned to Madrid
with a young creole of the Antilles and all the luxurious and expensive tastes of the colonies; fortunately, however, she was married to an old and
extremely-rich Spanish nobleman, Don Hijos,
Marquis of San-Réal, who, upon the occupation of
Spain by the French troops, had come to live at
Paris, where he inhabited a house in the Rue Saint-
Lazare. As much from his indifference to the subject as from any respect he had for the innocence of
youth, Lord Dudley did not acquaint his children
with the relationships that he created for them in
every quarter of the globe. This is one of the trifling drawbacks of civilization, but its advantages
are so numerous that we can forgive an occasional
fault in consideration of its many benefits. To have
done with Lord Dudley we will say that in 1816
he came to Paris, seeking a refuge there from the

persecutions of English justice, which in the East, it seems, casts the mantle of its protection only over merchandise. The noble traveler, seeing Henri one day, asked who he was, and on hearing his name:

"Ah! he is my son—what a pity!" he said.

Such is the history of the young man who, about mid-April, 1815, was nonchalantly strolling in the great alley of the Tuileries, after the manner of all animals who, conscious of their strength, walk the earth in their peaceful pride and majesty: the shop-keepers' wives turned their heads with frank admiration, for another look at him; the other women did not turn; they waited for him to retrace his steps, and then fixed in their memories, that they might evoke it at the proper season, that deli cious face, which could not have marred the appearance of the most beautiful among them.

"What are you doing here on a Sunday?" said the Marquis de Ronquerolles to Henri, as he passed.

"There are fish in the net," replied the young man.

This exchange of thought was effected by means of two significant glances, neither of the two men giving the least sign of being acquainted with the other. De Marsay continued to scan the promenaders with that rapidity and certainty of vision and hearing that are characteristic of the Parisian, who at first sight appears to see and hear nothing, but who in reality sees and hears everything. At this moment a young man came up to him and, taking him familiarly by the arm, said:

"De Marsay, my dear fellow, how goes it?"

"Very well, thanks," replied de Marsay with an air which, seemingly full of interest and affection, among the young men of Paris proves nothing, neither for the present nor the future.

The truth is, the young men of Paris are like the young men of no other city in the world. They may be divided into two categories: the young man who has something and the young man who has nothing, or the young man who thinks—*pense*—and he who spends—*dépense*. But, understand, we are speaking now only of those who, to the manner born, lead at Paris the agreeable life of a gentleman of elegant leisure. There are other young men indeed, but these are youths who have been long in mastering the ins-and-outs of Parisian existence, and remain its dupes. They do not speculate, they study, they "dig," as the others say. Finally, there are to be found there certain young men, rich or poor, who embrace a career and pursue it only; they resemble a little, Rousseau's Émile, material to make citizens of, and never show themselves in society. Diplomats, very impolitely, call them nobodies. Nobodies or not, they serve to increase the number of those mediocrities under whose weight France stoops. They are always on hand, always ready to temper public and private interests with their trowel of mediocrity, ever pluming themselves on their efficiency, which they call morality and probity. These specimens of animated social *rewards of merit* infest the administration, the army, the magistracy, the Chambers, the court. They diminish and detract from the glory and grandeur of the country, and form as it were a sort of lymph in the body politic, destroying its energy and making it limp and flaccid. According to these paragons of virtue, every man of talent is a rascal and a profligate. If the rascals are paid for their services, at all events they serve, while the others only muddle things and are respected by the multitude; but, fortunately for France, the gilded youth constantly brands them with the uncomplimentary epithet: dolts!

At the first glance, therefore, it is natural to suppose that the two species of young men who lead a life of leisure—to which agreeable corporation Henri de Marsay belonged—are entirely distinct and separate. To the observer, however, who looks beneath the surface, it soon becomes manifest that such differences as there are are purely moral, and that nothing is more deceptive than that pretty outer shell. Still, they all equally assert their superiority over the rest of mankind, talk at random of men, measures, literature and art, have at their tongue's end the political shibboleth of the year; they will interrupt a conversation by a bad pun and ridicule science and scientists; they affect a fine scorn for whatever is unknown to them or for anything they fear; they place themselves above everything by constituting themselves supreme judge and arbiter of everything. They would not hesitate to make their father the victim of a

practical joke, and on occasion are prepared to weep
crocodile tears on their mother's bosom; but as
a general rule they are skeptical of everything,
scout the idea of female virtue, or, affecting modesty, are in reality the obedient slaves of a design-
ing courtesan or some woman old enough to be their
grandmother. All alike are rotten to the core,
through calculation, through depravity, through
brutal selfishness and fierce desire of material success; if they were threatened with the stone and
the doctor should sound them, he would find it, in
every one of them—in the heart. In their normal
state they have the prettiest manners and behavior
imaginable, parade their politeness at every opportunity, abound with hospitalities and offers of service. One unvarying style of persiflage is the
keynote of their changing jargon; they aim at out-
landish effects in their attire, delight in repeating
the silly gags of the actor who is the favorite of
the hour, and when presented to a stranger, with
cool assurance stare him out of countenance or
silence and disgust him with their impertinence; but
woe to him who does not know how to lose one eye
for the sake of depriving them of two. The misfortunes and calamities of their country leave them
entirely unconcerned. They remind one, in a word,
of the pretty foam-wreath that crests the wave
when the storm rages. They dress, dine, dance
and enjoy themselves on the day of Waterloo, while
the cholera is raging, or during a revolution. Finally, they all live under the same expense; but

here begins the parallel. Some have the money in hand to pursue this pleasant but expensive way of living, while others have it only in expectation; both classes patronize the same tailors, but in the case of the last-named class, bills are unpaid. Again, if some, like sieves, receive all sorts of ideas and retain none, there are others who sift and compare, accepting the good and rejecting the bad. If there are some who, thinking they know everything, know nothing and are cock-sure on every question, if they lend to those who are comfortably circumstanced and refuse the needy, there are others who make a secret study of their neighbors' foibles and so shape their course that their money as well as their indiscretions shall yield them good returns. Some retain no lasting impression of events, because their mind, like a mirror dimmed by long use, has ceased to reflect images; others husband their faculties and life while appearing, like the former, to throw them out of the window. One class of men, guided by the star of a fallacious hope, devote themselves without conviction to a cause which to them seems sailing merrily upstream, impelled by the breeze of popular favor, but they make haste to jump aboard another political craft when they see their own beginning to lose headway; the other class weighs the future and, having drawn its deductions, adheres to them consistently, beholding in political fidelity what the English see in commercial probity, an element of success. But while the young man who has

something will celebrate a change of government
by letting off a pun or exploding a *bon mot,* you
will see the young man who has nothing plotting
and contriving until, by fair means or foul, he
comes to the top while giving his friends a hand.
The former never give other men credit for
ability; they look on all their ideas as brand new,
as if the world were made the day before yesterday,
have unlimited confidence in their powers, and are
in reality their own worst enemy. But the latter
judge men in accordance with their merit, and are
far more likely to err on the side of distrust than of
credulity; they have thoughts that they are deep
enough not to communicate to the friends whom
they are exploiting, and when at night they lay
their head upon their pillow they weigh men as the
miser weighs his gold-pieces. These fire up at a
fancied insult from an equal or inferior and receive
with equanimity the kicks and cuffs of the shrewder
intellects which use them and pull the principal
string that moves these puppets, their vanity;
those know how to make themselves respected and
select their victims and their protectors. Thus it
comes about that some day those who had nothing
have something, and those who had something
have nothing. The latter look on their comrades
who have prospered as sly fellows, false friends,
but also as able men. "He is very able!" is the
supreme eulogium passed on those who have,
quibuscumque viis, succeeded in politics, gallantry
or money-making. Among those who play this rôle

are certain young men who started on their
career with debts, and it is hardly necessary to say
that these are far more dangerous than those who
began life without a sou.

The youth who styled himself Henri de Marsay's
friend was a rattle-pated young spendthrift, lately
come up to town from his province, whom his Parisian associates were, according to fashion, instruct-
ing how to squander a patrimony with neatness
and despatch; he had one cake still to devour, however, in the shape of an old manor in the country.
He was neither more nor less than an heir who,
from his scanty allowance of a hundred francs a
month, had leaped at a bound into the entire paternal fortune, and who, if he had not sufficient sense
to see that he was being gulled, was shrewd enough
to call a halt when he found that he had made ducks
and drakes of two-thirds of his property. At the
cost of sundry thousand-franc notes he had laid in
at Paris a stock of varied and useful information:
among other things he knew what was the correct
thing in harness and horse-trappings, and was
aware that it is bad form to wear soiled gloves,
was up in the intricacies of the servant question,
how to hire his people, what to pay them, and on
what pretexts they may be discharged; in speaking
of his horses and Pyrenean dog it was a matter of
pride with him to use exactly the right terms and
no other; one glance at a woman's apparel, her
boot, her gait and bearing, sufficed to tell him to
what class she belonged; he had made an exhaustive

study of écarté and stored his memory with several
words of the slang current in fashionable circles;
he had acquired a discriminating taste in tea and
English silverware, which would make him an
authority in introducing those articles among his
neighbors on his return to the country and give him
the right to treat everything about him with contempt, for the remainder of his days.   De Marsay
had taken him up, thinking he might use him in
society, as a daring speculator makes use of a confidential clerk.   De Marsay's friendship, genuine
or feigned, gave social standing to Paul de Manerville, who, on his side, took to himself great credit
for his astuteness in exploiting in his own way, his
intimate friend.   He lived in Henri's reflected light,
walked under his umbrella, trod in his shoe-leather,
gilded himself with his rays.   His air, when standing or walking beside de Marsay, seemed to say:
"Be careful how you tread on our toes; we are
regular tigers."   He often fatuously said: "If I
were to ask Henri for a thing I should be sure to
get it, for he is my friend."   But he took good
care never to ask for anything.   He feared his
friend, and his fear, though not manifested visibly,
reacted on the others and was serviceable to de
Marsay.

"A great man, de Marsay is," said Paul.   "Just
let him alone—whatever he wants he'll get, you
see if he doesn't.   I shouldn't be surprised to see
him minister of foreign affairs some day.   Nothing
daunts him."

And then he would invoke de Marsay's name, as Corporal Trim was wont to call on his nightcap:

"Ask de Marsay—you'll see!" or:

"We were hunting the other day, de Marsay and I, and I jumped a hedge without falling off my horse—ask de Marsay!" or:

"De Marsay and I were in company with some women, and I give you my word of honor, I was—" etc.

So we see that Paul de Manerville must be set down as belonging to the great, puissant and illustrious family of nobodies. He was to be a deputy some day. In the meantime he was not even a young man.

His friend de Marsay defined him in these terms: "You ask me what Paul is. Paul?—why, he's Paul de Manerville."

"I am surprised, old man," he said to de Marsay, "to see you here of a Sunday."

"I was about to make the same remark to you."

"An intrigue?"

"An intrigue."

"Bah!"

"I can tell you that much without fear of compromising my passion. And then, you see, a woman who visits the Tuileries on Sunday is of no account, socially speaking."

"Ah, ah!"

"Be silent, or I won't speak another word. You laugh too loud, people will think we have been breakfasting too well. Last Thursday I was strolling on the Terrasse des Feuillants, right where we are now, thinking of nothing in particular. On reaching the exit at the Rue de Castiglione, however, by which I was intending to leave the garden, I came face to face with a woman, or rather a young person, who seemed restrained less by decorum from embracing me then and there, than by one of those electric shocks of surprise which paralyse arms and legs and running down the spinal column to the soles of your feet root you to the ground. I have often produced effects of that kind; it is a species of animal magnetism that becomes very powerful when the reciprocal affinities are strongly developed. But, my dear boy, it was not a case of stupefaction, nor was she a commonplace girl. Her expression seemed to say: 'What, is it thou, my ideal, the being of my reveries, of my sleeping and waking dreams! How happens it thou art here? why this morning? why not yesterday? Take me, I am thine,' et cætera. 'Good,' I say to myself, 'another!' Then I proceed to scrutinize her. My dear fellow, I assure you, from a physical standpoint, I never set eyes on a woman more adorably feminine. She is of that species which the Romans classified as *fulva, flava,* the woman of fire. And first of all, what struck me most at the time and still sticks in my memory was a pair of eyes yellow as the tigers'—yellow as the real, glittering gold that chinks and jingles in your fob!"

"That is an old story you're giving us, my boy," cried Paul. "She comes here occasionally; she is *the Girl with the Golden Eyes.* We gave her that name. She is a young person about twenty-two years of age; I remember seeing her here when the Bourbons were on the throne; but at that time she was accompanied by a woman who was worth a thousand of her."

"Hold your tongue, Paul! There is not a woman upon earth who can begin to compare with that girl; she is coaxing and winsome as a kitten that comes and rubs against your legs—a clear-faced, black-haired girl, delicate in appearance, but who should have tufts like downy threads on the third joints of her fingers and on her cheeks, commencing at the ears and running down into the neck, a white down, luminous in the sunshine."

"Ah! but you should have seen the other, de Marsay. She has black eyes that know not what it is to weep, but that burn into your soul; black eyebrows that meet and would give her an expression of severity were it not for the arch and voluptuous mouth upon whose lips ruddy and glowing, no kiss could stay; a Moorish complexion in which a man may bask as in the sunlight; but, now I think of it, she resembles you—"

"You flatter her."

"—A stately, slender figure with graceful sweeping contour, like that of a corvette built for privateering, which swoops down on the unsuspecting merchantman with French impetuosity, rams her amidships with her prow, and sends her to the bottom in a trice."

"But what is to me the woman whom I never saw?" rejoined de Marsay. "Since I first began to make a study of woman, my unknown beauty is the only one whose virgin bosom and voluptuous contours have realized the ideal of my dreams. She is the original of the delirious picture called *The Woman Caressing her Chimera*, the most fervid and most infernal inspiration of ancient art; a sacred poem prostituted by those who have copied it in their frescoes and mosaics, or in miniature as a trinket, which this cameo appears to be to the herd of vulgar bourgeois who wear it pendent from their watch-chain; though it portrays the sum, the all of woman, a fathomless abyss of pleasures, though it represents the ideal woman as she is sometimes seen in Spain, in Italy, but rarely ever in France. Well, I again encountered this Girl with the Golden Eyes, this Woman Caressing her Chimera; I saw her again, here, on Friday last. I had a presentiment that she would not let a day go by without revisiting the spot; I was not mistaken. It was a pleasure to me to follow her, unseen by her, and watch the movements, so leisurely and graceful, of the idle woman, but which revealed the depths of passion that only slumbered. She turned about, she saw me; again she disclosed her adoration, again she started and trembled. Then I first noticed the veritable Spanish *duenna* who guarded the treasure, a female hyena in woman's attire, a she-devil paid by a jealous husband or lover to watch over this delicious creature. The sight of

23

the duenna did not cool my ardor, but it aroused my
curiosity.   Saturday, I was there again—no result!
And here I am to-day, awaiting the girl whose
chimera I am, and shall like nothing better than to
play the part of the monster in the painting."

"There she is now," said Paul.   "Everyone is
turning for a look at her."

The stranger blushed; her eyes flashed as she
caught sight of Henri; she closed them and passed
on.

"Did you say she noticed you?" Paul de Manerville sarcastically asked.

The duenna scrutinized the two young men nar-
rowly.   When next the stranger and Henri met in
the course of their promenade, the young girl
pressed closely up against him and, taking his
hand in hers, she pressed it tenderly.   Then she
turned and smiled at him provokingly, but the old
woman hurried her away in the direction of the
Rue de Castiglione.   The two friends followed the
young woman, admiring the magnificent carriage
of her neck, with which her head was connected
by a combination of vigorous lines, and on which
stubborn little curls stood out.   The Girl with the
Golden Eyes had that firmly shaped, small, high-
arched foot that is so appetizing to luxurious imaginations.—She was, moreover, accounted daintily
shod and wore a short dress.   On her way to the
gate she turned again and again for a look at Henri,
and was manifestly reluctant to follow the duenna,
of whom she appeared to be at one and the same

time both mistress and slave: she could have her flogged, but could not discharge her. That was self-evident. The two friends came to the gate. Two footmen let down the steps of an elegant but quiet-looking coupé, whose panels bore a coat-of-arms. The Girl with the Golden Eyes got in first, seated herself on the side where she would be visible when the carriage turned, and resting her hand on the window-ledge, and unseen by the duenna, and careless of the comments of the bystanders, waved her handkerchief, thus expressing to Henri as plainly as if she had spoken: "Follow me!"

"Did you ever see the handkerchief more prettily thrown?" said Henri to Paul de Manerville.

Then, perceiving a cab that had just landed a fare and was preparing to go away again, he hailed the driver.

"Follow that coupé, see where it goes, what house it stops at; it will be worth ten francs to you.—Adieu, Paul."

The cab followed the coupé. The coupé entered the Rue Saint-Lazare and discharged its inmates into one of the finest mansions of the quarter.

De Marsay never acted rashly. Another young man would, obeying his impulse, have set to work at once to collect all the information he could, in regard to a woman who seemed the embodiment of all the fervid poetry of the Orient, but he, too adroit to endanger his future prospects in that way, told his driver to continue along the Rue Saint-Lazare and set him down at his residence. The

next morning, about the time when the letters are
distributed, his first valet de chambre, a lad named
Laurent, as artful and sly a fellow as the Frontin of
the old comedy, was loitering in the vicinity of the
house of which the fair stranger was an inmate.
That he might be less liable to suspicion while prac-
tising his vocation as a spy he had purchased from
a second-hand dealer a disguise, the cast-off suit of
an Auvergnat, whose stupidity of face and manner
he imitated as well as he could.   When the letter-
carrier whose route that morning embraced the Rue
Saint-Lazare came along, Laurent, feigning to be a
messenger, and unable to recall the name of the
person to whom he was to deliver a package, applied
to him for advice and assistance.   The functionary,
generally wide-awake enough, was deceived at first
by appearances, and Laurent elicited from him the
information that the house in which the Girl with
the Golden Eyes resided was owned by Don Hijos,
Marquis de San-Réal, a Spanish grandee.   Of course
the Auvergnat had no business with the marquis.

"My package is for the marquise," said he.

"She is not at home," the postman replied.
"Her letters are forwarded to her at London."

"Is not the marquise a young lady, who—"

"Ah!" said the letter-carrier, interrupting and
eyeing him sharply, "you are a porter—as much as
I am a dancing-master."

Laurent displayed some gold-pieces which brought
a smile to the face of the man in the cocked hat.

"There you have the full style and title of the

game you are pursuing," said he, extracting from his leather box a letter which bore the London postmark and whose address: *Mademoiselle Paquita Valdès, Hôtel San-Réal, Rue Saint-Laʒare, Paris,* betrayed a feminine calligraphy in its minute and elongated characters.

"What do you say to a bottle of Chablis, accompanied by a nice *filet sauté* with mushrooms and preceded by a dozen or two of oysters?" said Laurent, who desired to cultivate the valuable friendship of the carrier.

"At half-past nine, after I have got through with my deliveries. Where?"

"At the *Puits sans Vin,* at the corner of the Rue de la Chaussée-d'Antin and the Rue Neuve-des-Mathurins," Laurent replied.

"Listen to me, friend," said the postman an hour later, when he and the valet de chambre were seated at table together, "if your master is in love with that girl he has laid out a fine job for himself! I doubt if you succeed in as much as getting a peep at her. I have been a letter-carrier in Paris for ten years now, off and on, and during that time have struck up against many systems of doors, but I tell you this, without fear of contradiction by any of my comrades, Monsieur de San-Réal's door beats them all for mysteriousness. There is a secret password without which no one can get into the hotel; and furthermore you will observe that the house is detached, so that there is no possibility of communication between it and the houses on each side.

The porter is an old Spaniard who does not speak a word of French, but who scrutinizes people like a Vidocq, for fear they may be robbers. If you were a lover or a thief—excuse me for mentioning your name in such a connection—and succeeded in eluding the vigilance of the first Cerberus, you would find in the first apartment—which has glazed doors—surrounded by a crowd of lackeys, a major-domo, a truculent old fellow, even more savage and intractable than the porter. The moment anybody puts his foot across the porte-cochère out starts Mr. Major-domo from his den, awaits the intruder in the vestibule, and subjects him to an examination in regular police-court style. The thing happened to me, who am only a poor letter-carrier. He took me for a *hemisphere* in disguise," said he, laughing at the far-fetched idea. "As for the domestics, you need not hope to get anything out of them.—I believe they were born dumb; not a soul in the quarter ever heard the sound of their voices; I don't know what wages they get for keeping their mouth shut and not drinking, but the fact is they are unapproachable. Either they are afraid they will be shot or lose a tidy sum of money in case they tell tales. If your master's love for Mademoiselle Paquita Valdès is sufficient to surmount all these obstacles, he certainly will not get the best of Doña Concha Marialva, the duenna who always accompanies her and would tuck the young lady under her petticoats if she thought she were about to get away from her. Those two women are as inseparable as though they were sewed together."

"What you tell me, estimable man of letters," replied Laurent after he had tossed off a glass of wine, "only confirms what I have already learned. I thought the people were making game of me, upon my honor, I did. The orange-woman across the street told me they let loose savage dogs in the garden at night, hanging chunks of meat from poles at such a height that the animals cannot reach them, and should anyone attempt to scale the wall the vicious brutes, thinking he is coming to rob them of their food, are ready to pounce on him and rend him limb from limb. You will tell me that they might be given a dose of little pills, but it seems they are trained to take nothing except from the hand of the porter."

"The porter of the Baron de Nucingen, whose garden adjoins the garden of the hotel San-Réal, told me the same thing," remarked the carrier.

"Good! my master knows the baron," said Laurent to himself. "I want you to know," he continued, looking steadily at the postman, "that the master I serve is a man of mettle, and if he should take it in his head to kiss the soles of an empress's feet, she would have to make up her mind to submit to the operation. If he should require your services, as I hope he may, for he is extremely generous, could he depend on you?"

"Damme, Monsieur Laurent, my name is Moinot.

It is sounded exactly as they speak sparrow—*moineau* —M-o-i-n-o-t, Moinot.''

''I see,'' said Laurent.

''I live at No. 11, Rue des Trois-Frères, fifth floor,'' Moinot went on; ''I have a wife and four children. If what you desire of me does not conflict too seriously with my conscience and my official duties,—you understand—I am at your service.''

''You are a fine fellow,'' said Laurent, shaking him by the hand.

''It is more than probable that Paquita Valdès is the mistress of the Marquis de San-Réal, King Ferdinand's friend,'' said Henri when his valet de chambre had reported the result of his investigations. ''Only a dried-up old Spanish mummy past eighty would think of all those precautions.''

''Monsieur,'' said Laurent, ''unless he drops into it from a balloon, no one will ever see the interior of that hotel.''

''You are an ass! To possess Paquita is it necessary to enter the hotel, since Paquita is free to leave it?''

''But the duenna, monsieur—how about her?''

''We'll put your duenna under lock and key for a few days.''

''Good—then we shall have Paquita!'' exclaimed Laurent, rubbing his hands.

''You rascal!'' Henri replied; ''if you have the impudence to speak in that manner of a woman before I have had her I will condemn you to the

embraces of old Concha. Help me to dress; I am
going out.''

Henri abandoned himself for a moment to his
pleasant thoughts. To the praise of womankind be
it said, he obtained as many of the sex as he condescended to desire. What would we think of a
woman who, being without a lover, could resist a
young man armed with good looks, wit and above
all, strength of purpose and wealth, which last are
the only two really efficient forces? But de Marsay, while triumphing thus easily, was bound to
weary of his triumphs, and accordingly, for some
two years past, he had been the victim of ennui.
He dived to the bottom of the sea of pleasure and
brought up more mud than pearls. Thus, like
kings and conquerors, he had come to that pass
where he implored fortune to grant him an obstacle
to vanquish, an enterprise that should call into play
once more his disused powers of mind and body.
Although Paquita Valdès presented to him an en-
semble of perfections such as he had only enjoyed
in detail hitherto, the element of passion was almost
wanting in him. Satiety had nearly extinguished
in his heart the sentiment of love. Like old men
and those who have drained the cup of life to the
lees he had only extravagant caprices and ruinous
fancies, which left no pleasurable impressions on
his heart. In the young, love is the noblest of sentiments; it gives life to the soul, in its all-pervading
sunshine, the finest inspirations, the grandest
thoughts expand and bloom; the first fruits of

everything are always sweetest. In men love becomes a passion; strength leads to abuse. In old
men it degenerates into vice; impotence leads to
excess. Henri was at the same time an old man, a
man, and a young man. To recover the emotions of
a genuine love he required, like Lovelace, a Clar-
issa Harlowe. Without the transforming reflection
from such a pearl of great price, all he could look to
have was passions whetted by Parisian vanity,
wagers with himself as to the depth of corruption
to which he could reduce some woman of his acquaintance, or adventures that stimulated his curiosity. After the report made by Laurent, his valet
de chambre, the Girl with the Golden Eyes assumed
an inestimable value to him. He would have a foe
in ambush to contend with who was apparently as
dangerous as he was adroit, and to come off victorious
would engage all the resources that Henri could
command. He was about to take a part in that
everlasting old comedy which will be always new,
and the characters in which are an old man, a
pretty woman, and a lover: Don Hijos, Paquita,
and de Marsay. If Laurent was a good Figaro, the
duenna appeared to be incorruptible. So we see
that the cast given by Chance to this living comedy
was stronger than any ever given by a dramatic
author. But after all, is not Chance a man of
genius?

"It is necessary to play cautiously," said Henri
to himself.

"Well," said Paul de Manerville, appearing at

the door, "how is the world using us? I have come
to breakfast with you."

"Very good," said Henri. "You won't be
shocked if I make my toilet in your presence?"

"What a notion!"

"We are getting to be so English in our ways of
late," said Henri, "that it wouldn't surprise me to
see us all turn prudes and hypocrites, like them."

Laurent had brought out such a wealth of toilet
apparatus that Paul felt obliged to say:

"The process will last a couple of hours, I suppose?"

"No! two and a half," replied Henri.

"Now we are alone together and can speak our
minds to each other. I should like to know why it
is that a man of your supreme ability can waste so
much time on a frivolous performance that must be
alien to his nature. Why spend two hours and a
half on your precious person when you might pop
into a bath, dress and comb your hair, all in fifteen
minutes? Come, explain yourself."

"It shows the affection I must have for you, you
great numskull, that I consent to talk with you on
matters of such importance," said the young man,
whose feet were at that moment being treated with
a lather of English soap, applied with a soft brush.

"But I have dedicated to you my most sincere
attachment," replied Paul de Manerville, "and
I love you while acknowledging you to be my
superior—"

"You must have noticed, if indeed you are capable

of noticing a moral phenomenon," said de Marsay, without acknowledging Paul's protestation otherwise than by a look, "that women love a coxcomb. Do you know the reason of that fact? My friend, it is because coxcombs are the only men who give attention to their persons. Now is it not clear that he who gives this minute attention to the outer man is at the same time contributing to the comfort of others? The man who does not claim to belong to himself is the very man whom women covet. Love has an essentially thievish disposition. I am not speaking now of that excessive neatness in which they so delight. Did you ever see one enamored of a sloven, even though he might be a man of mark? If you did, the fact must be ascribed to those strange fancies that frequently possess a woman's mind during pregnancy, to those foolish thoughts which enter people's heads. Again, I have seen men of the highest reputation sacked remorselessly for no other reason than their untidiness. A fop whose thoughts are entirely of his person has his mind occupied with a trifling thing, an absurdity. And what is woman? is she not a trifling thing, a bundle of absurdities? Two words lightly spoken suffice to employ her thoughts for four hours. She is sure that the fop will think of her, because he has no great ideas to occupy his mind. She will never find herself neglected for glory, ambition, art, politics; those great wantons whom she looks on as her rivals. Then the coxcomb is sufficiently courageous to make himself ridiculous for the sake of pleasing woman, and her heart is rich in compensation for the man who is ridiculed through love. Finally, a coxcomb cannot be a coxcomb unless he has good and sufficient grounds for being so. It is the women who give us that type. The coxcomb is a colonel of Love's forces; he has his conquests, he has his regiment of women to command. My dear fellow, at Paris everyone's affairs are known, and no one need try to pass for a coxcomb who has not the necessary qualifications. You, who have but one mistress, and perhaps are right in having only one, try to play the coxcomb— why, you won't be ridiculous merely, you will be dead, you will be tried, convicted and sentenced as one of those men condemned unremittingly to do one single thing. Your name will be synonymous with imbecility, as Monsieur de Lafayette's name is synonymous with America—Liberty—Monsieur de Talleyrand's with diplomacy; Désaugiers' with poetry; Monsieur de Ségur's with romance. Let any of these men step outside of his class, no one will grant there is any merit in his work. That is the way with us Frenchmen, always supremely unjust! For all we know Monsieur de Talleyrand may be a great financier, Monsieur de Lafayette a tyrant, and Désaugiers an administrator. Next year you may have forty mistresses, the public don't acknowledge you have one. So you see, friend Paul, that foppishness is the outward sign and token of an unquestionable power gained over the female sex. A man who has the love of several women is credited with possessing superior qualities, and then it is a fight who shall own him, wretched mortal! Do you think, moreover, it counts for nothing to have the right of entering a salon, staring around you at the company over your high cravat or through your monocle, and withering with your scorn the eminent savant whose waistcoat is old-fashioned?—Laurent, you are hurting me!—After breakfast, Paul, we will go to the Tuileries and see if we can catch a glimpse of the adorable Girl with the Golden Eyes.''

When, after an excellent repast, the two young men had explored the Terrasse des Feuillants and the great alley of the Tuileries, they found no trace of the sublime Paquita Valdès, on whose account fifty young men, the most elegant dandies of Paris, were there, all perfumed, having high cravats, top boots and spurs, cracking their whips, walking, talking, laughing and devoting themselves to all the devils.

''We have our labor for our pains,'' said Henri, ''but I have the best idea in the world. The young person is in the habit of receiving letters from London; we must bribe the postman or make him drunk, get possession of a letter, open it—and read it, of course—slip a little *billet doux* inside the envelope, and seal it up again. The old tyrant, *crudel tiranno*, doubtless knows the writer of the London letters and won't suspect anything.''

The next day de Marsay again took an airing on the Terrasse des Feuillants and saw Paquita there;

under the influence of his passion she seemed to
him more beautiful than before.   Those eyes, that
seemed to partake of the brilliancy of the sun's rays
and whose glances betokened the ardor of that perfect form whose every fibre spoke of pleasure, he
already doted on.   As they paced up and down the
public promenade, each time they met, the young
man burned to touch the garment of the entrancing
girl, but all his attempts were fruitless.   At last,
when he had passed the duenna and Paquita with
the intent that when he turned he should be on the
side of the Girl with the Golden Eyes, Paquita,
no less impatient than he, swerved suddenly toward
him and de Marsay felt her press his hand so
quickly and passionately that it seemed to him he had
received an electric shock.   In a moment, all the
emotions of youth came surging to his heart.   When
the two lovers looked at each other Paquita
appeared ashamed; she lowered her eyes in her desire not to meet Henri's, but as her glance fell she
did not fail to note the feet and figure of him whom
women, previous to the Revolution, were wont to
call *their conqueror*.

"Really, I must have that girl for my mistress,"
said Henri to himself.

He followed her to where the terrace ends in
the Place Louis XV., and there caught sight of
the old Marquis de San-Réal, leaning on the arm
of his valet and walking with the painful and
halting step of one afflicted with gout and caco-
chymia.   Doña Concha, who evidently mistrusted

Henri, placed Paquita between herself and the old man.

"Oh! as for you," said de Marsay, with a contemptuous look at the duenna, "if there is no way of bringing you to terms we'll put you to sleep with a little opium. We have read our mythology and haven't forgotten the fable of Argus."

Before she took her place in the carriage the Girl with the Golden Eyes gave her lover a glance or two, whose meaning there was no mistaking and which threw Henri into raptures, but the duenna intercepted one and spoke a few sharp words to Paquita, who flung herself into the coupé with a look of vexation. Several days passed during which Paquita came no more to the Tuileries. Laurent, who, in pursuance of orders from his master, went and reconnoitred the premises in the Rue Saint-Lazare, learned from the neighbors that since the day when the duenna had intercepted the glance between Henri and her charge neither the two women nor the old Marquis had left the house. Thus the slender tie that united the pair of lovers was already broken.

A few days afterward, by mysterious methods for which no one could account, de Marsay had attained his end: he had a seal and sealing-wax exactly like those that sealed the missives which came to Mademoiselle Valdès from London, writing-paper similar to that employed by the foreign correspondent, and, finally, counterfeit stamps with which to affix the English and French postmarks. He indited the following epistle, which outwardly had every appearance of having come from London:

"DEAR PAQUITA,

"I shall not attempt to depict in words the passion with which you have inspired me. If, to my everlasting happiness, it is reciprocated by you, know that I have discovered a way by which we may communicate with each other. My name is Adolphe de Gouges, and I live at No. 54, Rue de l'Université. If you are so closely watched as to be unable to write, or if you have not pen and paper, I shall know it by your silence. To-morrow, therefore, between the hours of eight in the morning and ten at night, my confidential man will be on the lookout in the Baron de Nucingen's garden; if, within that time, you shall not have thrown a letter over the wall, on the following morning, at ten o'clock, my trusty agent will pass to you over the wall, by means of a cord, two phials. Try to be walking in your garden about that time. One of the phials will contain opium to quiet your Argus—six drops will be enough to give her; the other will hold ink. The ink-bottle is of cut glass, the other is plain. Both are flat and thin, to admit of concealment beneath your corset. What I have done thus far to open a correspondence between us should prove to you how deeply I love you. Do not doubt me; to obtain an interview of an hour I declare to you I would give my life.'

"They always swallow that bait, the poor creatures!" said de Marsay to himself, "but they are right. What should we think of a woman who would refuse to be ensnared by a love-letter supported by such corroborative testimony?"

The letter was delivered to the porter of the San-Réal mansion the following morning, about eight o'clock, by our friend Moinot, the postman.

24

De Marsay, in order that he might be near the field of battle, had come to take breakfast with Paul, who lived in the Rue de la Pépinière. At two o'clock, just as the two friends were laughing over the troubles of a young man who had been trying to make a splurge on a slender fortune that his companions obligingly consented to spend for him, Henri's coachman came to Paul's door inquiring for his master and, being admitted, presented a mysterious person who insisted on speaking with de Marsay in person. This individual was a mulatto, whom Talma, had he ever come across him, would certainly have taken as the model for his make-up in Othello. All the traits of the Moor were there in that African face and figure—the quick suspicion, the grandeur of his vengeance, the rapidity with which action followed decision, his Moorish strength and childish impulsiveness. His black eyes had the steady, fixed look which characterize those of a bird of prey and, like the vulture's, were surrounded by a bluish membrane destitute of hairs. His low, narrow forehead had in it something menacingly repulsive. It was clear that the man was the slave of a single overmastering idea. His sinewy arm was not his own. He was accompanied by a person whom everyone, from the shivering hyperboreans to the perspiring slaves of the Gold Coast, may best depict to their imaginations by means of this phrase: *He was an unhappy man.* By this expression all the world will understand him, each nation will picture him to itself in accordance with its own ideal of deepest misery. But whose fancy is vivid enough to portray his poor wrinkled, pasty-white face, red at its extremities, and his long ragged beard? who is capable of beholding in his mind's eye his yellowish cravat tied like a rope, his frayed and dirty collar, his shiny hat, his faded coat now of greenish hue, his sorry trousers, his shrunken waistcoat, his pinchbeck breast-pin, his wretched shoes whose strings had dangled in the mud? who shall comprehend him in all the immensity of his distress, past and present? Who? only the Parisian. The pauper of Paris is the man whose cup of misery is full, for he still sees sufficient pleasure to realize the full extent of his wretchedness. The mulatto reminded one of an executioner of the time of Louis XI. with a patient in his clutches.

"What brings those two knaves here?" said Henri.

"Angels and ministers of grace defend us! but one of them makes my flesh creep," exclaimed Paul.

"You, who have a little more the appearance of a Christian than the other, who are you?" said Henri, looking at the man of rags and tatters.

The mulatto stood gazing at the two young men, evidently comprehending nothing, but trying to obtain an inkling of what was said from their gestures and the movement of their lips.

"I am an interpreter and public writer. My name is Poincet, and my residence the Palais de Justice."

"Good—and that fellow!" said Henri to the writer, pointing at the mulatto.

"I don't know who he is; he speaks only a kind of Spanish jargon, and brought me here to assist in communicating with you."

The mulatto took from his pocket the letter written by Henri to Paquita and handed it to the former, who tossed it into the fire.

"Well, the mystery begins to clear a little," said Henri to himself. "Paul, leave us for a few moments."

"I made a translation of that letter for him," the interpreter continued when they were alone. "When I had completed it he went off somewhere, I don't know where. Then he came back to get me and bring me here, promising me two louis for my pains."

"What have you to say to me, Chinaman?" asked Henri.

"I did not say he was a Chinaman," the interpreter volunteered while waiting for the mulatto's answer. "He says, monsieur," Poincet continued when he had received his unknown companion's communication, "that you are to be on the Boulevard Montmartre, near the café, to-morrow night at half-past ten. You will find a carriage waiting there with a lackey standing by the door; you will say to the man *cortejo*—which is a Spanish word signifying lover," Poincet added with a congratulatory glance at Henri; "then he will let down the steps and you will get in."

"All right!"

The mulatto man tendered two louis to the interpreter, but de Marsay insisted on paying; during the operation the mulatto spoke a few words.

"What is he saying?"

"He is warning me," replied the man of the sorrowful countenance, "that unless I keep my tongue between my teeth he will strangle me—and faith, I think the beauty has very much the appearance of a man who would do it."

"I am quite certain of it," Henri replied; "he will do as he says."

"He desires me to say further," the interpreter added, "that the person on whose behalf he is acting entreats you, for her sake as well as for your own, to observe the greatest prudence in your behavior; otherwise the poniards that threaten you and her would infallibly be buried in both your hearts, and no earthly power would avail to save you."

"Did he say that? So much the better—the game will be all the more interesting.—You may come in, Paul!" he shouted to his friend.

The mulatto, who had never once taken his eyes off Paquita Valdès' lover, went his way, accompanied by the interpreter.

"At last here is an adventure that gives promise of a little romance," said Henri to himself when Paul returned. "After participating in a considerable number I at last have the good fortune of lighting on an intrigue in this great city of Paris

that has its accompaniment of considerable peril.
The deuce! What a daring, resolute, inflexible being
a woman becomes in the face of danger! Attempt
to coerce a woman, to thwart her inclination, and
you give her a pretext and the courage to overleap
in an instant barriers that for years have held her
in restraint. Pretty creature, leap! She'll die?
poor child! Poniards? a woman's weak imagin-
ings! They all feel the need of making their little
comedy as tragic as possible. However, Paquita,
we'll remember your warnings! we'll think of
them, my girl! Deuce take me if I don't believe
the adventure has lost a portion of its piquancy,
now that I know that delicious girl, nature's fairest
handiwork, is mine."

The young man was uppermost again in Henri,
notwithstanding the apparent cynicism of his reflections. To get through the day without too much
weariness of spirit while waiting for the morrow
he had recourse to extravagant pleasures: he gamed,
dined and supped with his friends; drank like a
hack-driver, ate like a German, and won ten or
twelve thousand francs. He left the *Rocher de
Cancale* at two o'clock in the morning, slept like a
baby, awoke the next day fresh and rosy, and
dressed to go to the Tuileries, proposing to take a
horseback ride after he had seen Paquita and thus
create an appetite for dinner, thereby helping to
kill time.

At the hour specified Henri was on the boulevard,
recognized the carriage, and gave the password to

a man whom he took to be the mulatto. On hearing the password the man made haste to open the door and let down the steps. The young man was whirled along the streets of Paris at such a rattling pace and his thoughts were so absorbed in other matters that he failed to recognize either the avenues through which the carriage passed or the locality where it stopped. The mulatto ushered him into a house where the staircase was near the porte-cochère. The stairs were dark, as was the landing on which Henri was obliged to wait while the mulatto was opening the door of a damp, malodorous and unlighted apartment, whose rooms, dimly illuminated by the candle that his guide discovered in the ante-chamber, presented the forsaken, half-furnished appearance that houses have whose occupants are traveling. He was reminded of the sensation he had experienced in reading one of Anne Radcliffe's novels, in which the authoress conducts her hero through the long suite of cold, dark, untenanted rooms of some old, ruinous and deserted castle. Finally the mulatto threw open the door of a salon. The condition of the old furniture and faded draperies imparted to the room a resemblance to the salon of an equivocal resort. There was the same garish attempt at elegance, the same collection of ill-assorted, tawdry ornaments, and everywhere the same dust and dirt. Seated on a sofa covered with red Utrecht velvet, beside a smoking chimney whose fire was smothered in its own ashes, was a poorly-clad old woman, wearing one of those turbans that English women have the faculty of making when they reach a certain age, and which would have an immense success in China, where the trend of artistic genius is toward the monstrous. The salon, the old woman, the cold hearth, of themselves would have sufficed to congeal love had not Paquita been there, seated on a sofa, her form wrapped in a voluptuous dressing-gown, free to bestow her glance of gold and fire, free to pose her arched foot, free in her luminous movements. This first interview was what such events always are between two passionate beings who, at a bound, have surmounted the barriers separating them and who, not being acquainted, desire each other ardently. It is impossible that there should not be a certain discordant note in a situation trying enough until the two souls become keyed to the same pitch. If desire gives to the man audacity and disposes him to a lack of gentleness, the woman, on the other hand, risking her womanliness, however deep may be her love, is frightened to find herself so quickly at her journey's end and confronted by the necessity of making that surrender which, to many women, means a leap in the dark into an abyss at whose bottom they know not what they shall find. The involuntary coldness of such a woman is in sharp contrast with her avowed passion, and necessarily reacts upon the warmest lover. Hence these ideas, which often float in a nebulous, ill-defined shape in people's minds, superinduce there a sort of temporary

malady. In the agreeable journey undertaken by
two congenial souls through the delightful domain of
Love this period may be likened to a sandy waste,
alternately hot and cold, full of burning sands
intersected by marshes and unrelieved by tree or
shrub, beyond which lie the rose-decked groves
where Love and his train of pleasures sport uncon-
fined upon the flower-enameled turf. It often happens that a stupid laugh is the only reply that a
man of wit and intelligence can find to make; his
wit is in a sense benumbed and chilled by the icy
constriction of his desires. It is quite supposable
that two beings, equally beautiful, gifted and passionate, should at first talk the silliest and vapidest
commonplace, until chance—a word, a quivering
look—the spark that touches off the magazine,
brings about the thrice-happy transformation that
conducts them into the flowery path down which
they walk or rather glide deliciously. This mental
state is always in direct ratio to the violence of the
sentiments. A man and woman, whose love for
each other is feeble, experience nothing of the sort.
The effect of this crisis may further be compared
to that produced by a blazing sun in a clear sky.
At first sight nature seems shrouded in a gaseous
veil, the blue of the firmament appears black, the
intensest light resembles darkness. In Henri and
in the fair Spaniard passion asserted itself with
equal violence, and that law of statics by virtue
of which two forces of equal value neutralize each
other in meeting, might be accepted as true in the

moral kingdom also. Then, too, the old mummy's
presence added materially to the embarrassment of
the situation. Love is disconcerted or emboldened
by everything; everything is to it a presage of
good or evil. The decrepit hag was there as pre-
figuring a possible dénouement, and to their eyes
was the horrible fish's tail which Greek symbolism
has given to the sirens and chimeras, so fair and
alluring as far down as their waist, even as all passions are in their inception. Although Henri was
not an *esprit fort* in the ironical sense which the
term generally carries with it, he was a man of
immense force of character, as great as a man can
be who is without belief; yet the concurrence of all
these circumstances impressed him deeply. Besides, the men of strongest mental powers are
naturally the most impressionable and consequently
the most superstitious, if indeed that may be called
superstition which is the disposition to act intui-
tively on the impulse of the moment, which may
be and doubtless is the perception of effects resulting from causes concealed from others' eyes, but
visible to theirs.

Paquita took advantage of this moment of silent
constraint to abandon herself to that ecstasy of
adoration which fills the heart of a woman who
loves passionately and finds herself at last in the
presence of the idol for whom she has long vainly
hoped. Joy and happiness were in her eyes; they
seemed to emit living sparks. She was spell-
bound, and abandoned herself without fear, to the

intoxication of a felicity she had long dreamed of.
She appeared then to Henri so marvelously beautiful
that the old woman and all the horrid phantasmagoria of rags, antiquated, rusty, worn draperies,
the green straw cushions of the arm-chairs, the red
foot-stool much worn, all this miserable luxury
vanished entirely. The salon suddenly became
brilliant with light, and he saw but dimly, as
through a cloud, the frightful harpy, mute and
motionless on her red sofa, whose yellow eyes
betrayed the servility that owes its existence to
misfortune, or is caused by a vice that has mastered
one and lashes him with the relentless severity
with which an eastern despot scourges his unhappy
slaves. Her eyes had the cold lustre of those of a
caged tiger, who knows his powerlessness and is
obliged to swallow his murderous inclinations.

"Who is that woman?" said Henri to Paquita.

But Paquita did not answer. She indicated by a
sign that she did not speak French, and asked Henri
if he understood English. De Marsay repeated his
question in that language.

"She is the only woman whom I can trust,
although she sold me once," Paquita tranquilly
replied. "My dear Adolphe, she is my mother,
and was a slave, purchased in Georgia for her sur-
passing beauty, of which few traces remain to-day.
She only speaks her mother tongue."

The woman's attitude and her acute anxiety to
divine by her daughter's and Henri's gestures and
expression what was going on between them, were

suddenly made clear to the young man, whose mind was easier after the explanation.

"Paquita," he said to her, "when shall we be free?"

"Never!" she sadly answered. "Indeed, we have but a few days that we can call our own."

She lowered her eyes and looked at her hands, then counted with the right upon the fingers of the left, displaying to Henri's gaze the most beautiful pair of hands he had ever seen.

"One, two, three—"

She counted up to twelve.

"Yes," said she, "we have twelve days."

"And then?—"

"Then," said she, with the absorbed air of a weak woman kneeling to receive the axe of the executioner, and suffering death in advance from a cruel terror that robbed her of that superb energy which nature seemed to have endowed her with only that she might intensify pleasure and transform the coarsest delights into endless poems. "Then—" she repeated.

Her eyes were fixed, she seemed to be contemplating some menacing object in the distance.

"I do not know," she said.

"The girl is losing her senses," Henri mentally remarked, himself indulging in a singular train of thought.

Paquita seemed to him occupied by some thought foreign to himself, like a woman constrained equally by remorse and passion. Perhaps she had in her heart another love that she remembered and forgot in turn. In a moment's time Henri was assailed by a thousand conflicting thoughts. The girl was becoming a mystery to him, but as he contemplated her with the experienced eye of the veteran voluptuary, thirsting for new pleasures—like that king of the Orient who commanded that a fresh sensation be created for him—a horrible longing to which great natures are liable—Henri recognized in Paquita the richest organization that nature had delighted to frame for love. The presumed working of the machine, leaving the soul out of the question, would have frightened another than de Marsay; but he was fascinated by this promise of abundant harvests of pleasure, this constant variety in happiness, the dream of every man, and that every loving woman aims at also. He was transported with the idea of infinity made palpable and applied to the service of the creature in his excesses of enjoyment. He saw all these things in this girl more distinctly than he had seen them yet, for she was pleased to be admired and with delight submitted to his inspection. De Marsay's admiration rose almost to the point of frenzy, and he betrayed it all in a look that the Spaniard understood, as if glances of that nature were familiar to her.

"If you were not to be mine, mine only, I would kill you!" he cried.

Paquita, hearing these words, hid her face in her hands and naïvely exclaimed:

"Ah! holy Virgin, into what hands have I fallen!"

She rose, crossed the room, and cast herself down on the red sofa, where she buried her face in the rags that covered her mother's bosom and wept. The old woman received her daughter without stirring from her position or manifesting the least emotion. The mother possessed in the highest degree that gravity peculiar to savage races, that statuesque impassibility before which the keenest observer is at fault. Did she, or did she not, love her daughter? there was no answer. Beneath that impenetrable mask all human sentiments, good and evil, lay hidden, and anything might be expected from this creature. Her look wandered slowly from her child's beautiful hair, which covered her like a mantle, to Henri's face, which she observed with unutterable curiosity. She seemed to be asking herself by what witchcraft he was there, by what caprice nature had made so seductive a man.

"Those women are making a fool of me!" said Henri to himself.

At that moment, Paquita raised her head and cast on him one of those looks that penetrate the soul and set it afire. She appeared to him so lovely that he vowed to possess himself of that treasure of beauty.

"My Paquita! be mine!"

"Would you kill me?" she said, fearful, trembling, anxious, but drawn to him by a mysterious force.

"I kill you?" said he, smiling.

Paquita uttered a cry of fear and spoke a word to

the old crone, who authoritatively took Henri's hand
and that of her daughter, examined them closely,
then released them, tossing her head with horrible
significance.

"Be mine, now, this instant, go with me and
never leave me, I implore you, Paquita! Do you
love me? Come!"

In a moment he poured forth a thousand insen-
sate phrases, with the rapidity of a mountain torrent dashing over its rocks, repeating the same idea
in a hundred different forms.

"It is the same voice," said Paquita sadly, but
in a tone too low for de Marsay to hear, "and—the
same ardor," she added.—"Well, yes!" she said
with an abandon of passion which words fail to express. "Yes! but not to-night. I gave too little
opium to la Concha this evening, Adolphe; she
might awake, and I should be lost. The entire
household believes now that I am sleeping soundly
in my chamber. Be at the same place in two days,
repeat the same word to the same man. That man
is my foster-father; Cristemio adores me, and
death by torture could not extract from him a word
to my injury. Adieu," she said, grasping Henri
around the body and twining about him like a serpent.

She pressed her body against his, in closest contact, she pillowed his head on her bared bosom, she
offered him her lips, snatched and received a kiss
so ravishingly that both their heads swam and de
Marsay thought the earth was opening to swallow

him; then, in a voice that showed how little she was mistress of herself, Paquita cried, "Be gone!" But while repeating "Be gone" she still kept him in her passionate embrace, and with lingering steps conducted him to the staircase.

There the mulatto, whose white eyes glowed at the sight of Paquita, took the candle from his idol's hand and escorted Henri to the street. Depositing the candle in the archway, he opened the door, placed Henri in the carriage, and set him down in the Boulevard des Italiens in an incredibly short time. The horses seemed to have a demon in their bodies.

The entire scene was like a dream to de Marsay, but one of those dreams which, in vanishing, leave behind them a sensation of unearthly bliss, that a man hungers after and pursues during the remainder of his life. One single kiss had been sufficient. Never had assignation passed off more properly, more chastely, more coldly, perhaps, in a place more horrible in its associations, in presence of a more hideous goddess; for the mother had remained in Henri's imagination as something fiendish, debased and disgusting: a skinny, squalid, vicious and spiteful fury such as poet's or artist's fancy had never yet conceived. And yet never had an interview more stirred his senses, revealed more adventurous delight nor caused the spring of love to gush forth and shed, as it were, its atmosphere around a man. There was in it something sombre and sweet, mysterious and tender, restrictive and expansive—a linking together of the horrible and celestial, of paradise and hell, that intoxicated de Marsay. He was no longer himself, and yet he was able to resist the allurements of pleasure.

That the reader may understand his behavior in the dénouement of this narrative, it is necessary to explain why his mental powers had increased instead of diminishing at the age when most young men's faculties are contracted by excessive commerce with women. His character had been enlarged by a combination of occult circumstances which were the means of investing him with an immense secret power. The young man wielded a sceptre more powerful than that of modern kings, almost all restrained by law in the exercise of their least inclinations. De Marsay's dominance was the autocratic authority of an oriental despot. But this power, so stupidly exerted in Asia by ignorant and degraded men, was let loose by European intelligence and French *esprit;* the keenest and most vigorous of all intellectual instruments. Henri, in regard to his amusements and vanities, was limited only by his desires. This invisible influence on the social world, without boasting, invested him with a real but secret majesty, locked in his own bosom. The opinion he had of himself was not that which a monarch like Louis XIV. may have entertained of his personality; it was rather like that which the proudest of the caliphs, a Pharaoh, a Xerxes, who claimed divine descent, held of themselves, when in imitation of the Supreme Being

25

they veiled themselves before their subjects, alleging that to look on them was to die. Thus, with no sentiment of remorse that he was at the same time judge and plaintiff, de Marsay coolly condemned to death the man or woman who had injured him. The sentence, though often pronounced inconsiderately in trifling moods, was irrevocable. If there was a mistake it was as irreparable as the action of the undiscriminating thunderbolt, which spares the old coachman on the box and annihilates the happy girl within the coach while being driven to an appointment with her lover. The caustic and profound irony that marked the young man's conversation was a source of terror to almost everyone; no one cared to provoke it. Women have unbounded admiration for those men—self-styled pashas who walk the earth seemingly accompanied by their lions and executioners and other fearful paraphernalia. The result is that these men betray in their looks and bearing a firmness, a self-reliance, a consciousness of power, a leonine spirit which realize to the feminine mind the type of force of which all women dream. Such a man was de Marsay.

Happy now in his prospects for the future, he was once more a young and tractable man, and when he retired to rest his dreams were all of love. He dreamed of the Girl with the Golden Eyes, as dream only young men in love. There were fantastic visions, impalpable marvels, bathed in glorious light and revealing unseen worlds, but never completely, for a veil interposed changes the optical conditions. The next day and the day following Henri disappeared and none of his friends knew where he was. His strange power was his only on certain conditions, and, fortunately for him, during those two days he was simply a private soldier in the service of the demon from whom he held his talismanic existence. But at the appointed hour, in the evening, on the boulevard, he was awaiting the arrival of the carriage, which was not long in making its appearance. The mulatto came up to Henri and said to him in French a few words which he had apparently learned by heart:

"She tell me, if you want come, must let eyes be bandaged."

And Cristemio displayed a large white silk handkerchief.

"No!" roared Henri, his high-mightiness suddenly aroused.

He would have entered the carriage, but the mulatto made a sign and it rolled away.

"Yes!" cried de Marsay, furious at the thought of losing a promised pleasure.

Besides, he saw the futility of wasting words on a slave as habituated to blind obedience as a hangman. And then was it fitting that his anger should fall on this passive instrument?

The mulatto gave a shrill whistle and the carriage returned. Henri bounded into it and took his seat.

Already some curious idlers had gathered on the

boulevard. Henri was strong; he determined to try conclusions with the colored man. When the carriage started at a sharp trot he seized his guide and keeper by the wrists, thinking that by over-powering him he would be able to preserve the use of his faculties and thus learn in what direction he was being carried. The attempt was fruitless. The mulatto's eyes scintillated in the obscurity. He emitted a hoarse roar that his rage made inartic-ulate, released himself, threw de Marsay down with a hand of iron, and pinned him, as it were, on to the floor of the vehicle; then, with his free hand, he drew forth a three-edged poniard and gave another whistle. The driver heard the signal and stopped. Henri was unarmed, there was nothing for it but to yield; he stretched out his head to receive the handkerchief. This evidence of submission pacified Cristemio, who adjusted the bandage with a respect and gentleness that evinced a sort of veneration for the person of the man who possessed his idol's love. But before taking this precaution, mistrustful, he slipped his poniard into a side-pocket, and but-toned himself to the chin.

"The confounded Chinaman, he would have mur-dered me!" remarked de Marsay to himself.

The carriage again set off, at a rapid pace. For a young man as thoroughly acquainted with Paris as Henri was there was one means of knowing in what direction he was going: all he had to do was to give strict attention and count by the gutters they crossed, the intersecting streets as long as

their course lay straight along the boulevard.   In
this way he could distinguish the side street that
the carriage entered when it diverged, either
toward the Seine or the Heights of Montmartre, and
judge the name of the street, or the location to which
his guide conducted him.   But the great excitement
which followed his struggle with the mulatto, the
rage he felt because of his compromised dignity, the
schemes of vengeance which he pondered over, the
suppositions suggested by the infinite precaution
taken by that mysterious girl in getting him to her,
all concurred to distract his attention and prevent
the concentration of his thoughts and a perfect clear-
ness of memory.   When the carriage stopped, after
a course of half an hour, it was no longer on the
pavements.   The mulatto and the coachman took
Henri in their arms, lifted him out, placed him on
a kind of litter, and carried him through a garden, —
for he smelt the flowers and the peculiar odor of
trees and grass.   The silence that prevailed there
was so profound that he could distinguish the sound
of the dew dripping from the moist leaves.   The
two men bore him up a staircase, then set him on
his feet, led him by the hand through several apartments, and finally left him in a room which, he
perceived, was luxuriously carpeted and whose
atmosphere was perfume-laden.   A woman's hand
pressed him down upon a divan and removed the
handkerchief.   Henry saw Paquita before him,
Paquita in all the glory of a voluptuous woman.

The part of the boudoir in which Henri now

found himself, described a sweeping and graceful curve, while the further end of the apartment was quite square, where there was a mantle-piece resplendent in its white marble and gold. He had entered by a side door which was concealed by a rich portière of tapestry, facing which was a window. The horseshoe space was furnished with a genuine Turkish divan, a mattress, so to speak, laid on the floor, large as a bed; this divan was fifty feet around and was covered with white cashmere, and tufted with knots of black and crimson silk arrayed in the form of lozenges. The back of this huge bed rose several inches above the numerous cushions that still further enriched and beautified it by the exquisite taste of their colors and arrangement. The boudoir was draped with a red fabric overlaid with Indian muslin fluted, like a Corinthian column, by folds alternately raised and depressed, that ended at floor and ceiling in a strip of flame-colored material embroidered in black with arabesque designs. Seen through the muslin the red became pink, the color of love, which was repeated in the window curtains, likewise of Indian muslin, lined with pink taffeta and edged with a fringe in a combination of black and crimson. Six silver-gilt sconces, each holding two wax candles, projected from the tapestried wall at equal distances to illuminate the divan. The ceiling, from the middle of which was suspended a chandelier in dull gold, was dazzlingly white, and the cornice was gilded. The carpet could only be compared to an

Oriental shawl; it exposed the designs and recalled the poetry of Persia, where it had been woven by the hands of slaves. The furniture was covered with white cashmere, set off by black and crimson trimmings. The clock, the candelabra, and other ornaments were all in white marble and gold. The single table in the apartment had a white cashmere cover. Elegant jardinières were filled with roses of every variety, with flowers that were either red or white. In a word, every detail seemed to have been the object of a care impelled by love. Never had wealth been more temptingly subordinated to elegance, to express taste and inspire pleasure. Everything there was calculated to warm and animate the coldest nature. The shifting play of color in the draperies, whose lines were continually changing, at one moment all pink and the next entirely white according to the direction whence the eye fell on them, harmonized agreeably with the effects of light imprisoned in the diaphanous folds and plaits of the muslin, producing nebulous appearances. The soul has an undefinable attachment for white, love delights in red, and gold flatters the passions, for it has power to realize their fancies. Thus all that is vague and mysterious in man, all his unexplained affinities were gratified in their involuntary sympathy. In this perfect harmony there was a concert of color to which the soul replied with half-formed, floating voluptuous thoughts. It was here, surrounded by a vaporous atmosphere laden with exquisite perfumes that Henri now saw, Paquita, robed in a white dressing-gown, bare-footed, and with sprays of orange-blossoms in her black hair, kneeling before him as the god of that temple which he had condescended to enter. De Marsay, although accustomed to the refinements of Parisian luxury, was surprised by the elegance of this retreat, comparable only to the shell from which Venus sprang. Whether it was the result of the contrast between the darkness from which he had just emerged and the light in which he now basked, or of a rapid comparison between his present surroundings and those of the former interview, the tender sensation he experienced was such as true poetry inspires. His anger, his revengeful feelings, his wounded vanity, all surrendered as in the midst of this bower, which might have sprung into existence at the touch of a fairy wand, he beheld that masterpiece of creation, her whose warm-tinted complexion, whose soft skin, enriched by the reflection of red colors, and by a permeating influence as of some subtle love vapor, and who was resplendent as if herself reflecting all light and color. Like an eagle swooping on his prey he seized her by the waist and placed her on his knee, enjoying an unspeakable delight in the rapturous pressure of this girl, whose charms, so generously developed, now sweetly encircled him.

"Come, Paquita!" he whispered.

"Speak aloud, and have no fear," she said. "This retreat was built for love. No sound can escape its precincts; so great is the desire to jealously preserve the accents of the loved voice. However loud may be the cry it could not be heard beyond these walls.   Murder might be done here, the victim's shrieks would avail him no more than if he were in the middle of Sahara.''

"Who was he, who so well understood jealous love and its requirements?''

"You are never to question me on that point,'' she replied, loosing with an indescribably pretty gesture the young man's cravat, doubtless that she might see more of his neck.

"Yes, there it is, the neck I love so!'' she cried. "Will you do something to please me?''

This question, asked in a tone which rendered it almost lascivious, aroused de Marsay from the reverie in which he was plunged by the peremptory manner in which Paquita had forbidden all enquiry as to the unknown entity who hovered like a cloud above them.

"And if I should insist on knowing who is ruler here?''

Paquita trembled as she looked at him.

"Is it not I?'' he said, rising and disengaging himself from the girl, who fell over backward on the divan.   "Where I am I submit to share no man's rule.''

"Alas! alas!'' exclaimed the poor slave, overcome by terror.

"For whom do you take me then?—answer, will you?''

Paquita rose meekly, her eyes streaming with

tears, went to one of the two ebony cabinets that were in the room, took from it a poniard, and presented it to Henri with an air of gentle submissiveness that would have softened the heart of a tiger.

"Give me a feast such as men give when they love," she said, "and then, while I am sleeping, kill me, for I cannot answer your question. Listen! I am not free, I am bound as some poor animal is tethered to its stake; I cannot understand how I managed to bridge the gulf that separates us. Stupefy me with love, then kill me. Oh, no, no!" she cried, clasping her hands, "do not kill me! life is beautiful to me, I love it! If I am a slave I am also a queen. I might beguile you with fond words, I might tell you that I love you only, prove it, and availing myself of my brief empire over you say, 'Take me, as one passing through the garden of a king stops for a moment to breathe the perfume of a flower.' Then, when I had displayed a woman's crafty eloquence and stretched the wings of pleasure; when my thirst for pleasure was fully quenched, I could have you thrown down a well, constructed for the purpose of satisfying private vengeance without fearing the reprisals of justice, where no one would ever find you, where the quicklime would consume you and there would not be left an atom of your being. You would remain buried in my heart, mine forever."

Henri looked on the girl unflinchingly, and his fearless look filled her with joy.

"But no, I will not do that! It is not into a trap you have fallen here, but into the heart of a woman who loves you fondly, and I it is who will be cast into the well."

"All this has a prodigiously queer look to me," said de Marsay, eyeing her closely. "But you appear to me to be a nice girl,—only a little strange and incomprehensible. On my honor you're a living charade, and it is very difficult for me to find the explanation."

Paquita did not comprehend a word of what the young man said; she gazed at him with soft, wondering eyes that could never appear stupid so long as their voluptuous expression remained.

"Come, my love," said she, coming back to her original idea, "do you wish to afford me a pleasure?"

"I will do whatever you wish, and even what you don't wish," laughingly replied de Marsay, who had resolved to let himself go with the current of his new adventure without looking where it might lead, and had recovered all his foppish freedom. Perhaps too, he counted on his force of will and his experience acquired in many successful love passages, to conquer the girl a few hours later and learn all her secrets.

"Well," said she, "let me dress you up according to my fancy."

"Dress me any way you please," Henri replied.

Paquita, delighted, went to one of the two cabinets and drew forth a red velvet gown with which she proceeded to invest de Marsay, then she put a woman's bonnet on his head and wrapped a shawl about him.   While giving herself up to these buffooneries, with all the innocence of a child she laughed hysterically and seemed like a bird fluttering its wings; but she saw nothing beyond the present.

If it is impossible to picture the unheard of delights shared by those two splendid beings created by heaven in one of its joyous moods, it may be necessary to give some idea metaphysically of the strange and almost fantastic impressions received by the young man.   People of de Marsay's social status and who lead the life he led find it an easy matter to decide on the innocence of a girl.   But, strange to say, if the Girl with the Golden Eyes was a virgin, she certainly was not innocent.   The strange union of the mysterious and the palpable, of light and darkness, of the beautiful and the hideous, of pleasure and peril, of heaven and hell, that had thus far characterized this adventure was continued in the capricious and charming creature whom de Marsay dallied with.   All the resources of the most refined voluptuousness, all that was known to Henri of that poetry of the senses which is called love, was surpassed by the treasures unfolded by that girl whose sparkling eyes belied none of the promises they gave.   It was an oriental poem, glowing with the sunlight that Hafiz and Saadi have infused into their impassioned verse. But neither Saadi's nor Pindar's rhythm was capable of expressing the desolation that overtook the delicious girl when the illusion had passed in which an iron hand compelled her to dwell.

" I am dead, dead!" she cried. "Adolphe, bear me away to the ends of the earth, to an island where we are unknown. Let there be no traces of our flight! We should be pursued even to hell.— Good God, daylight!—fly, be gone. Shall I ever behold you again? Yes, to-morrow, I must see you, even if to taste this happiness I should have, with my own hands, to slay all my guardians.— Farewell—until to-morrow."

She clasped him to her bosom in an embrace that had in it the bitter fear of death. Then she touched a button that evidently connected with a bell and begged de Marsay to let himself be blindfolded.

"Suppose I refuse—suppose I insist on remaining here?"

"It would only be advancing the moment of my death," said she, "for now I am certain of dying for your sake."

Henri submitted to her wish. In the man freshly satiated with pleasure there is too often seen a certain ingratitude, an inclination to forget, a desire for freedom, a fancy for taking exercise, a tinge of scorn and possibly of disgust for his erstwhile idol —inexplicable sentiments, in fine, which are base and unworthy. Doubtless it was the perception of this confused, but real affection in hearts not warmed by that celestial fire nor perfumed with that holy incense which gives us constancy in love that suggested to Rousseau the adventures of Milord Édouard, which form the conclusion of the *Nouvelle Héloïse*. If Rousseau was evidently inspired by Richardson's great work, he has departed from his model in a thousand instances which give his work a character of splendid originality; he has recommended it to posterity by profound thoughts that we find it difficult to analyze when, in our youth, we read the work with the object of finding in it ardent descriptions of our most physical passions, while serious and philosophic writers never employ its images except to illustrate and enforce some great thought. The adventures of Milord Édouard are one of the most charmingly European conceptions of the book.

Thus Henri found himself under the influence of that mongrel sentiment that does not comprehend true love.

With him it was essential that a woman should shine by comparison, and the irresistible allurements of memories were necessary to attach him to a woman. True love rules especially by memories. The woman whose image is not graven on her lover's heart, either by the satiety of pleasure or by depth of sentiment, can she ever be loved? Unconsciously to Henri, Paquita had established herself in his affection by both these methods. But at the present moment, conscious only of the fatigue resulting from an excess of happiness—that delicious melancholy of the body—he was unable to analyze his heart by recalling to his lips the suave

taste of the keenest pleasures he had ever plucked.
Day was just breaking when he found himself on
the Boulevard Montmartre, idly watching the reced-
ing carriage; he took two cigars from his pocket,
lighted one of them at the lantern of a worthy
woman who was selling brandy and coffee to the
laborers, butcher-boys, market-gardeners and others
of the Parisian populace who are astir before daybreak, then went his way, his hands in his trousers'
pockets and smoking his cigar with an indifference
that was really shameful.

"There is a heap of comfort in a good cigar," he
said to himself.   "That's something which never
palls on a man."

And the poor Girl with the Golden Eyes, over
whom half the gilded youth of Paris were going
wild in those days, he scarce so much as gave her
a thought!   To refer to death in the midst of their
pleasures,—the fear of which had more than once
darkened the face of the beautiful creature, who
might claim kinship with the houris of Asia through
her mother, with Europe through her education,
and with the tropics through her birth,—seemed to
him one of those artifices which all women employ
with an eye to making themselves interesting.

"She is from Havana, the most essentially Spanish city of the New World; that accounts for her
affecting terror instead of thrusting upon me tales
of trial and tribulation, her coquetries, her reflections on duty, as a Parisian woman would have
done.   By her eyes of gold! I'm sleepy."

He saw a hackney cabriolet standing at the corner before Frascati's on the chance of picking up some belated gamester; he aroused the sleeping driver, was driven home, went to bed, and slept the sleep of the wicked, which, for some unaccountable reason that no sonneteer has yet taken the trouble to explain, is as sweet and salubrious as that of the just. Possibly it is an effect of the proverbial saying, *Extremes meet.*

About noon de Marsay awoke, stretched his arms and became aware of the gnawings of one of those canine appetites that any old soldier will remember having experienced on the day after a great victory. It was with pleasure therefore that he saw Paul de Manerville before him, for nothing is more agreeable on such occasions than to have a companion in eating.

"Well," said his friend, "we all supposed that you and the Golden-eyed one had been secluding yourselves together for the last ten days."

"The Girl with the Golden Eyes! I've given up thinking of her. Faith, I've other fish to fry."

"Oh, oh! you wish to be discreet."

"And why shouldn't I be?" said de Marsay with a laugh. "My friend, discretion is an excellent trait in a man's character, as well as a profitable one. Listen—but no, I shall not say a word. You never teach me anything, and I don't mean to squander the treasures of my wisdom on you, getting nothing in return. Life is a river down which we sail to build up commerce. By all I hold most

sacred upon earth, by my cigars! I will not be a
professor of social economy to a class of blockheads.
Come to breakfast.   It is less expensive to give
you an omelet and tunny than to waste the grey
matter of my brain.''

"Do you haggle with your friends?''

"My dear boy,'' said Henri, who rarely let slip
an opportunity of airing his sarcasm, "as it may
sometime happen to you, just as to any other man,
to be in need of discretion, and as I entertain a very
sincere affection for you—Yes, I love you! I give
you my word of honor, if all you wanted to keep
you from blowing out your brains was a thousand
franc note, you would find it right here—for we
haven't yet mortgaged anything down yonder, eh,
Paul?—If you were going to fight a duel to-morrow
I would pace off the distance and load your pistols
in order that you might be killed according to
regulation.   And if anybody, except myself should
see fit to speak evil of you behind your back, he
would find that he had the extremely tough customer who lives in my skin to deal with.   That's
what I call friendship—proof against everything.
Well, little one, when you are in want of discretion,
you must know there are two kinds of discretion:
discretion active and discretion passive.   Passive
discretion is that used by fools, who employ silence,
negation, a frowning air, the discretion of shut doors,
true feebleness! Active discretion proceeds by
affirmation. If I should say this evening at the club:
'Faith of an honest man, the Girl with the Golden

26

Eyes was not worth what she cost me!' everybody would say as soon as I was outside the door: 'Did you hear that coxcomb de Marsay, who would have us believe that he has already had the Girl with the Golden Eyes? He takes that way of ridding himself of his rivals—he's not a fool!' But this is a vulgar and dangerous subterfuge. No matter how far-fetched our remarks there are always idiots enough to believe them. The best kind of discretion is that employed by a clever woman when she wants to pull the wool over her husband's eyes. It consists in insinuating things against a woman for whom we do not care, or whom we do not possess, in order to preserve the honor of the woman whom we love sufficiently to respect. That is what I call the *woman-screen*. Ah! here comes Laurent. —What have you brought us?"

"Ostend oysters, Monsieur le Comte."

"You will find out some day, Paul, the amusement there is in fooling the world by concealing from it the secret of our affections. I find a tremendous pleasure in escaping from the stupid jurisdiction of the multitude, which never knows what it wants or thinks it wants, takes the means for the end, cuddles and curses you alternately, and builds up one day only to tear down the next. How delightful to impose emotions on it and receive none from it, to bridle it, to never yield obedience to it! If there is anything we have a right to be proud of, is it not that self-acquired power of which we are at once cause and effect, beginning and end.

No man knows whom I love or what is my purpose.
Perhaps it will be known some day whom I have
loved, what I have purposed, just as the plot of the
play is known when the curtain is rung down; but
let the bystanders look into my hand while the
game is going on?—that would be weakness,
idiocy! I know nothing more contemptible than
strength foiled by cunning. I am initiating myself
in a small way into the mysteries of the ambassa-
dorial profession, you see—but is diplomacy a more
difficult study than life? I doubt it. Are you ambitious? Would you become somebody?"

"You are laughing at me, Henri—as if my abil-
ities were not mediocre enough to raise me to any
position."

"Good, Paul! If you keep on laughing at yourself you will soon be in a position to laugh at everybody else."

By the time the cigars were reached de Marsay
had begun to view the events of his night in a
strange light. Like many great minds, his perspi-
cacity was not spontaneous; he did not get at once
to the marrow of things. Like all natures gifted
with the power of living mainly in the present—
squeezing the orange, so to speak, and gulping
down its juice—his second-sight required an interval of slumber to identify itself with causes. Car-
dinal de Richelieu was such a man, but it did not
preclude in him the gift of foresight necessary to
the conception of great measures. De Marsay was
furnished with such a mental equipment, but in the

beginning he used his weapons only in furtherance
of his pleasures, and it was not until he was satiated with those pleasures that occupy the mind of
every young man possessed of wealth and power
that he became one of the shrewdest politicians
of the time.   Man steels and hardens himself in
that way; he uses women that women may not use
him.   De Marsay, then, looking at the sum total of
the events of that night, whose pleasures had begun
by trickling in a modest stream and had ended in a
raging torrent, perceived that he had been duped
by the Girl with the Golden Eyes.   He could now
read that page so brilliantly effective, and divine
its hidden meaning.   Paquita's purely physical
innocence, the surprise of her delight, some words,
unintelligible at first but now clear, that had escaped
her in the midst of her delirium, all showed him
that he had posed for another person.   As he was
thoroughly familiar with social corruption in all its
forms, and as he professed perfect indifference in
regard to all kinds of caprices and believed them to
be justified from the very fact that they can be satisfied, he did not take fright and shy at vice; he
knew it as we know a friend, but he could not endure
the thought of having acted as its food.   If his suppositions were correct he had been outraged in the
tenderest spot of his nature.   The mere suspicion
of such a thing roused him to fury; he roared as
might a tiger if taunted by a gazelle, a tiger which
to the power of the brute united the intelligence of
the demon.

"Well, what ails you now?" asked Paul.

"Nothing!"

"If you were asked if you had anything against me I shouldn't like to hear you answer with a *Nothing!* like that: it would probably involve a duel next day between you and me."

"I have given up fighting," said de Marsay.

"That sounds even still more tragic. You assassinate perhaps?"

"You misinterpret the words. I execute."

"My dear friend," said Paul, "your jokes are of an infernally dark complexion this morning."

"What would you have! pleasure leads on to ferocity. Why? I don't know, and I am not curious enough to seek the cause.—These cigars are prime. Give your friend a cup of tea.—Are you aware, Paul, that I am leading the life of a brute? It is high time to select a career and devote one's energies to something worth the anxiety of living for. Life is a strange comedy. I am frightened, and I laugh at the inconsistencies of our social order. The government chops off the head of a poor devil who kills one man and ennobles the individual who, being a doctor, sends to their last account a dozen fellow-creatures in a winter. Morality is powerless against a score of vices that are undermining society and which there is no way of punishing.—Another cup, if you please—'Pon my honor! man is a buffoon dancing on the brink of a precipice. They talk of the immorality of *Liaisons Dangereuses* and I know not what other novels with titles designed to inflame the imaginations of cooks and chambermaids, but there is a horrible, filthy, frightful, disgusting book, always open, whose covers will never be closed, to-wit, the great book of the world. And there is another book, a thousand times worse, which comprises all that men speak in each other's ears or that women whisper behind their fans of an evening, at the ball."

"Henri, something unusual has certainly come over you; you can't conceal it, for all your active discretion."

"Yes—I wish I knew how to kill time until this evening. Let's go and try our luck at cards—perhaps I shall be fortunate enough to lose."

De Marsay rose, completed his toilet, took a handful of bank notes and stuffed them in his cigarcase, and utilized Paul's carriage to convey him to the Salon des Etrangers, where he passed the time until dinner in those thrilling alternations of loss and gain which are the last resource of powerful organizations when they are compelled to do something to kill time. Later, in the evening, at the usual hour, he was at his former rendezvous, and submitted without resistance to be blindfolded. Then, with that concentration of the will that only a vigorous intellect can command, he devoted his attention and intelligence to making out the streets through which the carriage passed. He was almost certain that he was driven to Rue Saint-Lazare, and set down at the private door of the garden of the Hôtel San-Réal. When, as on the previous

occasion, he passed that door and was placed on a
litter borne, doubtless, by the coachman and the
mulatto, as he heard the gravel creak beneath their
feet he saw why such extreme precaution was observed. Had he been free or afoot he might have
plucked a bough from a shrub or examined the
nature of the soil that adhered to his boots, but,
being conveyed aërially, if one may so speak, into
a house whose locality was unknown to him, his
adventure must remain what it had been hitherto,
a dream. But to man's despair all that he does,
whether for good or evil, is done imperfectly. All
his works, physical and intellectual, are marked
with the sign of destruction. It had rained slightly,
the ground was damp. Certain vegetable odors are
much stronger by night than by day, so that Henri
caught the fragrance of mignonette in the alley
along which he was borne. This trifling circumstance might enlighten him in the investigation he
proposed to make as to the location of the hotel that
contained Paquita's bower. In the same way he
noted in memory the various turns his bearers made
within the house and thought he should be able to
recall them. At the termination of his journey he
found himself, as on the preceding evening, seated
on the divan, with Paquita before him unfastening
his bandage—but she was pale and greatly changed.
She had been weeping. Kneeling before him like
an angel at her prayers, but sorrowful, dejected,
profoundly melancholy, the poor girl had little in
common with the curious, eager and impulsive

creature who had taken de Marsay on her wings and borne him aloft to the seventh heaven of bliss. The despair concealed under the veil of pleasure was so manifestly genuine that even de Marsay, hardened as he was, felt himself admiring this new masterpiece of nature and for the time being quite forgot the principal object of the rendezvous.

"What is troubling you, my Paquita?"

"My love," said she, "take me away this very night. Place me in some retreat where no one, seeing me, shall say, 'That is Paquita,' or 'That is the girl with the golden glance and long hair.' There I will give you pleasures as long as you are willing to receive them from me. Then, when the time comes that you no longer love me, you will leave me; I shall not complain, I will not say a word; and my abandonment need cause you no remorse, for one day spent with you, a single day, during which I shall have beheld you, will be dearer to me than all a lifetime. But if I remain here I am lost."

"I cannot leave Paris, my child," Henri replied. "I am not my own master; I am bound by an oath to the destiny of several persons, who are devoted to me as I to them. But I can give you a refuge in Paris where no earthly power can harm you."

"No," she said; "you forget what a woman is capable of doing."

Never did words spoken by human lips express more deadly terror.

"Who or what can harm you, if I stand between you and the world?"

"Poison!" she exclaimed. "Already Doña Concha suspects you. And anyone can see," she continued, making no effort to check the big tears that trickled slowly down her cheeks, "that I am no longer what I was. Well, abandon me to the fury of the monster that will devour me, so let it be! But come, let us crowd the delights of a lifetime into our one night of love. Besides, I will plead, I will weep, I will scream, I will defend myself—perhaps I shall succeed in escaping."

"To whom will you plead?" he asked.

"Silence!" said Paquita. "If I secure my pardon it will perhaps be owing to my discretion."

"Give me my velvet gown," Henri soothingly said.

"No, no!" she earnestly replied; "remain what you are, one of those angels whom I was taught to hate and whom I used to regard as monsters, while all earth holds no object so beautiful as you," she said, stroking Henri's hair. "You cannot conceive what a poor ignorant thing I am. I have learnt nothing. Since I was twelve years old I have been kept under lock and key and not allowed to see a living soul. I can neither read nor write, and the only languages I speak are English and Spanish."

"How comes it then that you receive letters from London?"

"My letters?—see, here they are" said she, fetching from a tall Japanese vase some written sheets.

She held out for de Marsay's inspection some of

the letters, on which the young man saw with surprise odd figures, similar to those of a rebus, traced in blood, and all expressing the utmost intensity of passion.

"Why," he exclaimed, while wonderingly examining those hieroglyphics, the creation of a watchful jealousy, "you must be in the clutches of an infernal spirit?"

"Infernal, that is the word."

"But how did you manage to leave the house?"

"Ah!" she said, "that was my destruction. I managed it by placing before Doña Concha the fear of immediate death and future wrath. I had the curiosity of a demon. I wished to destroy the brazen barrier that had been erected between me and the world, I wished to see what young men were like, for of men I knew only the Marquis and Cristemio. Our coachman and the valet who accompanies us are old mummies—"

"But you were not always kept a prisoner? Your health required—"

"Yes," she replied, "we went out in the carriage now and then, but it was by night and in the country, along the banks of the Scine, where we could not see or be seen."

"Are you not proud to be loved so devotedly?"

"No," she rejoined, "not I! However well supplied, that cloistered life is as darkness compared to light."

"What do you call light?"

"You, my beautiful Adolphe! you, for whom I

would lay down my life.   All of passion that was ever spoken to me or that I have inspired I feel for thee!   For some time I knew nothing of existence, but now I know what it is to love; heretofore I was loved; I did not love.   I would leave all for your sake—take me.   Take me as your plaything, if you will, only let me be with you until you tire of me and break me.''

"Are you sure you would have no regrets?''

"Not one!'' she said, suffering him to read in her eyes, whose golden purity remained untroubled.

"Am I the object of her preference?'' Henri asked himself, who, if he had an inkling of the truth, was disposed to condone the offense in favor of a love so candid and ingenuous.   "I will see about it,'' he thought.

If Paquita owed him no explanation of her past, the most trivial recollection became in his eyes a crime.   So he had the miserable weakness to harbor selfish thoughts, to judge his mistress, to study her while revelling in the most delirious pleasures that ever Peri descended from the skies invented for the object of her love.   Nature seemed to have created Paquita for love, and to have devoted special pains to her task.   From one night to the next her woman's instincts had developed wonderfully.   Great as were the young man's powers and his recklessness in regard to his pleasures, in spite of his satiety of the night before, he found in the Girl with the Golden Eyes that seraglio that the amorous woman knows how to create and

of which the man never wearies. Paquita responded
to that passion for the infinite which is felt by all
really great men, that mysterious passion so dra-
matically expressed in *Faust*, so poetically described
in *Manfred*, and that induced Don Juan to explore
the heart of woman hoping to find there that
boundless thought to the discovery of which so
many visionaries devote themselves, that the
savant thinks he catches glimpses of in science, and
the mystic finds only in God. De Marsay was
enraptured by the notion that at last he had found
the ideal being with whom the struggle might be
carried on indefinitely without wearying, and for the
first time in years he opened his heart. His nerves
relaxed their tension, his coldness melted in the
atmosphere of that ardent soul, his bitter views took
wing and happiness colored his existence as with
the rosy and white tints of Paquita's bower. Under the spur of a masterful delight he was carried
beyond the limits within which he had hitherto
confined his passion. He did not wish to be surpassed by this girl whom a love, in some sense
artificial, had formed in advance to meet the
requirements of his nature, and thus, in that vanity
which urges a man to conquer in everything, he
found strength sufficient to subdue the girl; but,
then, too, forced over the line within which the
soul is her own mistress, he lost himself in those
delicious realms so foolishly called by the vulgar
imaginary space. He was tender, kind, and commu-
nicative. He almost drove Paquita wild.

"Why might we not go to Sorrento, to Nice, or
to Chiavari, and pass our life thus? Will you?"
he said to Paquita in a thrilling voice.

"Need you ever say to me 'Will you?'" she
exclaimed. "Have I a will? I am only something
separate from yourself in order to be a source of
pleasure to you. If you would select a retreat
worthy of us, Asia is the only land where Love can
spread his wings."

"You are right," Henri replied. "We will go to
India, where spring reigns eternal, where the earth
is spread with a perennial carpet of flowers, where
a man may display all the magnificence of a
sovereign, and not be talked of, as he would be in
those stupid countries where the people seek to
realize the insipid dream of equality. Let us go
to the land where we shall live among slaves,
where the sun will always shine on an ever-white
palace, where perfumes are scattered in the air,
the birds sing of love, and where people die when
they no longer have the power to love.

"And where the lovers die together!" exclaimed
Paquita. "But let us not wait, let us go now, at
once—and we will take Cristemio."

"Faith, I know of no happier dénouement to the
drama of life than pleasure. We will go to India;
but in order to go, my child, a great deal of money
will be required, and to get that money I must settle my affairs."

She was entirely ignorant of such matters.

"There are piles of gold here in the house—as

high as that," she said, holding her hand at a distance from the floor.

"It is not mine."

"What difference does that make?" she rejoined. "If we have need of it let us take it."

"It does not belong to you."

"Belong!" she replied.   "Did you not take me? When we have taken that, it will belong to us."

He laughed.

"Poor innocent! it's little you know of the things of this world."

"No, but here is what I do know," she cried, drawing Henri down upon her.

De Marsay, oblivious to everything, was contemplating the prospect of making the fair creature his own for ever when suddenly, in the very midst of his transports, he received a poniard stroke that pierced his heart, then for the first time humiliated. Paquita, who by main strength had raised his form in air as if to gaze on him, exclaimed:

"Oh! Margarita!"

"Margarita!" cried the young man in a terrible voice, "I know now what I wished still to doubt."

He made one bound and reached the cabinet that contained the long poniard; fortunately for Paquita and himself the door was locked.   His fury was intensified on finding his purpose thwarted, but he controlled himself, went and got his cravat and came toward her with such an expression of fell determination on his face that Paquita, without knowing of what crime she was guilty, saw that her

life was at stake. She started up, and to escape
the fatal noose that de Marsay was about to place
about her neck, at a single bound sprang to the further end of the apartment. There was a struggle.
The combatants were well matched in point of
dexterity, agility and strength. To end the conflict
she threw a cushion between her lover's legs and
tripped him, then availed herself of her temporary
advantage to touch the button of the bell that com-
municated with the ante-chamber. The mulatto
came rushing in. Cristemio threw himself on de
Marsay, and in less time than it takes to tell it had
brought him to the floor, and had his foot upon his
chest, the heel toward his throat. The young man
saw that if he attempted to resist the life would be
crushed out of him in an instant at a signal from
Paquita.

"Why did you wish to kill me, my love?" she
said to him.

De Marsay made no reply.

"What have I done to displease you?" she continued. "Speak, let us explain."

Henri preserved the unconcerned air of a brave
man in defeat, cold of mien, silent, a manner wholly
English, asserting his dignity consciously even in
his momentary resignation. He had already reflected, moreover, notwithstanding the madness of
his rage, that there was little prudence in killing
the girl on the spur of the moment, and that it
would be the part of wisdom to so arrange the murder as to secure his own immunity from justice.

"My beloved," Paquita went on, "speak to me; do not leave me thus without a last love-farewell! It would pain me to retain in my heart the fear that you have implanted therein—Will you speak?" she cried, with an angry stamp of the foot.

For all reply de Marsay cast on her a look that said so clearly *You shall die!* that Paquita came and threw herself on his bosom.

"Do you wish to kill me, then? Kill me, if my death will afford you pleasure!"

She made a sign to Cristemio, who lifted his foot from the young man's chest and stepped back a little way. Whether he approved or condemned Paquita's action no one could have told: his face was inscrutable.

"That is a man!" said de Marsay, gloomily, pointing toward the mulatto. "There is no true devotion save that which obeys a friend's commands without discussing them. You have in that man a true friend."

"I will present you with him if you will have him," she replied. "He will serve you as faithfully as he has served me if I tell him it is my wish."

She waited a moment for an answer, then went on in a tone of tenderness:

"Adolphe, speak to me one kind word!—See, the day is breaking."

Henri was silent. The young man had an odious characteristic, for we are prone to admire everything that resembles strength of mind, and men

often make a fetish of exaggeration. Henri was
incapable of forgiving. The power of forgiving
which is certainly one of the soul's graces, was
mere nonsense to him. The ferocity of the North-
men, with which English blood is strongly tainted,
had been transmitted to him by his father. He
was immutable, alike in his good sentiments and in
his evil. Paquita's exclamation was the more horrible to him that he had been despoiled of the
sweetest conquest that had ever gratified his masculine vanity. Hope, love, all the senses had flour-
ished rampant in him, everything in his heart and
his intelligence, had kindled into flames; then those
flames, lighted to cheer and illuminate his life, had
suddenly been extinguished by a cold wind. Paquita, in her grief and stupefaction, had barely
strength to give the signal for departure.

"This is no longer of use," said she, throwing
aside the handkerchief that had been employed to
bandage Henri's eyes; "if he has ceased to love
me, if he hates me, all is at an end."

She waited for a look from him and, not obtaining
it, fell back fainting. The mulatto darted at Henri
a glance of such venomous significance that for the
first time in his life the young man—whose courage
no one had ever questioned—felt a shiver run
through his frame. "Unless you love her well, if
you cause her the least suffering, I will kill you!"
was the meaning of that quick glance. De Marsay
was conducted with the most obsequious attention
along a dimly-lighted inside corridor, upon reaching

27

the end of which he emerged by a secret door, upon a private stairway that led to the garden of the San-Réal mansion. Here, still under the mulatto's guidance, he traversed cautiously the entire length of a long alley of lindens, which terminated at a small door that opened on a narrow street, deserted at that hour. De Marsay took note of everything; the carriage was waiting; the colored man did not accompany him on this occasion, and when Henri put his head out of the window of the vehicle for a last glimpse of the hotel and its grounds he encountered the white eyes of Cristemio, with whom he exchanged a look. On each side it was a challenge, a defiance, a declaration of war according to savage methods, a war in which civilized customs were to be discarded, in which treachery and guile are acknowledged weapons. Cristemio knew that Henri had sworn to have Paquita's life. Henri knew that Cristemio would try to kill him before he could kill Paquita. The two men understood each other perfectly.

"The plot thickens and is growing interesting," said Henri to himself.

"Where shall I set monsieur down?" inquired the coachman.

De Marsay directed him to drive him to Paul de Manerville's.

For more than a week Henri was not to be found at his lodgings and for all that space of time none of his friends knew either how he was occupying himself or where he had taken up his abode. This retirement saved him from the fury of the mulatto, and resulted in the death of the poor creature who had centred all her hopes in him whom she loved as never woman loved on earth. At the expiration of the week, about eleven o'clock at night, Henri appeared in a carriage at the small door of the garden of the Hôtel San-Réal. Four men accompanied him. The driver was evidently one of his friends, for he stood up on his box alertly listening, like a faithful sentinel, to catch the slightest sound. One of the three others posted himself in the street, just outside the door, the second remained in the garden, leaning against the wall, and the last, who held in his hand a bunch of keys, accompanied de Marsay.

"Henri," his companion said to him, "we are betrayed."

"By whom, my worthy Ferragus?"

"They are not all asleep," replied the leader of the *Dévorants;* "it must surely be that someone in the house has not eaten or drunk—Look there, see that light!"

"Whence does it proceed? We have the plan of the house."

"I can tell without the plan," Ferragus replied. "It comes from the chamber of the Marquise."

"Ah!" ejaculated de Marsay. "She must have arrived to-day from London. That woman has robbed me of my vengeance! But if she has, my good Gratien, we will hand her over to the law."

"Listen, listen!—the deed is done," said Ferragus to Henri.

The two friends strained their ears and caught
the sound of feeble, plaintive cries that would have
softened a tiger's heart.

"Your Marquise forgot that the sounds would
escape through the chimney," the leader of the
Dévorants said, with such a smile as a critic gives
on discovering a fault in a great work.

"We, and we alone, know how to provide for
everything," said Henri. "Wait for me. I will
go and see what is going on upstairs; I shall be
glad to learn how they manage their family quarrels
—By God! I believe she is roasting her at a slow
fire."

De Marsay leaped lightly up the stairs that were
familiar to him and found his way to the boudoir.
On opening the door he experienced that involuntary shudder which no man, even the bravest, can
repress at the sight of fresh-spilled blood. The spectacle that met his eyes, moreover, was calculated
to astonish him in more respects than one. The
Marquise was a woman; she had planned her vengeance with that thoroughness of perfidy that char-
acterizes the weaker animals. She had dissembled
her anger in order to be certain of the crime before
she punished it.

"Too late, my own beloved!" said the expiring
Paquita, turning her fading eyes upon de Marsay.

The Girl with the Golden Eyes lay dying,
drowned in blood. The lighted candles, a delicate
perfume that pervaded the apartment, a certain disorder in which a man of experience in such matters

SAN-RÉAL AND PAQUITA

---

*Some animals, when roused to fury, leap on their
enemy, despatch him, and then, tranquil in their hour
of victory, seem to have forgotten their momentary
madness. There are others that wheel and turn
about their victim, watching jealously lest someone should come and rob them of the carcass—like
Homer's Achilles—three times making the circuit of
Troy's walls dragging his vanquished foe attached
by the feet to his war-car. So it was with the Marquise. She did not see Henri.*

Louis Edouard Fournier

R. de Los Rios, sc

might recognize the excesses common to all the passions, announced that the Marquise had not proceeded with her investigations without intelligent forethought. The white boudoir, where the crimson blood harmonized so well, told of a protracted conflict. The cushions bore the imprint of Paquita's hands. Everywhere she had clung to life, struggling bravely to defend and preserve it, and everywhere she had been stricken by the fatal weapon. There were large pieces of the fluted muslin draperies that had been torn away in long strips by her bleeding hands. She seemed to have attempted to scale the walls; there were marks of her bare feet on the back of the divan, along which she had doubtless run. Her body, gashed by the poniard in her slayer's hand, told with what fury she had fought to save a life that Henri had made so dear to her. She lay on the floor and with her last remaining strength had bitten through the muscles of the instep of Madame de San-Réal, who still held in her hand the blood-stained poniard. The Marquise had had much of her hair torn out by the roots, she was covered with wounds—many were still bleeding—inflicted by her adversary's teeth, and her torn gown disclosed her half-naked form, her lacerated breasts. She was sublime in all this. Her keen, fierce face exhaled an odor of slaughter, with parted lips she panted, her distended nostrils seemed insufficient for the work of giving air to her lungs. Some animals when roused to fury, leap on their enemy, despatch him, and then, tranquil in their hour of victory, seem to have forgotten their momentary madness. There are others that wheel and turn about their victim, watching jealously lest someone should come and rob them of the carcass—like Homer's Achilles—three times making the circuit of Troy's walls dragging his vanquished foe attached by the feet to his war-car. So it was with the Marquise. She did not see Henri. In the first place she was assured there was no one by to witness her actions, and next, had all Paris stood around her in a circle gazing, she was so frenzied by the odor of warm blood, so maddened by the strife, so carried beyond herself, that she would have been unconscious of its presence. A thunderbolt might have crashed through the ceiling, she would not have noticed it. She had not even heard Paquita's parting sigh, and believed that the dead woman's ears were open to her words.

"Die unconfessed!" she said, addressing her. "Down, down to hell, monster of ingratitude, and be the demon's leman! For the blood that thou hast given him thou owest me every drop of thine! Die, die, and suffer a thousand deaths! I was too kind: I was but a moment in despatching you; I should have made you suffer all the anguish that you have bequeathed to me. I shall still live! I shall live in sorrow! I have naught left to love save God!"

She stood gazing on the lifeless form.

"She is dead!" she said, after a pause, with a violent revulsion of feeling. "Dead!—Ah! I too shall die of grief!"

The Marquise, overcome by a despair that choked her voice, turned to throw herself on the divan and for the first time was able to see Henri de Marsay.

"Who are you?" she cried, darting forward with her poniard raised to strike.

Henri seized her arm, and they were thus able to eye each other face to face.   Then a horrible consternation overcame them, the blood seemed curdling in their veins, and their legs trembled like those of terror-stricken horses.   Two Menæchmi could not have resembled each other more closely. They spoke simultaneously, and each asked the same question:

"Lord Dudley is your father?"

Each bowed the head in affirmation.

"She was true to the instincts of her race," said Henri, glancing at Paquita.

"She was better than could have been expected from her surroundings," replied Margarita-Euphémia Porrabéril, throwing herself on Paquita's corpse with a cry of despair.   "Poor, poor girl! oh! that I could restore thee to life! I have done wrong, forgive me, Paquita! Thou art dead, and I survive —I am the more wretched."

At this juncture the repulsive face of Paquita's mother appeared in the doorway.

"You are about to say that you did not sell her to me that I might kill her," cried the Marquise. "I know the reason that brings you forth from your den. I will pay you for her a second time. Not a word."

She went to the ebony cabinet, took from it a sack of gold, and cast it contemptuously at the hag's feet. The chink of the gold brought a smile to the Georgian's impassive face.

"My coming was opportune, sister," said Henri. "The officers of justice will soon be on your trail—"

"It is nothing," replied the Marquise. "There is but one person who could demand an account of the girl's fate. Cristemio is dead."

"And the mother," said Henri, pointing to the old woman, "will she not be always pursuing you for blackmail?"

"She is from a country where the women are not beings but things that one does with as one will; they are bought and sold, they may be put to death —in a word, they are employed to gratify their masters' caprices, just as you make use here of your chairs and tables. Besides, she is controlled by one passion, which overmasters all others, and which, even had she loved her daughter, would have annihilated every trace of maternal affection, a passion—"

"For what?" Henri eagerly asked, interrupting his sister.

"For gaming, from which may God preserve you!" replied the Marquise.

"But whom will you get to help you," said Henri, pointing to the remains of the Girl with the Golden Eyes, "to remove the traces of this freak of yours, which justice will not be likely to overlook?"

"I have the mother," replied the Marquise,

pointing to the Georgian and signifying to her that she was not to leave the room.

"We shall meet again," said Henri, who reflected on his friends' probable alarm and felt he must be gone.

"No, brother," she said, "we shall never see each other more.   I shall return to Spain and enter the convent of *Los Dolores*."

"You are too young and beautiful for that," said Henri, taking her in his arms and kissing her.

"Adieu," she said; "nothing can console us for the loss of what we have looked on as the infinite."

A week later Paul de Manerville met de Marsay walking on the Terrasse des Feuillants in the garden of the Tuileries.

"Well, great rascal, what has become of your pretty Girl with the Golden Eyes?"

"She is dead."

"What ailed her?"

"Consumption."

Paris, March 1834–April 1835.

LIST OF ETCHINGS

VOLUME IV